REVISED EDITION

THE
COMPLETE
SCHOOL
ATLAS

HOLT, RINEHART AND WINSTON

Harcourt Brace & Company

Austin • New York • Orlando • Atlanta • San Francisco • Boston • Dallas • Toronto • London

Photo Credits

Front and Back Cover: Inset, Ralph Mercer/Tony Stone Images; Background, Frank Curry.

Title Page: Ralph Mercer/Tony Stone Images.

Pages 3–6, Frank Curry.

Pages 37–70, © Copyright General Electric Co. 1976.

Pages 71–100, Douglas Mazonowicz/Bruce Coleman, Inc.

Portions of this work were published in previous editions.

For permission to reprint copyrighted material, grateful acknowledgment is made to the following sources:

Macmillan Reference USA, a Division of Simon & Schuster: Adapted from map, "United States: Ethnic Population, 1980's" from *We the People: An Atlas of America's Diversity* by James Paul Allen and Eugene James Turner. Copyright © 1988 by Macmillan Reference USA, a Division of Simon & Schuster.

Printed in the United States of America

ISBN 0-03-050818-5

9   030   03 02 01

CONTENTS

WORLD AND REGIONAL MAPS 16

WORLD GEOGRAPHY 37

WORLD HISTORY 71

AMERICAN HISTORY 101

Introduction

The Complete School Atlas is a valuable source of geographical, historical, and statistical information. This classroom and research source has many useful features to aid you in your study:

▶ a **Skills Handbook** that explains how to read and to use different kinds of maps

▶ a selection of up-to-date physical and political maps of the world and the continents

▶ a **World Geography** section that contains information about various regions of the world, including full-color thematic maps that show economic, climate, and population characteristics

▶ easy-to-understand **World History** and **American History** maps that lead you from early world civilizations to the American Revolution and on to the turbulent changes of the twentieth century

▶ an **Appendix** that provides important statistical information about the countries of the world

▶ an **Index** that helps you locate places and directs you to maps about specific historical events

The Complete School Atlas packs a great deal of up-to-date information into one source. This easy-to-use atlas is a valuable resource for students and teachers trying to understand our ever-changing world.

SKILLS HANDBOOK

CONTENTS

Using an atlas requires the ability to understand how maps are created and how they are used. This Skills Handbook explains how to read and understand the maps in this atlas. You also will find examples of maps you will see on pages 41–70 of this atlas. These thematic maps are only some examples of the many kinds of maps you will find in this atlas and elsewhere.

7

MAPPING THE EARTH

The Globe

A globe is a scale model of the earth. It is useful for looking at the entire earth or at large areas of the earth's surface. **The** earth's land surface is organized into seven large landmasses, called **continents**, which are pictured in the four maps in Figure 1. Landmasses smaller than continents and completely surrounded by water are called **islands**. **G**eographers also organize the earth's water surface into parts, the largest of which is the world **ocean**. Geographers divide the world ocean into four oceans: the Pacific Ocean, the Atlantic Ocean, the Indian Ocean, and the Arctic Ocean. Lakes and seas are smaller bodies of water.

Figure 2 is a diagram of a globe. The pattern of lines that circle the earth in east-west and north-south directions is called a **grid**. The intersection of these imaginary lines helps us find the location of places on the earth. Some mapmakers label the lines with letters and numbers. The grid on many maps and globes, however, is made up of lines of **latitude** and **longitude**.

Lines of latitude are drawn in an east-west direction and measure distance north and south of the **equator**. The equator is an imaginary line that circles the globe halfway between the North Pole and the South Pole. Lines of latitude are called **parallels** because they are

NORTHERN HEMISPHERE

INDIAN OCEAN
ASIA
EUROPE
AFRICA
ARCTIC OCEAN
+ North Pole
PACIFIC OCEAN
ATLANTIC OCEAN
Equator
NORTH AMERICA

SOUTHERN HEMISPHERE

Equator
SOUTH AMERICA
PACIFIC OCEAN
ATLANTIC OCEAN
+ South Pole
ANTARCTICA
AFRICA
AUSTRALIA
INDIAN OCEAN

WESTERN HEMISPHERE

North Pole
NORTH AMERICA
ATLANTIC OCEAN
180°
Equator
PACIFIC OCEAN
SOUTH AMERICA
ANTARCTICA
South Pole

EASTERN HEMISPHERE

North Pole
EUROPE
ASIA
AFRICA
ATLANTIC OCEAN
Equator
INDIAN OCEAN
AUSTRALIA
Prime Meridian
ANTARCTICA
South Pole

▲ **Figure 1: The hemispheres**

always parallel to the equator. Parallels north of the equator are labeled with an *N*, and those south are labeled with an *S*.

Lines of longitude are drawn in a north-south direction and measure distance east and west of the **prime meridian**. The prime meridian is an imaginary line that runs through Greenwich, England, from the North Pole to the South Pole. Lines of longitude are called **meridians**.

▼ **Figure 2: Globe**

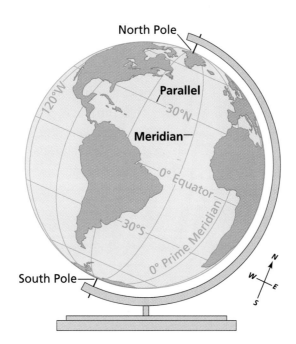

Parallels measure distance from the equator, and meridians from the prime meridian, in **degrees**. The symbol for degrees is °. Degrees are further divided into minutes, for which the symbol is '. There are 60 minutes in a degree.

Lines of latitude range from 0°, for locations on the equator, to 90°N or 90°S, for locations at the North Pole or South Pole. Lines of longitude range from 0° on the prime meridian to 180° on a meridian in the mid-Pacific Ocean. Meridians west of the prime meridian to 180° are labeled with a *W*. Those east of the prime meridian to 180° are labeled with an *E*.

Looking at the globe, you can see that the equator divides the globe into two halves, or **hemispheres**. See **Figure 1**. The half north of the equator is the Northern Hemisphere. The southern half is the Southern Hemisphere.

The prime meridian and the 180° meridian divide the world into the Eastern Hemisphere and the Western Hemisphere. Because the prime meridian separates parts of Europe and Africa into two different hemispheres, some mapmakers divide the Eastern and Western hemispheres at 20° W. This places all of Europe and Africa in the Eastern Hemisphere.

MAP-MAKING

A map is a flat diagram of all or part of the earth's surface. An **atlas** is an organized collection of maps in one book. **M**apmakers have different ways of presenting a round earth on flat maps. These different ways are called **map projections**. Because the earth is round, all flat maps have some distortion. Some flat maps distort size, especially at high latitudes. Those maps, however, might be useful because they show true direction and shape. Some maps, called equal-area maps, show size in true proportions but distort shapes. **M**apmakers must choose the type of map projection that is best for their purposes. Many map projections are one of three kinds: cylindrical, conic, or flat-plane.

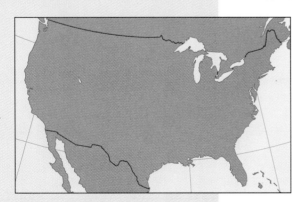

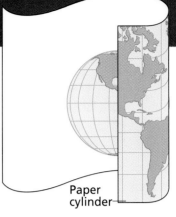

▶ **Figure 3a: Paper cylinder**

Cylindrical projections are designed from a cylinder wrapped around the globe. See **Figure 3a**. The cylinder touches the globe only at the equator. The meridians are pulled apart and are parallel to each other instead of meeting at the poles. This causes landmasses near the poles to appear larger than they really are. **Figure 3b** is a Mercator projection, one type of cylindrical projection. The Mercator projection is useful for navigators because it shows true direction and shape. The Mercator projection for world maps, however, emphasizes the Northern Hemisphere. Africa and South America are shown to be smaller than they really are.

▲ **Figure 3b: Mercator projection**

▼ **Figure 4a: Paper cone**

Conic projections are designed from a cone placed over the globe. See **Figure 4a**. A conic projection is most accurate along the lines of latitude where it touches the globe. It retains almost true shape and size. Conic projections are most useful for areas that have long east-west dimensions, such as the United States. See the map in **Figure 4b**.

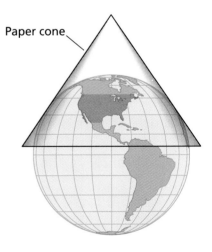

◀ **Figure 4b: Conic projection**

PANAMA
GULF OF PANAMA
LLANOS **VENEZUELA**
Orinoco River
Caroni R.
Angel Falls
ATLANTIC
Georgetown

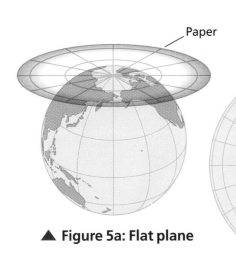

▲ **Figure 5a: Flat plane**

Flat-plane projections are designed from a plane touching the globe at one point, such as at the North Pole or South Pole. See **Figures 5a** and **5b**. A flat-plane projection is useful for showing true direction for airplane pilots and ship navigators. It also shows true area, but it distorts true shape.

◀ **Figure 5b: Flat-plane projection**

The Robinson projection is a compromise between size and shape distortions. It often is used for world maps, such as the map on pages 38–39. The minor distortions in size at high latitudes on Robinson projections are balanced by realistic shapes at the middle and low latitudes.

Drawing a straight line on a flat map will not show the shortest route between two locations. Remember, maps represent a round world on a flat plane. The shortest route between any two points on the earth is a **great-circle route**. See **Figures 6a** and **6b**. Any imaginary line that divides the earth into equal parts is a great circle. The equator is a great circle. Airplanes and ships navigate along great-circle routes.

▼ **Figure 6a: Great-circle route**

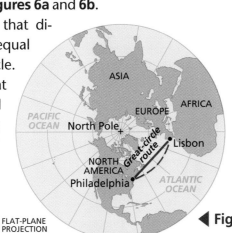

MERCATOR PROJECTION

FLAT-PLANE PROJECTION

◀ **Figure 6b: Great-circle route**

MAP ESSENTIALS

In some ways, maps are like messages sent out in code. Mapmakers provide certain elements that help us translate these codes to understand the information, or message, they are presenting about a particular part of the world. Almost all maps have several common elements: **directional indicators**, **scales**, and **legends**, or keys. Figure 7, a map of East Asia, has all three elements.

A directional indicator shows which directions are north, south, east, and west. Some mapmakers use a "north arrow," which points toward the North Pole. Remember, "north" is not always at the top of a map. The way a map is drawn and the location of directions on that map depend on the perspective of the mapmaker. Many maps in this atlas indicate direction by using a **compass rose ❶**. A compass rose has arrows that point to all four principal directions, as shown in **Figure 7**.

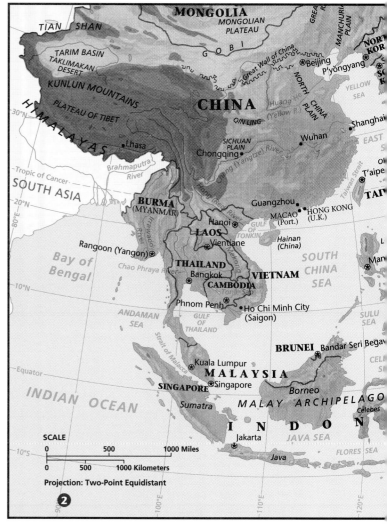

▲ Figure 7: East Asia—Physical–Political

Mapmakers use scales to represent distances between points on a map. Scales may appear on maps in several different forms. The maps in this atlas provide a line scale ❷. The scales give distances in miles and kilometers (km).

To find the distance between two points on the map in **Figure 7**, place a piece of paper so that the edge connects the two points. Mark the location of each point on the paper with a line or dot. Then, compare the distance between the two dots with the map's line scale. The number on the top of the scale gives the distance in miles. The number on the bottom gives the distance in kilometers. Because the distances are given in intervals, you will have to approximate the actual distance on the scale.

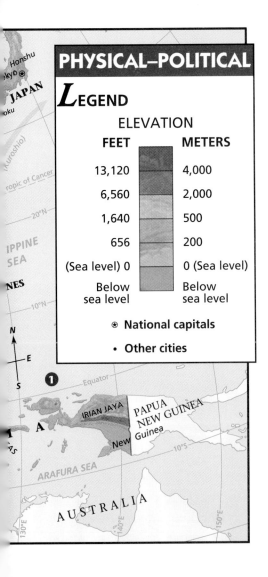

PHYSICAL–POLITICAL

*L*EGEND

ELEVATION

FEET		METERS
13,120		4,000
6,560		2,000
1,640		500
656		200
(Sea level) 0		0 (Sea level)
Below sea level		Below sea level

⊛ **National capitals**

• **Other cities**

The legend ❸, or key, explains what the symbols on the map represent. Point symbols are used to specify the location of things, such as cities, that do not take up much space on a large-scale map. Some legends, such as the one in **Figure 7**, show which colors represent certain elevations. Other maps might have legends with symbols or colors that represent things such as roads, economic resources, land use, population density, and climate.

Inset maps are sometimes used to show a small part of a larger map. Mapmakers also use inset maps to show areas that are far away from the areas shown on the main map. Maps of the United States, for example, often include inset maps of Hawaii. (See the map on page 41.) That state is too far from the other 49 states to accurately represent the true distance on the main map. Subject areas in inset maps can be drawn to a scale different from the scale used on the main map.

WORKING WITH MAPS

The maps on pages 16–36 include two kinds of maps: physical and political. On pages 41–70 you will find four kinds of maps. First is a physical–political map. Each of these maps is followed by a series of three thematic maps. These climate, population, and economic maps provide different kinds of information about each region of the world. Most maps after page 70 are historical maps. Historical maps use colors and symbols to show important events and places.

Mapmakers often combine physical and political features into one map. Physical–political maps, such as the one in **Figure 7** on pages 12 and 13, show important physical features in a region, including major mountains and mountain ranges, rivers, oceans and other bodies of water, deserts, and plains. Physical–political maps also show important political features, such as national borders, state and provincial boundaries, and capitals and other main cities.

▼ Figure 8:
East Asia—Climate

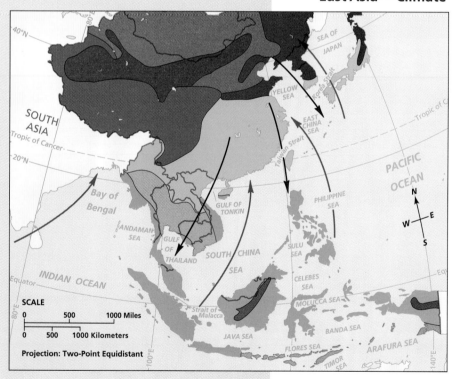

Mapmakers use climate maps to show dominant weather patterns in certain areas. Climate maps in this atlas use color to show the various climate regions of the world. See **Figure 8**. Colors that identify climate types are found in a legend that accompanies each map. Boundaries between climate regions do not indicate an abrupt change in dominant weather conditions between two climate regions. Instead, boundaries approximate areas of gradual change between two climate regions.

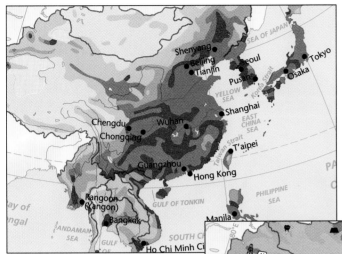

▲ Figure 9:
East Asia—Population

Population maps show where people live in a particular region and how crowded, or densely populated, regions are. Population maps in this atlas use color to show population density. See **Figure 9**. Each color represents a certain number of people living within a square mile or square kilometer. The population maps also use symbols to show metropolitan areas with populations of a particular size. These symbols and the color categories are identified in a legend.

Economic maps show the important resources of a region. See **Figure 10**. Various symbols and colors are used to show information about economic development, such as where major industry is located or where agricultural or ranching activities are most common. The meanings of each symbol and color are shown in a legend.

◀ Figure 10: East Asia—Economy

Some kinds of maps are not found in an atlas. Mental maps are those maps that we see in our minds. We use mental maps to help us make sense of the world around us. A person can, for example, visualize the community he or she lives in: the location and kinds of buildings there, the activities that take place there, and the surrounding environment. Similarly, mental maps help people structure what they know about any other place: the location and relative size of countries and continents, for example. As people learn more about places, they add more details to their mental maps of these places.

WORLD AND REGIONAL MAPS

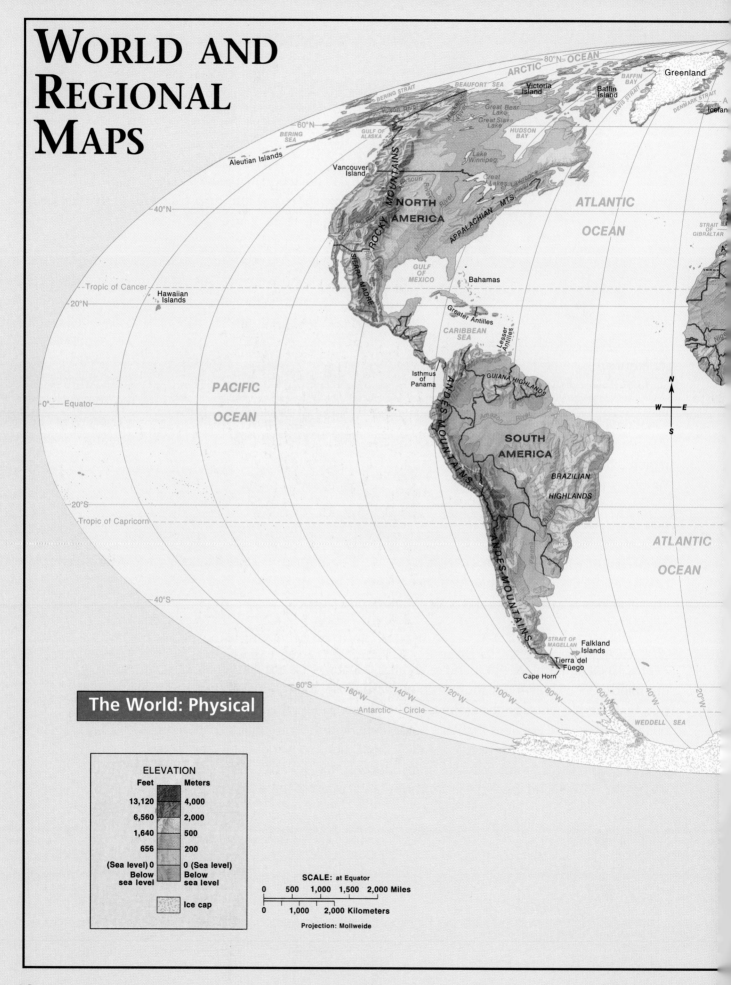

The World: Physical

ELEVATION

Feet	Meters
13,120	4,000
6,560	2,000
1,640	500
656	200
(Sea level) 0	0 (Sea level)
Below sea level	Below sea level

Ice cap

SCALE: at Equator

0   500   1,000 1,500 2,000 Miles

0   1,000   2,000 Kilometers

Projection: Mollweide

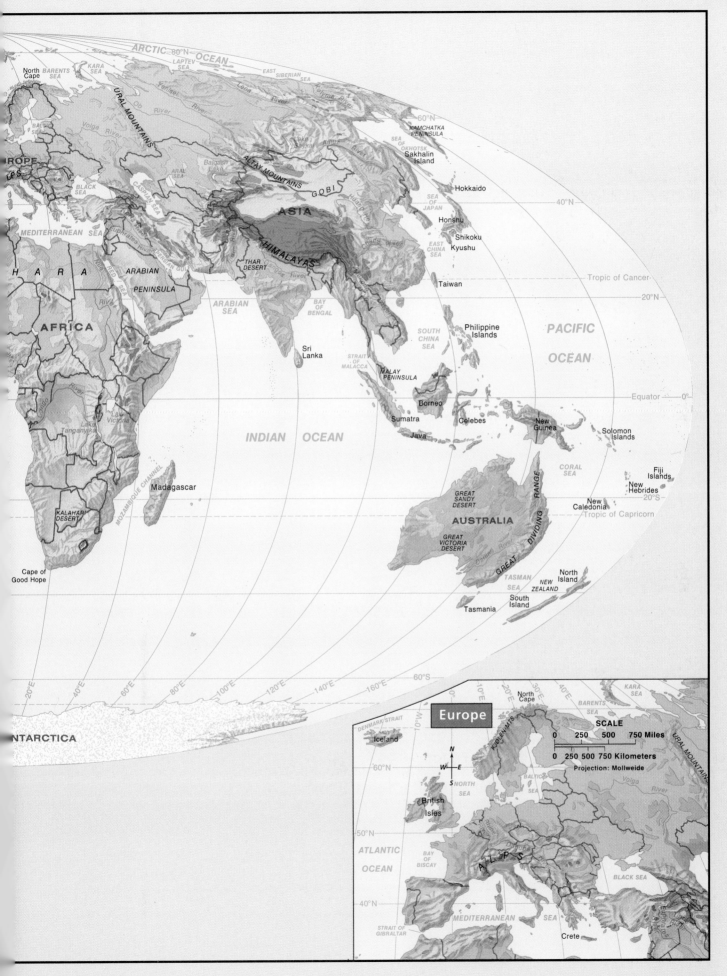

ARCTIC 80°N OCEAN

North Cape · BARENTS SEA · KARA SEA · LAPTEV SEA · EAST SIBERIAN SEA

URAL MOUNTAINS · Ob River · Yenisei River · Lena River · Kolyma River

60°N

KAMCHATKA PENINSULA · SEA OF OKHOTSK · Sakhalin Island

Lake Baykal · Amur River

Volga River · ARAL SEA · Balqash Lake · ALTAY MOUNTAINS · GOBI · Hokkaido

CASPIAN SEA · BLACK SEA

EUROPE · ALPS

40°N · SEA OF JAPAN · Honshu · Shikoku · Kyushu

ASIA · Huang He · Chang River · EAST CHINA SEA

MEDITERRANEAN SEA · HIMALAYAS · Taiwan · Tropic of Cancer

Euphrates River · PERSIAN GULF · THAR DESERT · 20°N

S A H A R A · ARABIAN PENINSULA · RED SEA · Nile River · ARABIAN SEA · BAY OF BENGAL · SOUTH CHINA SEA · Philippine Islands · PACIFIC OCEAN

AFRICA · Sri Lanka · STRAIT OF MALACCA · MALAY PENINSULA

Congo River · Equator 0°

Borneo · Celebes · New Guinea · Solomon Islands

Lake Victoria · Lake Tanganyika · Sumatra · Java

INDIAN OCEAN · CORAL SEA · Fiji Islands

Madagascar · MOZAMBIQUE CHANNEL · GREAT SANDY DESERT · New Hebrides · 20°S

KALAHARI DESERT · GREAT DIVIDING RANGE · New Caledonia · Tropic of Capricorn

AUSTRALIA · GREAT VICTORIA DESERT · Darling River · North Island

Cape of Good Hope · TASMAN SEA · NEW ZEALAND · South Island

Tasmania

20°E · 40°E · 60°E · 80°E · 100°E · 120°E · 140°E · 160°E · 60°S

ANTARCTICA

Europe

DENMARK STRAIT · 10°W · North Cape · 20°E · 30°E · 40°E · KARA SEA

Iceland · KJØLEN MTS · BARENTS SEA · URAL MOUNTAINS

SCALE
0   250   500   750 Miles
0   250 500 750 Kilometers
Projection: Mollweide

60°N · NORTH SEA · BALTIC SEA · Volga River

British Isles

ATLANTIC OCEAN · 50°N · BAY OF BISCAY · ALPS · BLACK SEA

40°N · MEDITERRANEAN SEA · Crete

STRAIT OF GIBRALTAR

The World: Political

ARCTIC OCEAN

GREENLAND (Denmark)

ICELA

ALASKA (US)

60°N

Aleutian Islands

Godthab

CANADA

Vancouver   Winnipeg

Ottawa   Montreal

NORTH AMERICA   Chicago   Toronto

New York City

40°N   **ATLANTIC**

UNITED STATES   Washington D.C.

OCEAN

Los Angeles

Houston

BERMUDA (UK)

Rab
Casablanc

MORO

Tropic of Cancer

THE BAHAMAS

WESTERN SAHARA (Sovereignty Disputed)

20°N

MEXICO

Havana

CUBA

DOMINICAN REPUBLIC

PUERTO RICO (US)

Nouakchott

MAURITAN

HAWAII (US)

Mexico City

ST. KITTS AND NEVIS

CAPE VERDE

SENEGAL

GUATEMALA   BELIZE

JAMAICA   HAITI

ANTIGUA AND BARBUDA

Dakar

Guatemala City

HONDURAS

VIRGIN ISLANDS (US, UK)

DOMINICA

GAMBIA   GUINEA

GUINEA-BISSAU

EL SALVADOR

NICARAGUA

ST. LUCIA   BARBADOS

Managua

GRENADA   ST. VINCENT AND THE GRENADINES

SIERRA LEONE

COSTA RICA   PANAMA

TRINIDAD AND TOBAGO

LIBERIA

Caracas

VENEZUELA   **GUYANA**

Bogotá   Georgetown   SURINAME

N

COLOMBIA   Paramaribo

FRENCH GUIANA (France)

W   E

Galápagos Islands (Ecuador)

Quito

S

0°   Equator

ECUADOR

KIRIBATI

PACIFIC

PERU

SOUTH AMERICA

OCEAN

BRAZIL

WESTERN SAMOA   AMERICAN SAMOA

Lima

Brasília

BOLIVIA

20°S   TONGA

La Paz   Sucre

Tropic of Capricorn

Rio de Janeiro

PARAGUAY

São Paulo

Asunción

CHILE

ATLANTIC

ARGENTINA

OCEAN

Santiago

URUGUAY

Buenos Aires   Montevideo

40°S

FALKLAND ISLANDS (UK)

SOUTH GEORGIA (UK)

SOUTH SAND ISLANDS (UK)

60°S   160°W   140°W   120°W   100°W   80°W   60°W   40°W   20°W

Antarctic Circle

⊛   **National capitals**

•   **Other cities**

SCALE: at Equator

0   500   1,000   1,500   2,000 Miles

0   1,000   2,000 Kilometers

Projection: Mollweide

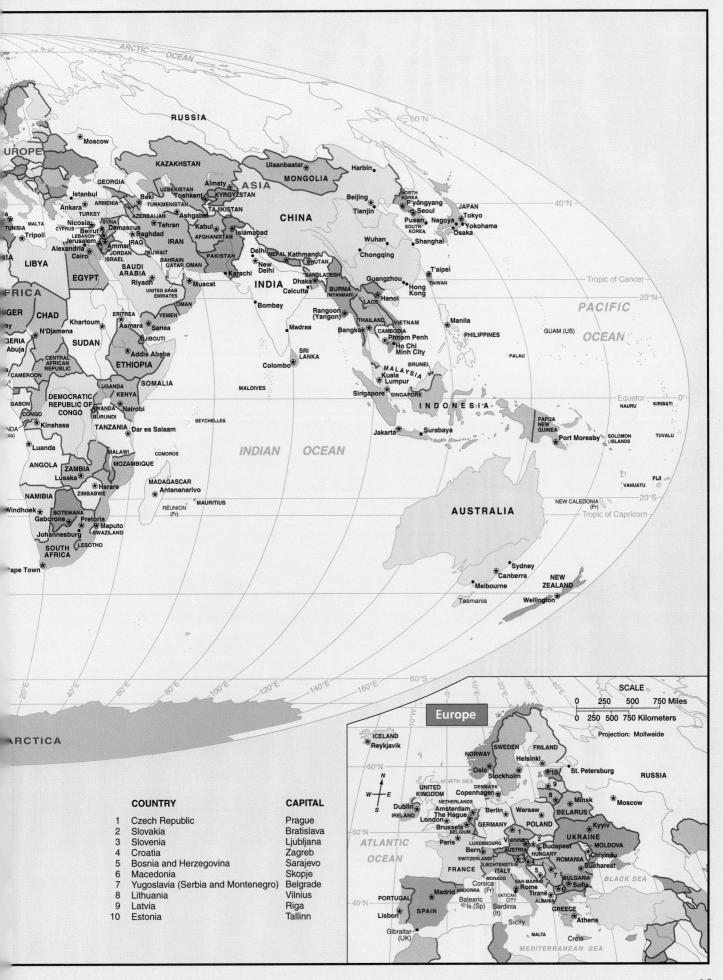

ARCTIC OCEAN

RUSSIA

60°N

Moscow

EUROPE

KAZAKHSTAN

ASIA

40°N

GEORGIA

Ulaanbaatar

MONGOLIA

Harbin

Istanbul

Almaty

Toshkent

KYRGYZSTAN

Beijing

NORTH KOREA

P'yŏngyang

JAPAN

Ankara

ARMENIA

Baki

UZBEKISTAN

TAJIKISTAN

Tianjin

Seoul

Nagoya

Tokyo

TURKEY

TURKMENISTAN

CHINA

Pusan

Yokohama

Nicosia

AZERBAIJAN

Ashgabat

Osaka

CYPRUS

SYRIA

Tehran

Kabul

SOUTH KOREA

Tripoli

MALTA

Damascus

Baghdad

AFGHANISTAN

Islamabad

Wuhan

Beirut

LEBANON

IRAQ

IRAN

Shanghai

Jerusalem

Amman

KUWAIT

PAKISTAN

Delhi

Chongqing

T'aipei

Alexandria

ISRAEL

JORDAN

BAHRAIN

Karachi

New Delhi

NEPAL

Kathmandu

Guangzhou

TAIWAN

Cairo

SAUDI

QATAR

OMAN

BHUTAN

Tropic of Cancer

LIBYA

EGYPT

ARABIA

Riyadh

UNITED ARAB EMIRATES

Muscat

INDIA

Calcutta

Dhaka

BANGLADESH

BURMA (MYANMAR)

Hong Kong

Hanoi

PACIFIC

20°N

NIGER

CHAD

Khartoum

ERITREA

Asmara

Sanaa

OMAN

Bombay

LAOS

OCEAN

N'Djamena

SUDAN

YEMEN

Rangoon (Yangon)

VIETNAM

Manila

GUAM (US)

NIGERIA

Abuja

DJIBOUTI

Madras

THAILAND

CAMBODIA

Bangkok

Phnom Penh

PHILIPPINES

CAMEROON

CENTRAL AFRICAN REPUBLIC

Addis Ababa

ETHIOPIA

SRI LANKA

Ho Chi Minh City

PALAU

GABON

UGANDA

Colombo

BRUNEI

DEMOCRATIC REPUBLIC OF CONGO

RWANDA

KENYA

Nairobi

MALDIVES

MALAYSIA

Kuala Lumpur

Equator

0°

NAURU

KIRIBATI

CONGO

BURUNDI

Singapore

SINGAPORE

Kinshasa

TANZANIA

Dar es Salaam

SEYCHELLES

INDONESIA

Luanda

PAPUA NEW GUINEA

TUVALU

ANGOLA

ZAMBIA

Lusaka

MALAWI

COMOROS

INDIAN OCEAN

Jakarta

Surabaya

Port Moresby

SOLOMON ISLANDS

20°S

Harare

MOZAMBIQUE

NAMIBIA

ZIMBABWE

MADAGASCAR

Antananarivo

MAURITIUS

FIJI

Windhoek

BOTSWANA

RÉUNION (Fr)

NEW CALEDONIA (Fr)

VANUATU

Gaborone

Pretoria

Maputo

AUSTRALIA

Tropic of Capricorn

Johannesburg

SWAZILAND

SOUTH AFRICA

LESOTHO

Sydney

Cape Town

Canberra

NEW ZEALAND

Melbourne

ANTARCTICA

Tasmania

Wellington

20°E 40°E 60°E 80°E 100°E 120°E 140°E 160°E 60°S

COUNTRY	CAPITAL
1 Czech Republic	Prague
2 Slovakia	Bratislava
3 Slovenia	Ljubljana
4 Croatia	Zagreb
5 Bosnia and Herzegovina	Sarajevo
6 Macedonia	Skopje
7 Yugoslavia (Serbia and Montenegro)	Belgrade
8 Lithuania	Vilnius
9 Latvia	Riga
10 Estonia	Tallinn

SCALE

0 250 500 750 Miles

0 250 500 750 Kilometers

Projection: Mollweide

Europe

ICELAND

Reykjavik

NORWAY

SWEDEN

FINLAND

60°N

Oslo

Helsinki

St. Petersburg

RUSSIA

NORTH SEA

Stockholm

10

9

UNITED KINGDOM

DENMARK

Copenhagen

8

Minsk

Moscow

Dublin

Amsterdam

Berlin

Warsaw

BELARUS

IRELAND

The Hague

NETHERLANDS

London

Brussels

GERMANY

POLAND

Kyyiv

50°N

BELGIUM

LUXEMBOURG

1

Vienna

2

UKRAINE

ATLANTIC OCEAN

Paris

Bern

AUSTRIA

Budapest

MOLDOVA

SWITZERLAND

LIECHTENSTEIN

3 4

HUNGARY

Chişinău

FRANCE

MONACO

SAN MARINO

5

7

ROMANIA

Bucharest

Corsica (Fr)

ITALY

BLACK SEA

Madrid

ANDORRA

VATICAN CITY

Rome

BULGARIA

Sofia

PORTUGAL

Balearic Is.(Sp)

Sardinia (It)

Tiranë

6

ALBANIA

40°N

SPAIN

Lisbon

Sicily

GREECE

Athens

Gibraltar (UK)

MALTA

Crete

MEDITERRANEAN SEA

19

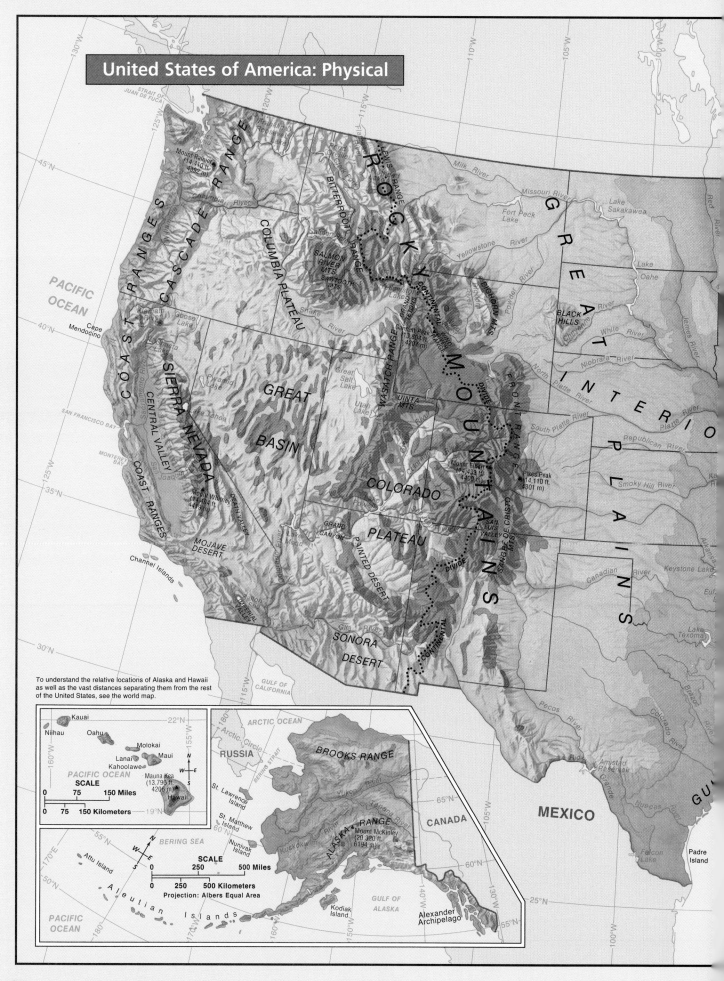

United States of America: Physical

STRAIT OF JUAN DE FUCA

PACIFIC OCEAN

Cape Mendocino

SAN FRANCISCO BAY

MONTEREY BAY

Channel Islands

COAST RANGES

CASCADE RANGE

COLUMBIA PLATEAU

SIERRA NEVADA

CENTRAL VALLEY

COAST RANGES

Mount Rainier (14,410 ft. 4392 m)

Mount Whitney (14,494 ft. 4419 m)

DEATH VALLEY

MOJAVE DESERT

IMPERIAL VALLEY

GREAT BASIN

Lake Tahoe

Pyramid Lake

Great Salt Lake

Utah Lake

Goose Lake

BITTERROOT RANGE

SALMON RIVER MTS.

SAWTOOTH MTS.

Snake River

R O C K Y

M O U N T A I N S

LEWIS RANGE

WASATCH RANGE

UINTA MTS.

Garnett Peak (13,804 ft. 4207 m)

CONTINENTAL DIVIDE

BIGHORN MTS.

FRONT RANGE

DIVIDE

Mount Elbert (14,433 ft. 4400 m)

Pikes Peak (14,110 ft. 4301 m)

SANGRE DE CRISTO MTS.

SAN LUIS VALLEY

COLORADO PLATEAU

GRAND CANYON

PAINTED DESERT

DIVIDE

CONTINENTAL DIVIDE

SONORA DESERT

Gila River

GULF OF CALIFORNIA

G R E A T

I N T E R I O R

P L A I N S

Milk River

Missouri River

Fort Peck Lake

Yellowstone River

Powder River

Cheyenne River

Lake Sakakawea

Lake Oahe

BLACK HILLS

White River

Niobrara River

North Platte River

South Platte River

Republican River

Platte River

Smoky Hill River

Keystone Lake

Arkansas River

Canadian River

Lake Texoma

Pecos River

Colorado River

Amistad Reservoir

Falcon Lake

Padre Island

Rio Grande

Brazos River

Nueces River

MEXICO

GULF

To understand the relative locations of Alaska and Hawaii as well as the vast distances separating them from the rest of the United States, see the world map.

Kauai

Niihau

Oahu

Molokai

Lanai

Kahoolawe

Maui

Mauna Kea (13,796 ft. 4206 m)

Hawaii

PACIFIC OCEAN

SCALE

0   75   150 Miles

0   75   150 Kilometers

ARCTIC OCEAN

Arctic Circle

RUSSIA

BERING STRAIT

St. Lawrence Island

St. Matthew Island

Nunivak Island

BROOKS RANGE

Yukon River

Kuskokwim River

Tanana River

ALASKA RANGE

Mount McKinley (20,320 ft. 6194 m)

CANADA

Kodiak Island

GULF OF ALASKA

Alexander Archipelago

BERING SEA

SCALE

0   250   500 Miles

0   250   500 Kilometers

Projection: Albers Equal Area

Attu Island

A l e u t i a n   I s l a n d s

PACIFIC OCEAN

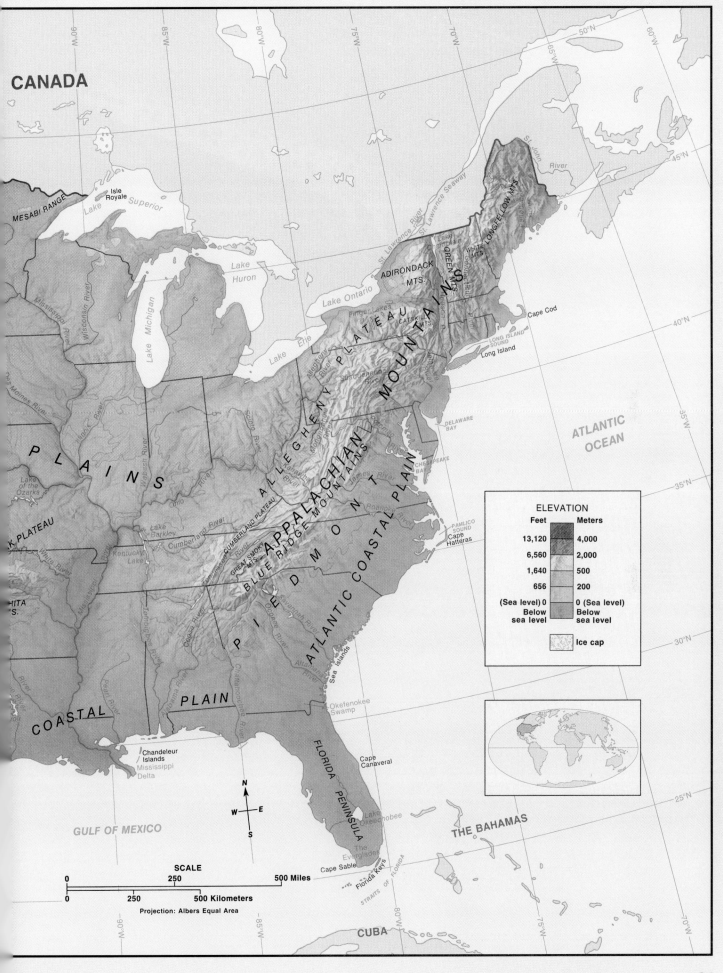

CANADA

MESABI RANGE

Isle Royale
Lake Superior

Lake Huron

Lake Michigan

P L A I N S

Des Moines River
Mississippi River
Wisconsin River
Illinois River
Lake of the Ozarks

K PLATEAU

HITA S.

Missouri River
White River
Mississippi River
Wabash River
Ohio River
Scioto River
Lake Barkley
Kentucky Lake
Cumberland River
Tennessee River

Lake Erie
Lake Ontario
Finger Lakes

ALLEGHENY PLATEAU

ADIRONDACK MTS.

Allegheny River
Susquehanna River
Monongahela River
Kanawha River

CUMBERLAND PLATEAU
GREAT SMOKY MTS.
BLUE RIDGE MOUNTAINS

A P P A L A C H I A N   M O U N T A I N S

GREEN MTS.
WHITE MTS.
LONGFELLOW MTS.
St. John River
St. Lawrence River
St. Lawrence Seaway
Lake Champlain
Hudson River
CATSKILL MTS.

Cape Cod
LONG ISLAND SOUND
Long Island

DELAWARE BAY

CHESAPEAKE BAY

James River
Roanoke River

P I E D M O N T

A T L A N T I C   C O A S T A L   P L A I N

PAMLICO SOUND
Cape Hatteras

ATLANTIC OCEAN

C O A S T A L   P L A I N

Pearl River
Mississippi Delta
Chandeleur Islands

Alabama River
Tombigbee River

Oconee River
Ocmulgee River
Altamaha River
Savannah River
Chattahoochee River

Sea Islands
Okefenokee Swamp

F L O R I D A   P E N I N S U L A

Cape Canaveral

Lake Okeechobee

The Everglades
Cape Sable
Florida Keys
STRAITS OF FLORIDA

GULF OF MEXICO

THE BAHAMAS

CUBA

ELEVATION

Feet		Meters
13,120		4,000
6,560		2,000
1,640		500
656		200
(Sea level) 0		0 (Sea level)
Below sea level		Below sea level

Ice cap

N
W   E
S

SCALE

0   250   500 Miles

0   250   500 Kilometers

Projection: Albers Equal Area

United States of America: Political

WASHINGTON

- Seattle
- Tacoma
- Olympia ★
- Spokane

STRAIT OF JUAN DE FUCA

PUGET SOUND

Franklin D. Roosevelt Lake

Pend Oreille

Flathead Lake

OREGON

- Portland
- Salem ★
- Eugene

Columbia River

PACIFIC OCEAN

Cape Mendocino

MONTANA
- Helena ★
- Billings

Fort Peck Lake

Missouri River

Yellowstone River

Yellowstone Lake

IDAHO
- Boise
- Pocatello

Snake River

NORTH DAKOTA
- ★ Bismarck
- Fargo

Lake Sakakawea

Red River

Lake Oahe

SOUTH DAKOTA
- ★ Pierre
- Sioux Falls

Mi

Shasta Lake

Goose Lake

Sacramento River

Pyramid Lake

NEVADA
- Reno
- Carson City ★
- Lake Tahoe

Great Salt Lake

Utah Lake

WYOMING
- Casper

- Salt Lake City ★
- Provo

UTAH

Green River

- Cheyenne ★

NEBRASKA

- Omah
- Lincoln

Platte River

CALIFORNIA

- Concord
- Berkeley
- Oakland
- San Francisco
- Hayward
- Sunnyvale
- Sacramento ★
- Stockton
- Modesto
- Fremont
- San Jose
- Fresno

SAN FRANCISCO BAY

MONTEREY BAY

San Joaquin River

- Bakersfield

- Lakewood
- Aurora
- Denver ★

- Colorado Springs

COLORADO

Lake Powell

KANSAS

- Topek
- Wichit

K

Arkansas River

- Las Vegas

Lake Mead

Colorado River

Salton Sea

- Oxnard
- Glendale
- Pasadena
- Los Angeles
- Pomona
- Inglewood
- San Bernardino
- Ontario
- Torrance
- Riverside
- Long Beach
- Fullerton
- Anaheim
- Santa Ana
- Garden Grove
- Huntington Beach
- San Diego

Channel Islands

ARIZONA

- Glendale
- Scottsdale
- Phoenix ★
- Mesa

- Tucson

Gila River

- Santa Fe ★
- Albuquerque

NEW MEXICO

- El Paso

- Amarillo

OKLAHOMA
- Oklahoma City ★

Canadian River

Keystone Lake

Eufa La

Le Te

- Lubbock

- Odessa

- Abilene

- Fort Worth
- Irving
- Arling

G
D.

TEXAS

Brazos River

Colorado River

- Waco

- Austin ★

Pecos River

GULF OF CALIFORNIA

Rio Grande

Amistad Reservoir

- San Antonio

- Hou
- Pas

MEXICO

- Laredo

- Corpus

Padre Island

To understand the relative locations of Alaska and Hawaii as well as the vast distances separating them from the rest of the United States, see the world map.

HAWAII
- Kauai
- Niihau
- Oahu
- Honolulu ★
- Molokai
- Lanai
- Maui
- Kahoolawe
- Hawaii

PACIFIC OCEAN

SCALE
0   75   150 Miles
0   75   150 Kilometers

22°N
19°N

ARCTIC OCEAN

Arctic Circle

RUSSIA

BERING STRAIT

- Nome

St. Lawrence Island

St. Matthew Island

Nunivak Island

- Fairbanks

Yukon River

ALASKA

- Anchorage

CANADA

65°N

60°N

GULF OF ALASKA

- Juneau ★

Kodiak Island

Alexander Archipelago

BERING SEA

- Attu Island

Aleutian Islands

PACIFIC OCEAN

SCALE
0   250   500 Miles
0   250   500 Kilometers
Projection: Albers Equal Area

55°N
50°N

25°N

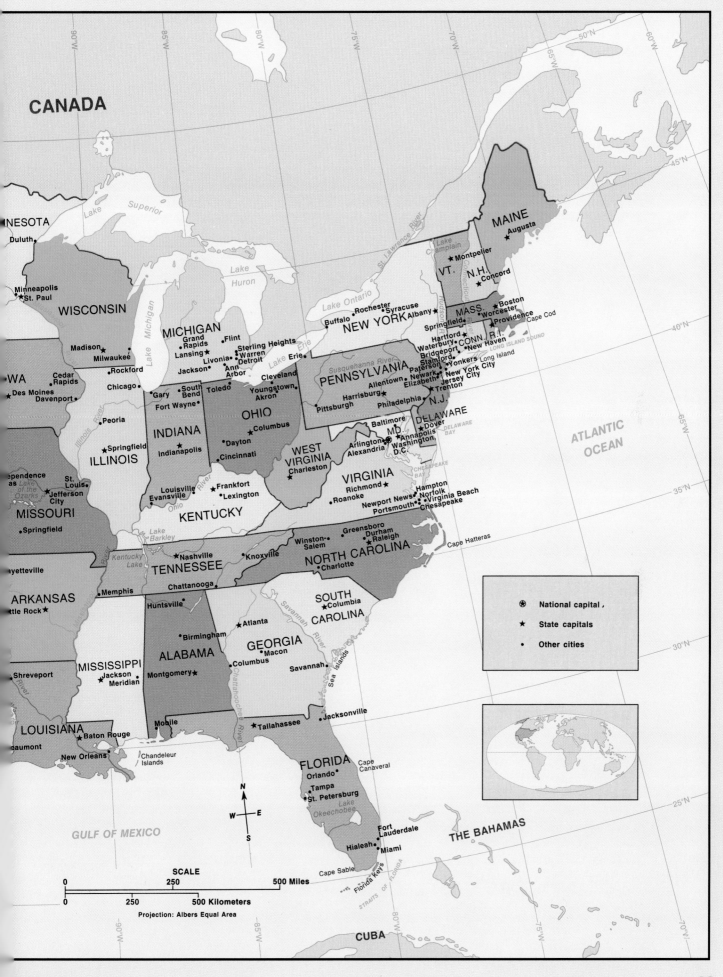

CANADA

NESOTA
• Duluth

WISCONSIN
• Minneapolis
★ St. Paul
• Madison ★
• Milwaukee
• Rockford

Lake Superior

Lake Michigan

Lake Huron

MICHIGAN
Grand Rapids • • Flint
Sterling Heights •
Lansing ★ • Warren
• Jackson • Livonia • Detroit
Ann Arbor

Lake Ontario
• Buffalo • Rochester • Syracuse
NEW YORK Albany ★
Springfield

Lake Erie

MAINE
Augusta ★
• Montpelier
VT. N.H.
• Concord
MASS. • Boston
• Worcester
Providence •
Hartford • Cape Cod
CONN. R.I.
Waterbury • New Haven
Bridgeport •
LONG ISLAND SOUND
Stamford •
Yonkers • Long Island
Paterson • New York City
Newark •
Jersey City •
Elizabeth •

WA
Cedar Rapids •
Des Moines ★
• Davenport

• Chicago
Gary • South Bend
Fort Wayne •
• Peoria

Toledo
Cleveland •
Youngstown •
Akron •

PENNSYLVANIA
Susquehanna River
Harrisburg ★
• Pittsburgh
Allentown •
Trenton ★
N.J.
Philadelphia •

DELAWARE
• Dover
DELAWARE BAY

INDIANA
★ Indianapolis
• Dayton

OHIO
• Columbus
• Cincinnati

ILLINOIS
★ Springfield

WEST VIRGINIA
Charleston ★

Baltimore •
MD.
Arlington • Annapolis ★
Alexandria • Washington, D.C.

ATLANTIC OCEAN

Independence
as
Lake of the Ozarks
★ St. Louis
Jefferson City ★
MISSOURI
• Springfield

Illinois River

Louisville •
Evansville •
Frankfort ★
Lexington •

Ohio River

KENTUCKY

VIRGINIA
Richmond ★
• Roanoke

Hampton •
Norfolk •
Newport News • Virginia Beach •
Portsmouth • Chesapeake •
CHESAPEAKE BAY

Lake Barkley
Kentucky Lake

ayetteville
ARKANSAS
ttle Rock ★

Missouri River

Kentucky River

★ Nashville
TENNESSEE
Chattanooga •
• Memphis

• Knoxville

Greensboro •
Winston-Salem • Durham •
Raleigh ★
NORTH CAROLINA
• Charlotte

Cape Hatteras

SOUTH CAROLINA
★ Columbia

Sea Islands

MISSISSIPPI
Jackson ★
• Meridian

• Huntsville

• Atlanta

• Birmingham
ALABAMA
Montgomery ★

GEORGIA
• Macon
• Columbus

Savannah River

• Savannah

LOUISIANA
★ Baton Rouge
eaumont
• New Orleans

Chandeleur Islands

• Mobile

Chattahoochee River

Tallahassee ★

• Jacksonville

• Shreveport

FLORIDA
• Orlando
Cape Canaveral

• Tampa
• St. Petersburg
Lake Okeechobee

GULF OF MEXICO

N
W E
S

Fort Lauderdale •
• Hialeah • Miami

Cape Sable
Florida Keys

THE BAHAMAS

STRAITS OF FLORIDA

CUBA

⊛ National capital
★ State capitals
• Other cities

SCALE
0   250   500 Miles
0   250   500 Kilometers
Projection: Albers Equal Area

23

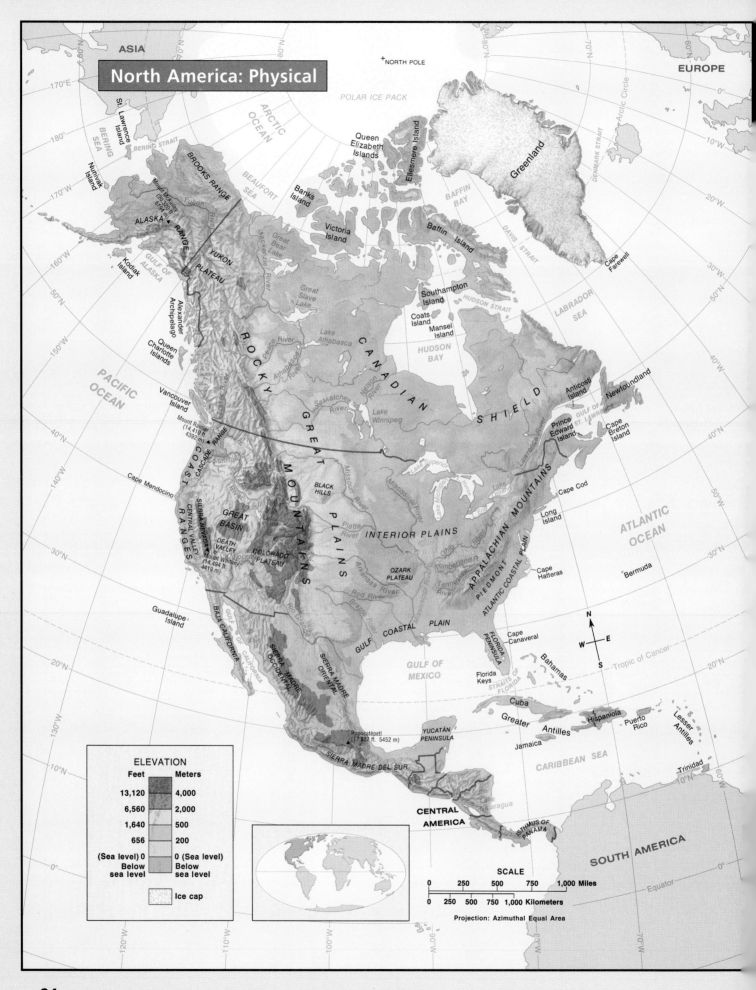

North America: Physical

ASIA

EUROPE

+NORTH POLE

POLAR ICE PACK

ARCTIC OCEAN

BERING STRAIT

BEAUFORT SEA

Queen Elizabeth Islands

Ellesmere Island

Greenland

St. Lawrence Island

BERING SEA

BROOKS RANGE

Banks Island

Victoria Island

Baffin Island

BAFFIN BAY

DENMARK STRAIT

Mount McKinley (20,320 ft. 6194 m)

ALASKA RANGE

Yukon River

YUKON PLATEAU

Great Bear Lake

DAVIS STRAIT

Cape Farewell

Nunivak Island

Mackenzie River

GULF OF ALASKA

Kodiak Island

Southampton Island

LABRADOR SEA

Alexander Archipelago

Great Slave Lake

HUDSON STRAIT

Coats Island

Mansel Island

PACIFIC OCEAN

Queen Charlotte Islands

Peace River

Athabasca River

Lake Athabasca

CANADIAN

HUDSON BAY

Anticosti Island

Newfoundland

Vancouver Island

Saskatchewan River

Nelson River

Lake Winnipeg

SHIELD

Prince Edward Island

GULF OF ST. LAWRENCE

Cape Breton Island

Mount Rainier (14,410 ft. 4392 m)

CASCADE RANGE

Columbia River

Missouri River

Lake Superior

St. Lawrence River

ROCKY

GREAT

Lake Michigan

Lake Huron

Cape Cod

Long Island

ATLANTIC OCEAN

Cape Mendocino

COAST RANGES

SIERRA NEVADA

CENTRAL VALLEY

GREAT BASIN

MOUNTAINS

PLAINS

BLACK HILLS

Snake River

Platte River

Lake Erie

Lake Ontario

APPALACHIAN MOUNTAINS

Ohio River

DEATH VALLEY

Mount Whitney (14,494 ft. 4419 m)

COLORADO PLATEAU

INTERIOR PLAINS

Arkansas River

OZARK PLATEAU

Mississippi River

Tennessee River

Cumberland R.

PIEDMONT

Cape Hatteras

Bermuda

Guadalupe Island

BAJA CALIFORNIA

GULF OF CALIFORNIA

Rio Grande

Red River

Brazos River

Mississippi River

ATLANTIC COASTAL PLAIN

FLORIDA PENINSULA

Cape Canaveral

SIERRA MADRE OCCIDENTAL

SIERRA MADRE ORIENTAL

GULF COASTAL PLAIN

GULF OF MEXICO

Florida Keys

STRAITS OF FLORIDA

Bahamas

Tropic of Cancer

Popocatépetl (17,887 ft. 5452 m)

YUCATÁN PENINSULA

Cuba

Greater Antilles

Jamaica

Hispaniola

Puerto Rico

Lesser Antilles

SIERRA MADRE DEL SUR

CARIBBEAN SEA

Trinidad

CENTRAL AMERICA

Lake Nicaragua

ISTHMUS OF PANAMA

SOUTH AMERICA

Equator

ELEVATION

Feet		Meters
13,120		4,000
6,560		2,000
1,640		500
656		200
(Sea level) 0		0 (Sea level)
Below sea level		Below sea level
	Ice cap	

SCALE

0   250   500   750   1,000 Miles

0   250   500   750   1,000 Kilometers

Projection: Azimuthal Equal Area

N W E S

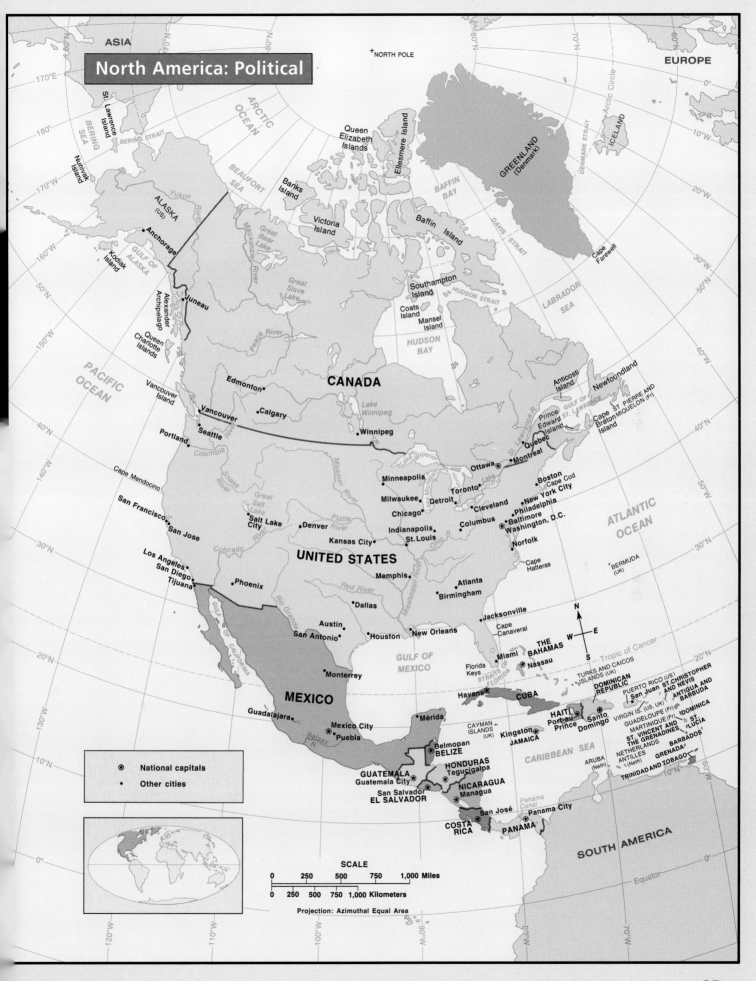

North America: Political

ASIA

EUROPE

+ NORTH POLE

ARCTIC OCEAN

Greenland
(Denmark)

ICELAND

St. Lawrence Island

BERING SEA

BERING STRAIT

Nunivak Island

BEAUFORT SEA

Banks Island

Queen Elizabeth Islands

Ellesmere Island

BAFFIN BAY

DENMARK STRAIT

ALASKA (US)

Yukon River

Victoria Island

Baffin Island

DAVIS STRAIT

Cape Farewell

Anchorage

Kodiak Island

GULF OF ALASKA

Mackenzie River

Great Bear Lake

Southampton Island

HUDSON STRAIT

LABRADOR SEA

Alexander Archipelago

Juneau

Great Slave Lake

Coats Island

Mansel Island

Peace River

CANADA

HUDSON BAY

Queen Charlotte Islands

Edmonton

Anticosti Island

Newfoundland

Cape Breton Island

ST. PIERRE AND MIQUELON (Fr)

Vancouver Island

Vancouver

Calgary

Lake Winnipeg

Prince Edward Island

GULF OF ST. LAWRENCE

Portland

Seattle

Winnipeg

St. Lawrence R.

Quebec

Columbia River

Snake River

Lake Superior

Ottawa ⊛

Montreal

Cape Mendocino

Minneapolis

Toronto

Lake Huron

Lake Ontario

Boston

Cape Cod

ATLANTIC OCEAN

San Francisco

Great Salt Lake

Salt Lake City

Milwaukee

Chicago

Detroit

Lake Erie

Cleveland

New York City

Philadelphia

San Jose

Platte River

Denver

Indianapolis

Columbus

Baltimore

Washington, D.C. ⊛

Colorado

Kansas City

St. Louis

Ohio R.

Norfolk

Los Angeles

UNITED STATES

Memphis

Cape Hatteras

BERMUDA (UK)

San Diego

Tijuana

Phoenix

Red River

Atlanta

Birmingham

Dallas

GULF OF CALIFORNIA

Austin

San Antonio

Rio Grande

Houston

New Orleans

Jacksonville

Cape Canaveral

N

Miami

THE BAHAMAS

W E

S

Phoenix

Monterrey

GULF OF MEXICO

Florida Keys

STRAITS OF FLORIDA

Nassau

Tropic of Cancer

Guadalajara

MEXICO

Mérida

Havana ⊛

CUBA

TURKS AND CAICOS ISLANDS (UK)

DOMINICAN REPUBLIC

PUERTO RICO (US)

San Juan

ST. CHRISTOPHER AND NEVIS

ANTIGUA AND BARBUDA

Mexico City ⊛

Puebla

CAYMAN ISLANDS (UK)

Kingston

JAMAICA

HAITI

Port-au-Prince

Santo Domingo

VIRGIN IS. (US, UK)

GUADELOUPE (Fr)

DOMINICA

MARTINIQUE (Fr)

ST. LUCIA

Balsas

Belmopan

BELIZE

CARIBBEAN SEA

ST. VINCENT AND THE GRENADINES

NETHERLANDS ANTILLES (Neth)

BARBADOS

GRENADA

GUATEMALA

Guatemala City ⊛

HONDURAS

Tegucigalpa

ARUBA (Neth)

TRINIDAD AND TOBAGO

San Salvador ⊛

EL SALVADOR

NICARAGUA

Managua ⊛

Panama Canal

COSTA RICA

San José ⊛

Panama City ⊛

PANAMA

SOUTH AMERICA

Equator

⊛ National capitals

• Other cities

SCALE

0 250 500 750 1,000 Miles

0 250 500 750 1,000 Kilometers

Projection: Azimuthal Equal Area

South America: Physical

CENTRAL AMERICA

CARIBBEAN SEA

Panama Canal

GULF OF PANAMA

Malpelo Island

Galápagos Islands

Margarita Island

Tobago

Trinidad

Orinoco River Delta

Angel Falls

Devil's Island

Cape Orange

Amazon River Delta

ATLANTIC OCEAN

LLANOS

GUIANA HIGHLANDS

Meta River

Orinoco River

AMAZON BASIN

Mount Tolima (18,425 ft. 5616 m)

Mount Chimborazo (20,561 ft. 6267 m)

0° Equator

Equator 0°

GULF OF GUAYAQUIL

Japura River

Negro River

Amazon River

Caqueta River

Putumayo River

Amazon River

Ucayali River

Juruá River

Purus River

Madeira River

Tocantins River

Xingu River

Tapajós River

Mount Huascarán (22,205 ft. 6768 m)

BRAZILIAN HIGHLANDS

10°S

MATO GROSSO PLATEAU

Ancohuma Peak (20,958 ft. 6388 m)

PACIFIC OCEAN

BRAZILIAN PLATEAU

CHACO

São Francisco River

Paraguay River

Salado River

20°S

ATACAMA DESERT

Tropic of Capricorn

Tropic of Capricorn

San Ambrosio Island

San Félix Island

ANDES MOUNTAINS

Pilcomayo River

Paraná River

Uruguay River

Paraguay River

Mount Aconcagua (22,834 ft. 6960 m)

Juan Fernández Islands

30°S

PAMPAS

Salado River

RÍO DE LA PLATA

ATLANTIC OCEAN

Chiloé Island

Chonos Archipelago

GULF OF SAN MATÍAS

PATAGONIA

ELEVATION

Feet		Meters
13,120		4,000
6,560		2,000
1,640		500
656		200
(Sea level) 0		0 (Sea level)
Below sea level		Below sea level

GULF OF SAN JORGE

Cape Tres Puntas

BAHÍA GRANDE

STRAIT OF MAGELLAN

Falkland Islands

South Georgia Islands

SCALE

0   250   500   750   1,000 Miles

0   250   500   750   1,000 Kilometers

Projection: Azimuthal Equal Area

Tierra del Fuego

Cape Horn

N
W   E
S

South America: Political

CENTRAL AMERICA

CARIBBEAN SEA

Barranquilla
Cartagena
Lake Maracaibo

⊛ Caracas

VENEZUELA

Orinoco River

Medellín

⊛ Georgetown

GUYANA

⊛ Paramaribo

Cayenne

SURINAME

FRENCH GUIANA (Fr)

⊛ Bogotá
• Cali

COLOMBIA

Malpelo Island (Colombia)

Río Negro

Amazon River

ATLANTIC OCEAN

Galápagos Islands (Ecuador)

0° Equator

⊛ Quito

ECUADOR

Amazon River

• Belém

Equator 0°

Guayaquil

Trujillo •

PERU

Ucayali River

BRAZIL

Recife •

São Francisco River

Callao ⊛ Lima

10°S

Salvador •

BOLIVIA

Lake Titicaca

Arequipa •

⊛ La Paz

⊛ Brasília

Lake Poopó

⊛ Sucre

Belo Horizonte •

San Ambrosio Island (Chile)

PARAGUAY

Campinas •
São Paulo •

Rio de Janeiro •

Tropic of Capricorn

San Félix Island (Chile)

⊛ Asunción

Curitiba •

Paraná River

N

Juan Fernández Islands (Chile)

Uruguay River

W   E

S

Pôrto Alegre •

Córdoba •

URUGUAY

30°S

Rosario •

Valparaíso •
Santiago ⊛

Buenos Aires
Morón ⊛
San Justo
Lomas de Zamora

⊛ Montevideo

RÍO DE LA PLATA

ATLANTIC OCEAN

PACIFIC OCEAN

CHILE

ARGENTINA

⊛ National capitals

• Other cities

FALKLAND ISLANDS (UK)

SCALE

0   250   500   750   1,000 Miles

0   250   500   750   1,000 Kilometers

Projection: Azimuthal Equal Area

STRAIT OF MAGELLAN

Tierra del Fuego

SOUTH GEORGIA ISLAND (UK)

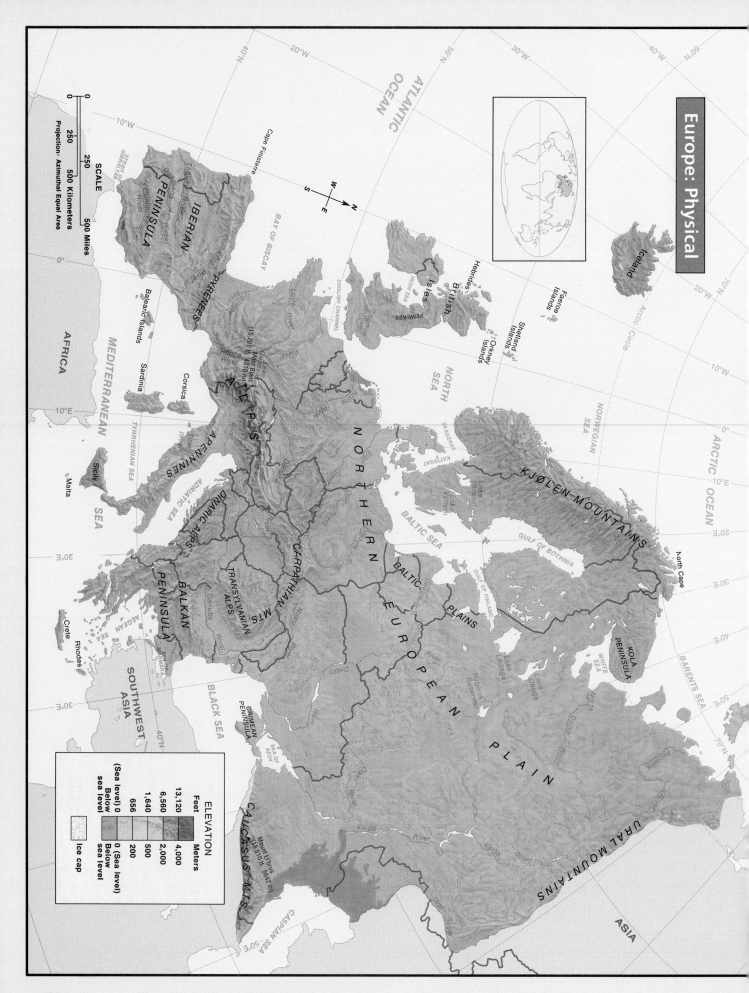

Europe: Physical

SCALE

0
250   500 Kilometers
0
250   500 Miles

Projection: Azimuthal Equal Area

ELEVATION

Feet	Meters
13,120	4,000
6,560	2,000
1,640	500
656	200
0 (Sea level)	0 (Sea level)
Below sea level	Below sea level

Ice cap

ATLANTIC OCEAN

AFRICA

MEDITERRANEAN SEA

IBERIAN PENINSULA

Cape Finisterre

BAY OF BISCAY

PYRENEES

Tagus River

Guadiana River

Ebro River

Guadalquivir River

STRAIT OF GIBRALTAR

Balearic Islands

Sardinia

Corsica

Sicily

Malta

TYRRHENIAN SEA

ADRIATIC SEA

ALPS

APENNINES

Mont Blanc (15,781 ft; 4810 m)

Rhône River

Loire River

Seine River

Rhine River

ENGLISH CHANNEL

British Isles

Hebrides

Thames River

IRISH SEA

PENNINES

Orkney Islands

Shetland Islands

Faeroe Islands

Iceland

NORTH SEA

NORWEGIAN SEA

Arctic Circle

ARCTIC OCEAN

North Cape

KJØLEN MOUNTAINS

KOLA PENINSULA

WHITE SEA

BARENTS SEA

ASIA

URAL MOUNTAINS

Pechora River

Kama River

Ural River

Volga River

Don River

Dnieper River

CAUCASUS MTS.

Mount Elbrus (18,510 ft; 5642 m)

CASPIAN SEA

BLACK SEA

SEA OF AZOV

CRIMEAN PENINSULA

SOUTHWEST ASIA

AEGEAN SEA

Crete

Rhodes

BALKAN PENINSULA

DINARIC ALPS

TRANSYLVANIAN ALPS

CARPATHIAN MTS.

Danube River

Elbe River

Oder River

Vistula River

BALTIC SEA

BALTIC PLAINS

GULF OF BOTHNIA

GULF OF FINLAND

Lake Vänern

Lake Vättern

Lake Ladoga

Lake Onega

Rybinsk Reservoir

SKAGERRAK

KATTEGAT

NORTHERN EUROPEAN PLAIN

Dvina River

Volga River

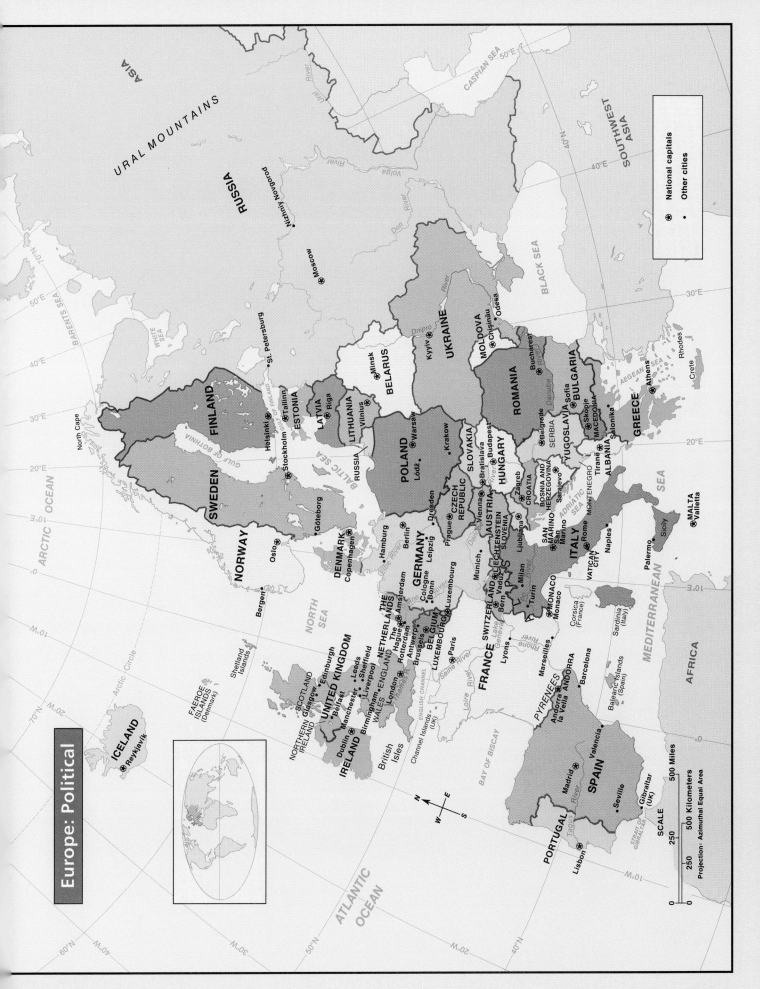

Europe: Political

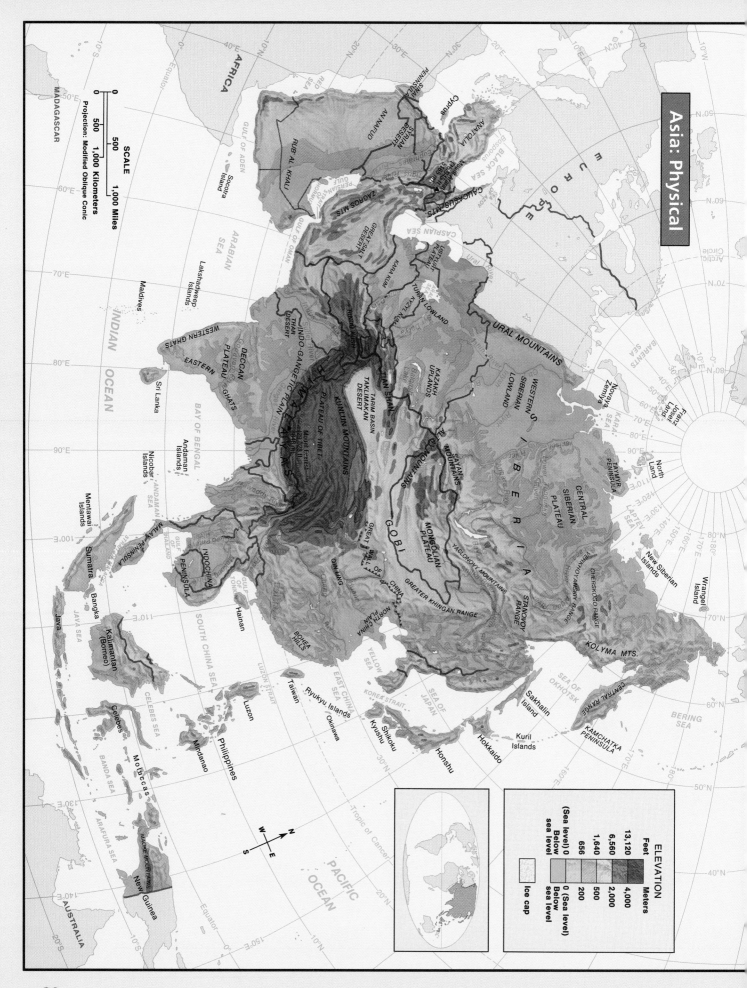

Asia: Physical

SCALE

0   500   1,000 Kilometers
0   500   1,000 Miles

Projection: Modified Oblique Conic

ELEVATION

Feet	Meters
13,120	4,000
6,560	2,000
1,640	500
656	200
0 (Sea level)	0 (Sea level)
Below sea level	Below sea level

Ice cap

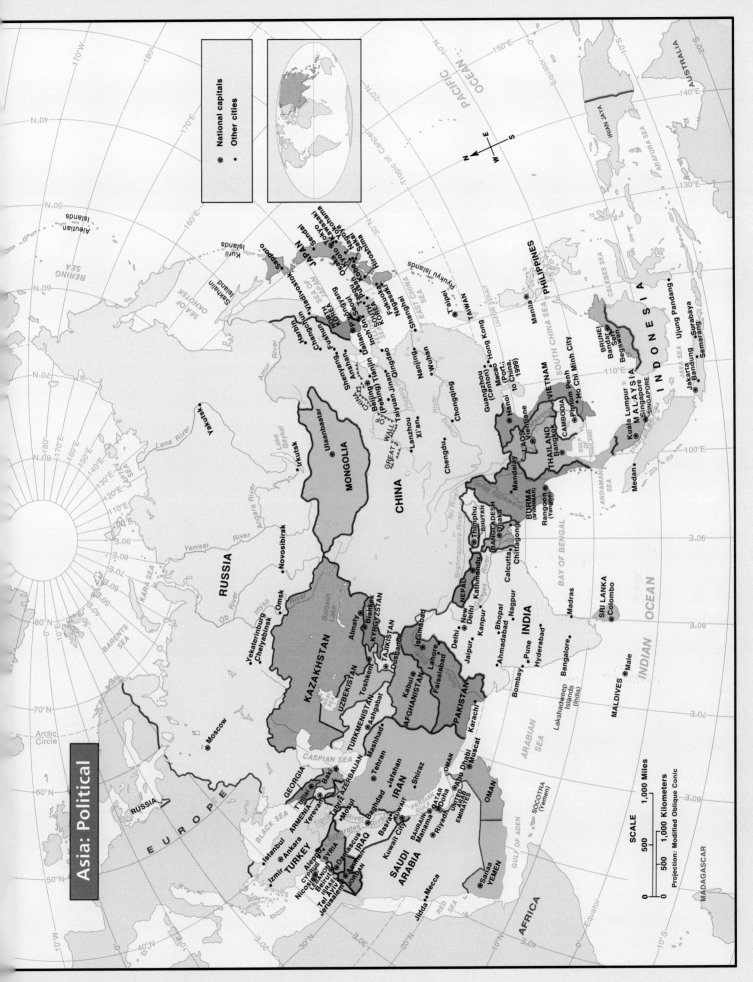

Asia: Political

National capitals ⊛
Other cities •

SCALE
1,000 Miles
1,000 Kilometers
500
0
500
Projection: Modified Oblique Conic

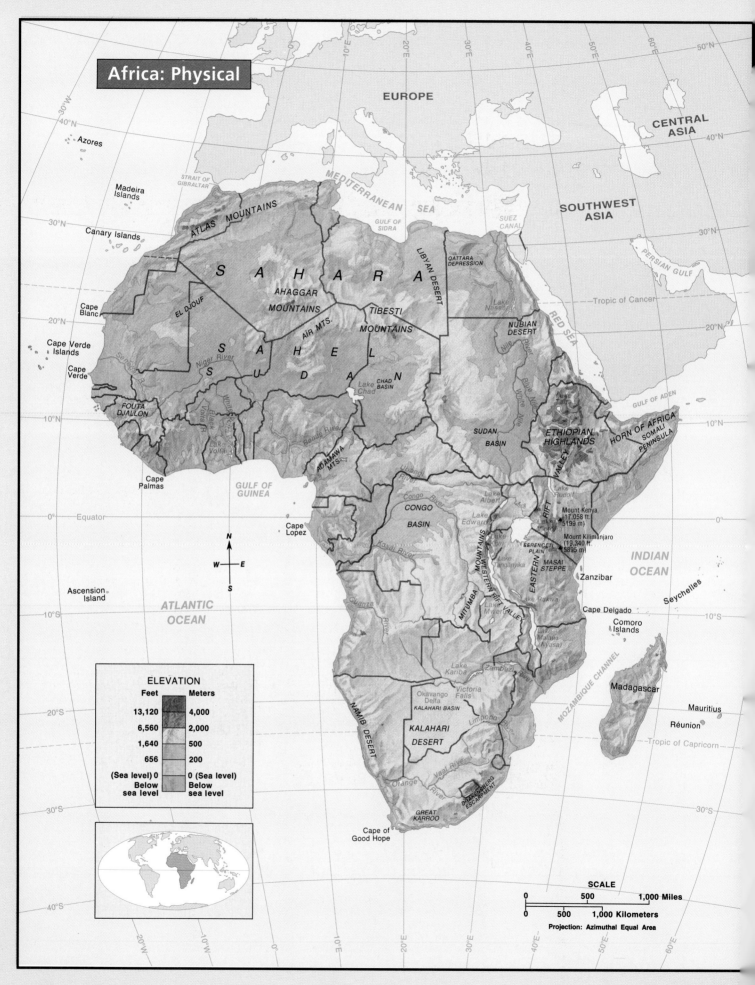

Africa: Physical

EUROPE

CENTRAL ASIA

SOUTHWEST ASIA

Azores

Madeira Islands

Canary Islands

MEDITERRANEAN SEA

STRAIT OF GIBRALTAR

GULF OF SIDRA

SUEZ CANAL

PERSIAN GULF

Tropic of Cancer

ATLAS MOUNTAINS

Cape Blanc

S A H A R A

AHAGGAR MOUNTAINS

TIBESTI MOUNTAINS

LIBYAN DESERT

QATTARA DEPRESSION

Lake Nasser

RED SEA

NUBIAN DESERT

EL DJOUF

AIR MTS.

S A H E L

SUDAN

Nile River

Cape Verde Islands

Cape Verde

Niger River

FOUTA DJALLON

White Volta

Black Volta

Benue River

Lake Chad

CHAD BASIN

Blue Nile

White Nile

GULF OF ADEN

Cape Palmas

GULF OF GUINEA

ADAMAWA MTS.

SUDAN BASIN

ETHIOPIAN HIGHLANDS

HORN OF AFRICA

SOMALI PENINSULA

Cape Lopez

CONGO BASIN

Ubangi River

Congo River

Lake Albert

Lake Edward

Lake Rudolf

Mount Kenya (17,058 ft. 5199 m)

Equator

Kasai River

RIFT VALLEY

Mount Kilimanjaro (19,340 ft. 5895 m)

SERENGETI PLAIN

Lake Kivu

Lake Victoria

INDIAN OCEAN

Ascension Island

ATLANTIC OCEAN

Cuanza

MITUMBA MOUNTAINS

WESTERN RIFT VALLEY

Lake Tanganyika

EASTERN RIFT VALLEY

MASAI STEPPE

Zanzibar

Cape Delgado

Seychelles

Comoro Islands

Lake Mweru

Lake Rukwa

Lake Malawi (Nyasa)

MOZAMBIQUE CHANNEL

Madagascar

NAMIB DESERT

Okavango Delta

KALAHARI BASIN

Victoria Falls

Lake Kariba

Zambezi River

Limpopo River

Mauritius

Réunion

Tropic of Capricorn

KALAHARI DESERT

Orange River

Vaal River

GREAT KARROO

DRAKENSBERG ESCARPMENT

Cape of Good Hope

ELEVATION

Feet		Meters
13,120		4,000
6,560		2,000
1,640		500
656		200
(Sea level) 0		0 (Sea level)
Below sea level		Below sea level

N
W E
S

SCALE

0   500   1,000 Miles

0   500   1,000 Kilometers

Projection: Azimuthal Equal Area

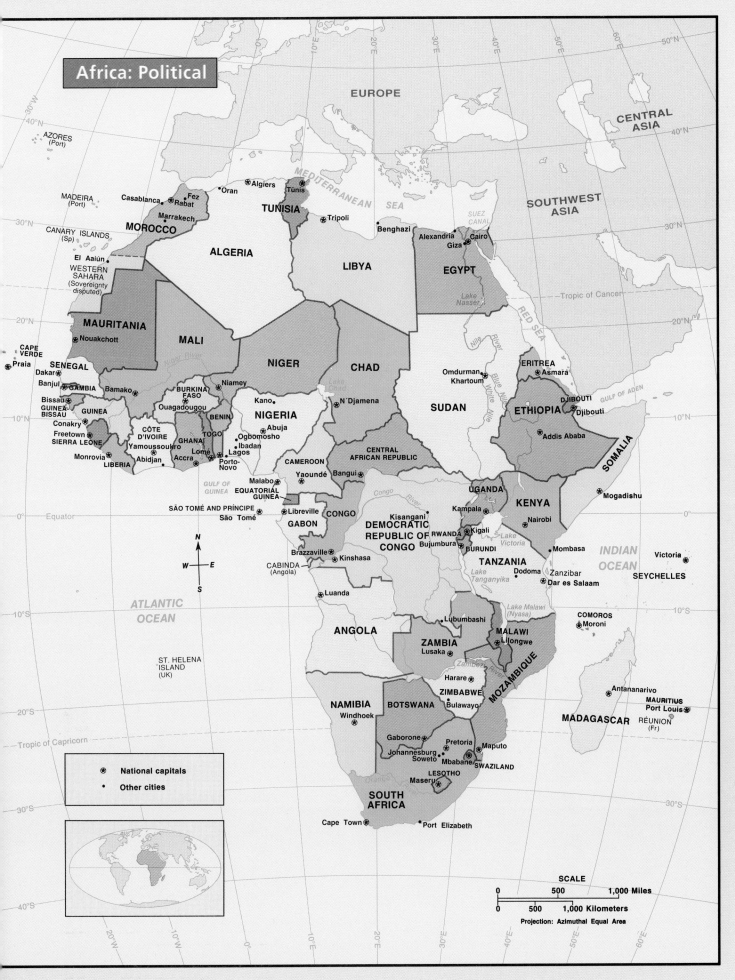

Africa: Political

EUROPE

CENTRAL ASIA

SOUTHWEST ASIA

AZORES (Port)

MADEIRA (Port)

CANARY ISLANDS (Sp)

MEDITERRANEAN SEA

⊛ Algiers
•Oran
•Tünis
TUNISIA
⊛ Tripoli
Benghazi
Alexandria ⊛ Cairo
Giza
SUEZ CANAL

Casablanca •Fez
•Rabat
Marrakech
MOROCCO

ALGERIA

LIBYA

EGYPT

Tropic of Cancer

El Aaiún •
WESTERN SAHARA (Sovereignty disputed)

Lake Nasser

CAPE VERDE
⊛ Praia

MAURITANIA
⊛ Nouakchott

MALI

NIGER

CHAD

RED SEA

Nile River

ERITREA
⊛ Asmara

SENEGAL
Dakar •
Banjul •
⊛ GAMBIA
Bissau ⊛
GUINEA-BISSAU
GUINEA
Conakry ⊛
Freetown ⊛
SIERRA LEONE
Monrovia ⊛
LIBERIA

Bamako ⊛

BURKINA FASO
Ouagadougou ⊛
BENIN
CÔTE D'IVOIRE GHANA TOGO
Yamoussoukro
Abidjan • Accra ⊛ Lomé
Porto-Novo

Niamey ⊛
Kano •
NIGERIA
⊛ Abuja
Ogbomosho •
•Ibadan
•Lagos

N'Djamena ⊛

Omdurman •
Khartoum ⊛

Blue Nile
White Nile

DJIBOUTI
⊛ DJIBOUTI
Djibouti •
GULF OF ADEN

SUDAN

ETHIOPIA
Addis Ababa ⊛

SOMALIA

CAMEROON
Yaoundé ⊛

CENTRAL AFRICAN REPUBLIC
Bangui ⊛

GULF OF GUINEA
Malabo ⊛
EQUATORIAL GUINEA

SÃO TOMÉ AND PRÍNCIPE
São Tomé •

Equator

Libreville ⊛
CONGO
GABON

Congo River

Brazzaville ⊛
Kinshasa ⊛
CABINDA (Angola)

DEMOCRATIC REPUBLIC OF CONGO
Kisangani •

UGANDA
Kampala ⊛
RWANDA ⊛ Kigali
Bujumbura ⊛ BURUNDI
Lake Victoria

KENYA
Nairobi ⊛
Mombasa •

Mogadishu ⊛

INDIAN OCEAN

SEYCHELLES
Victoria ⊛

TANZANIA
Dodoma ⊛ •Zanzibar
Dar es Salaam ⊛
Lake Tanganyika

N
W E
S

Luanda ⊛

ATLANTIC OCEAN

ST. HELENA ISLAND (UK)

ANGOLA

Lubumbashi •

Lake Malawi (Nyasa)

COMOROS
⊛ Moroni

ZAMBIA
Lusaka ⊛

MALAWI
Lilongwe ⊛

Zambezi River

Antananarivo ⊛

MAURITIUS
Port Louis ⊛

Tropic of Capricorn

Harare ⊛
ZIMBABWE
Bulawayo •

MOZAMBIQUE

MADAGASCAR

RÉUNION (Fr)

NAMIBIA
Windhoek ⊛

BOTSWANA

Gaborone ⊛
Johannesburg • Pretoria ⊛
Soweto • Maputo ⊛
Mbabane ⊛ SWAZILAND

Orange River

LESOTHO
Maseru ⊛

SOUTH AFRICA

Cape Town ⊛

•Port Elizabeth

⊛ National capitals
• Other cities

SCALE
0   500   1,000 Miles
0   500   1,000 Kilometers
Projection: Azimuthal Equal Area

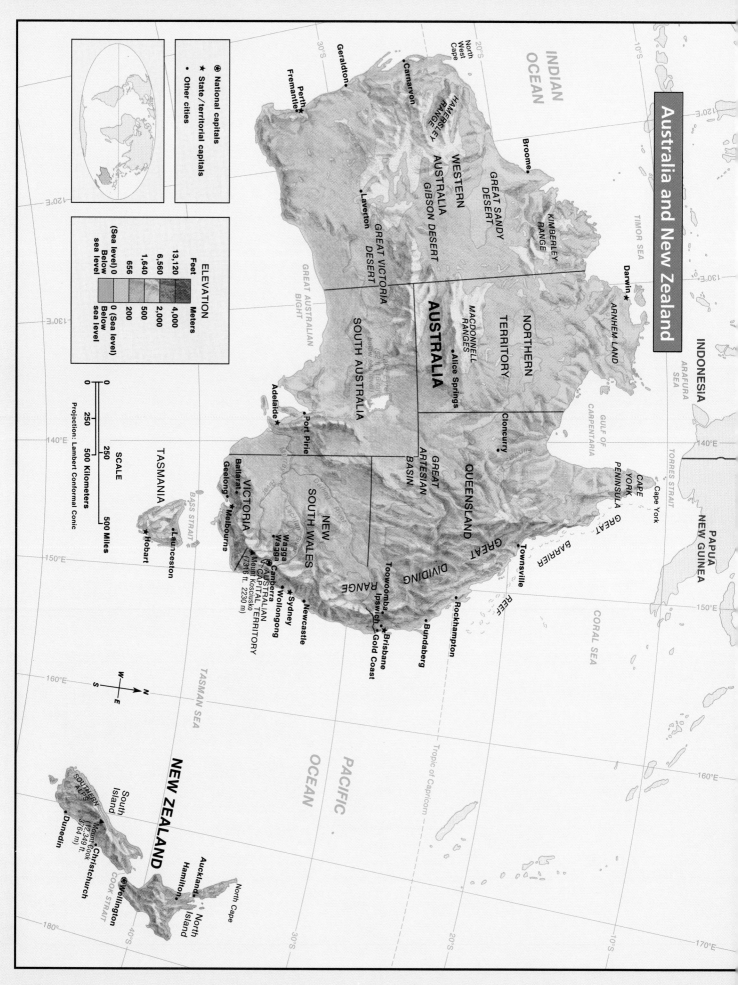

Australia and New Zealand

INDIAN OCEAN

INDONESIA

ARAFURA SEA

TIMOR SEA

PAPUA NEW GUINEA

TORRES STRAIT

GULF OF CARPENTARIA

Cape York

Torres Strait

CAPE YORK PENINSULA

CORAL SEA

North West Cape

Geraldton

Perth ★
Fremantle

Broome

HAMERSLEY RANGE

Carnarvon

WESTERN AUSTRALIA

GREAT SANDY DESERT

KIMBERLEY RANGE

Darwin ★

ARNHEM LAND

NORTHERN TERRITORY

MACDONNELL RANGES

Alice Springs

Cloncurry

QUEENSLAND

GREAT DIVIDING RANGE

GREAT BARRIER REEF

Townsville

Rockhampton

Bundaberg

Toowoomba

Ipswich Brisbane

Gold Coast

GIBSON DESERT

GREAT VICTORIA DESERT

Laverton

SOUTH AUSTRALIA

AUSTRALIA

GREAT ARTESIAN BASIN

GREAT AUSTRALIAN BIGHT

Adelaide ★

Port Pirie

NEW SOUTH WALES

Wagga Wagga

Canberra ✪ AUSTRALIAN CAPITAL TERRITORY

Mount Kosciusko (7316 ft. 2230 m)

Newcastle

Sydney

Wollongong

VICTORIA

Ballarat
Geelong ● Melbourne ★

BASS STRAIT

TASMANIA

Launceston

Hobart ★

TASMAN SEA

PACIFIC OCEAN

Tropic of Capricorn

NEW ZEALAND

North Cape

Auckland
Hamilton North Island

South Island

SOUTHERN ALPS

Mount Cook (12,349 ft. 3764 m)

Christchurch

Wellington ✪

COOK STRAIT

Dunedin

ELEVATION

Feet	Meters
13,120	4,000
6,560	2,000
1,640	500
656	200
0 (Sea level)	0 (Sea level)
Below sea level	Below sea level

⊛ National capitals
★ State/territorial capitals
• Other cities

SCALE

0 250 500 Kilometers

0 250 500 Miles

Projection: Lambert Conformal Conic

N
W E
S

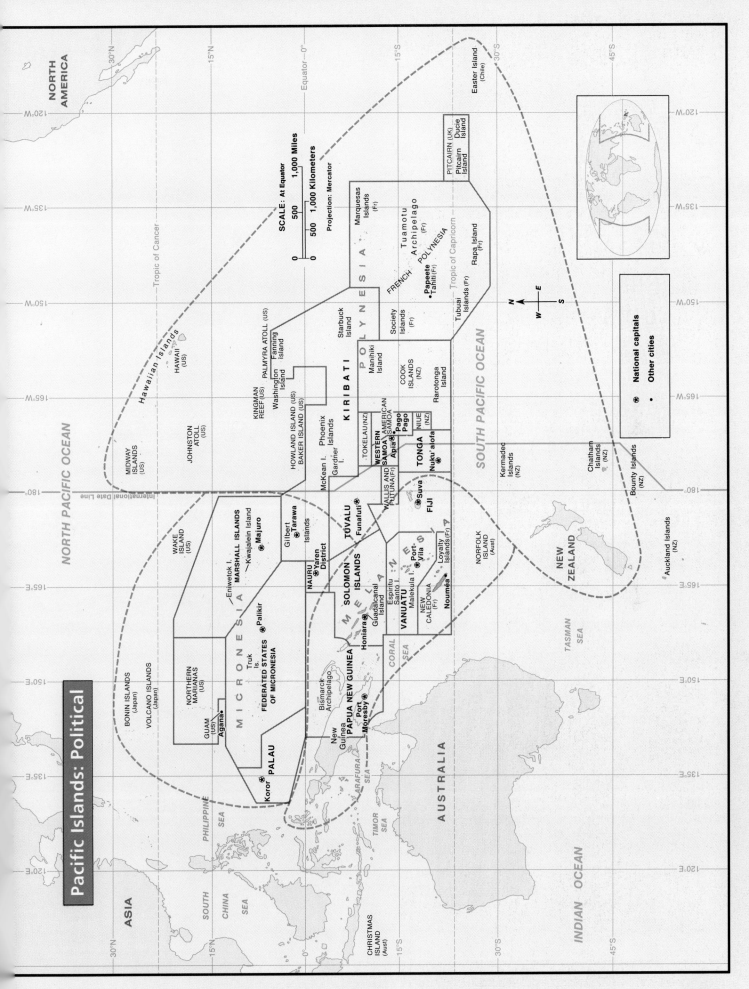

Pacific Islands: Political

SCALE: At Equator

Projection: Mercator

1,000 Miles
500

1,000 Kilometers
500
0

National capitals ⊛
Other cities •

NORTH AMERICA

ASIA

NORTH PACIFIC OCEAN

SOUTH PACIFIC OCEAN

PHILIPPINE SEA

SOUTH CHINA SEA

CORAL SEA

TASMAN SEA

ARAFURA SEA

TIMOR SEA

INDIAN OCEAN

AUSTRALIA

NEW ZEALAND

International Date Line

Tropic of Cancer

Equator—0°

Tropic of Capricorn

MICRONESIA

MELANESIA

POLYNESIA

KIRIBATI

BONIN ISLANDS (Japan)
VOLCANO ISLANDS (Japan)
NORTHERN MARIANAS (US)
GUAM (US) • Agana
PALAU • Koror ⊛
Truk Is.
FEDERATED STATES OF MICRONESIA ⊛ Palikir
Eniwetok I.
MARSHALL ISLANDS
Kwajalein Island
⊛ Majuro
WAKE ISLAND (US)
Gilbert Islands
⊛ Tarawa
NAURU ⊛ Yaren District
SOLOMON ISLANDS ⊛ Honiara
Guadalcanal Island
PAPUA NEW GUINEA ⊛ Port Moresby
New Guinea
Bismarck Archipelago
TUVALU ⊛ Funafuti
VANUATU
Espiritu Santo I.
Malekula I.
Port-Vila ⊛
NEW CALEDONIA (Fr)
Loyalty Islands (Fr)
Nouméa
WALLIS AND FUTUNA (Fr)
FIJI ⊛ Suva
TOKELAU (NZ)
WESTERN SAMOA ⊛ Apia
AMERICAN SAMOA
Pago Pago
NIUE (NZ)
TONGA ⊛ Nuku'alofa
COOK ISLANDS (NZ)
Rarotonga Island
Manihiki Island
Society Islands (Fr)
FRENCH POLYNESIA
Papeete • Tahiti (Fr)
Tubuai Islands (Fr)
Rapa Island (Fr)
Tuamotu Archipelago (Fr)
Marquesas Islands (Fr)
PITCAIRN (UK)
Pitcairn Island
Ducie Island
Easter Island (Chile)
Starbuck Island
Fanning Island
Washington Island
KINGMAN REEF (US)
PALMYRA ATOLL (US)
Phoenix Islands
McKean I.
Gardner Islands
HOWLAND ISLAND (US)
BAKER ISLAND (US)
JOHNSTON ATOLL (US)
MIDWAY ISLANDS (US)
Hawaiian Islands
HAWAII (US)
CHRISTMAS ISLAND (Aust)
NORFOLK ISLAND (Aust)
Kermadec Islands (NZ)
Chatham Islands (NZ)
Bounty Islands (NZ)
Auckland Islands (NZ)

30°N
15°N
15°S
30°S
45°S
120°W
135°W
150°W
165°W
180°
165°E
150°E
135°E
120°E

N W E S

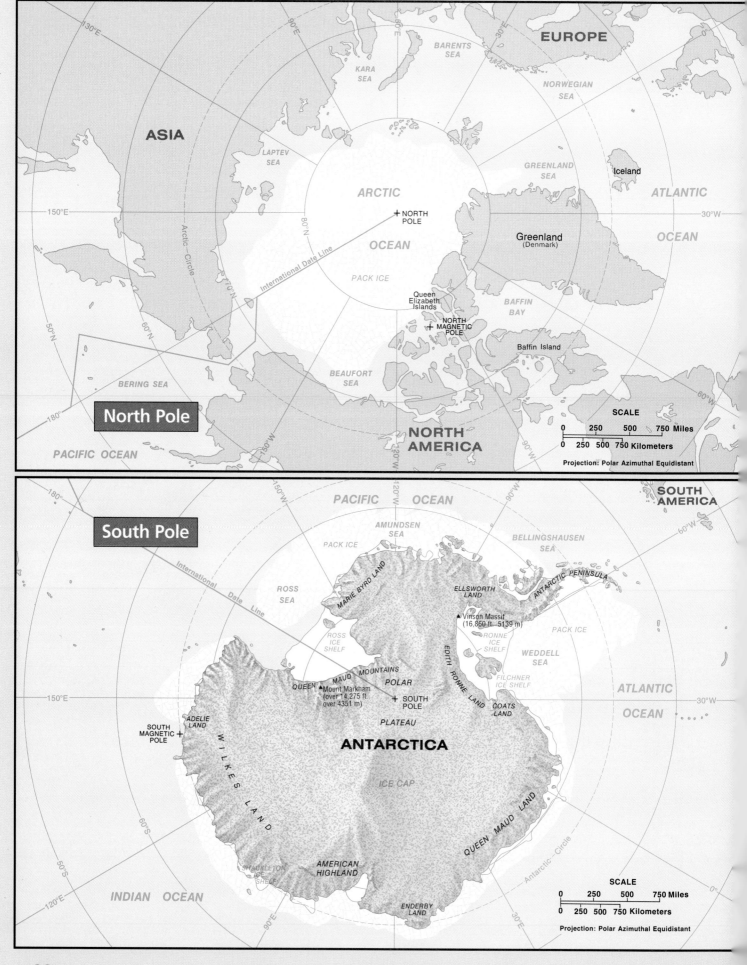

North Pole

ASIA

130°E

150°E

180°

PACIFIC OCEAN

BERING SEA

50°N

60°N

70°N

80°N

90°E

60°E

30°E

0
m

LAPTEV SEA

KARA SEA

BARENTS SEA

EUROPE

NORWEGIAN SEA

GREENLAND SEA

Iceland

ATLANTIC

30°W

OCEAN

Greenland (Denmark)

ARCTIC

+ NORTH POLE

OCEAN

Arctic Circle

International Date Line

PACK ICE

Queen Elizabeth Islands

+ NORTH MAGNETIC POLE

BAFFIN BAY

Baffin Island

60°W

BEAUFORT SEA

150°W

90°W

NORTH AMERICA

SCALE

0   250   500   750 Miles

0   250 500 750 Kilometers

Projection: Polar Azimuthal Equidistant

South Pole

180°

150°W

120°W

90°W

PACIFIC   OCEAN

SOUTH AMERICA

60°W

AMUNDSEN SEA

BELLINGSHAUSEN SEA

PACK ICE

ANTARCTIC PENINSULA

ROSS SEA

MARIE BYRD LAND

ELLSWORTH LAND

▲ Vinson Massif (16,860 ft. 5139 m)

RONNE ICE SHELF

PACK ICE

WEDDELL SEA

ROSS ICE SHELF

International Date Line

QUEEN MAUD MOUNTAINS

POLAR

EDITH RONNE LAND

FILCHNER ICE SHELF

ATLANTIC

30°W

150°E

QUEEN ▲ Mount Markham (over 14,275 ft. over 4351 m)

+ SOUTH POLE

COATS LAND

OCEAN

PLATEAU

SOUTH MAGNETIC POLE +

ADELIE LAND

ANTARCTICA

W I L K E S   L A N D

ICE CAP

60°S

QUEEN MAUD LAND

Antarctic Circle

0°

SHACKLETON ICE SHELF

AMERICAN HIGHLAND

ENDERBY LAND

30°E

INDIAN OCEAN

120°E

90°E

60°E

SCALE

0   250   500   750 Miles

0   250 500 750 Kilometers

Projection: Polar Azimuthal Equidistant

WORLD GEOGRAPHY

World Religions

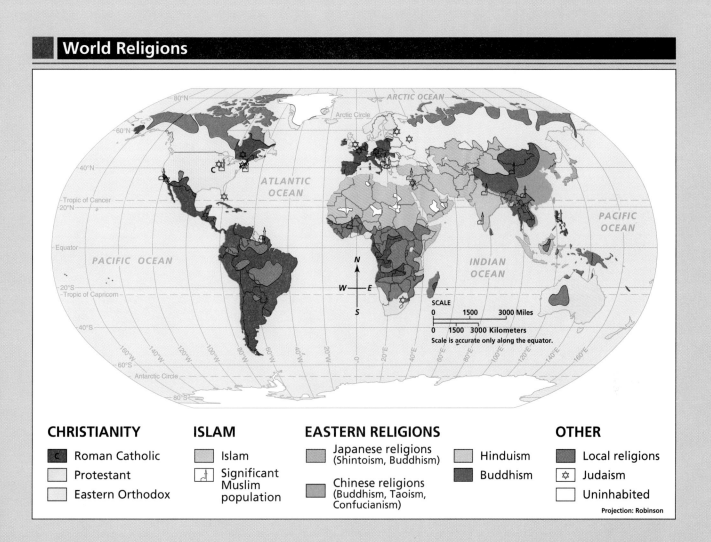

CHRISTIANITY
- C Roman Catholic
- Protestant
- Eastern Orthodox

ISLAM
- Islam
- Significant Muslim population

EASTERN RELIGIONS
- Japanese religions (Shintoism, Buddhism)
- Chinese religions (Buddhism, Taoism, Confucianism)
- Hinduism
- Buddhism

OTHER
- Local religions
- ✡ Judaism
- Uninhabited

Projection: Robinson

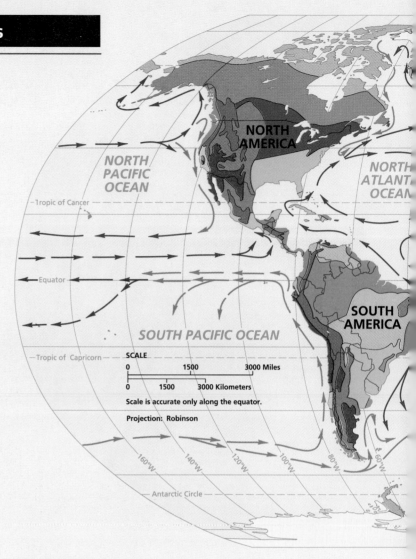

Legend

MONSOON AIR FLOW

← Wet monsoon

← Dry monsoon

MAJOR WORLD OCEAN CURRENTS

← Cool currents

← Warm currents

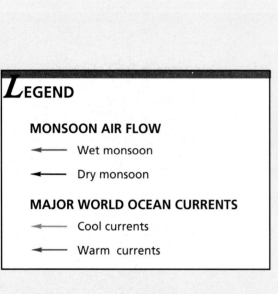

	Climate	Geographic Distribution	Major Weather Patterns	Vegetation
Low Latitudes	**HUMID TROPICAL**	along Equator; particularly equatorial South America, Congo Basin in Africa, Southeast Asia	warm and rainy year-round, with rain totaling anywhere from 65 to more than 450 in. (165–1,143 cm) annually; typical temperatures are 90°–95°F (32°–35°C) during the day and 65°–70°F (18°–21°C) at night	tropical rain forest
Low Latitudes	**TROPICAL SAVANNA**	between humid tropics and deserts; tropical regions of Africa, South and Central America, southern and Southeast Asia, Australia	warm all year; distinct rainy and dry seasons; precipitation during the summer of at least 20 in. (51 cm) and in some locations exceeding 150 in. (380 cm); summer temperatures average 90°F (32°C) during the day and 70°F (21°C) at night; typical winter temperatures are 75°–80°F (24°–27°C) during the day and 55°–60°F (13°–16°C) at night	tropical grassland with scattered trees
Dry/Semiarid	**DESERT**	centered along 30° latitude; some middle-latitude deserts in interior of large continents and along western coasts; particularly Saharan Africa, southwest Asia, central and western Australia, southwestern North America	arid; precipitation of less than 10 in. (25 cm) annually; sunny and hot in the tropics and sunny with great temperature ranges in middle latitudes; typical summer temperatures for lower-latitude deserts are 110°–115°F (43°–46°C) during the day and 60°–65°F (16°–18°C) at night, while winter temperatures average 80°F (27°C) during the day and 45°F (7°C) at night; in middle latitudes, the hottest month averages 70°F (24°C)	sparse drought-resistant plants; many barren, rocky, or sandy areas
Dry/Semiarid	**STEPPE**	generally bordering deserts and interiors of large continents; particularly northern and southern Africa, interior western North America, central and interior Asia and Australia, southern South America	semiarid; about 10–20 in. (25–51 cm) of precipitation annually; hot summers and cooler winters with wide temperature ranges similar to desert temperatures	grassland; few trees
Middle Latitudes	**MEDITERRANEAN**	west coasts in middle latitudes; particularly southern Europe, part of southwest Asia, north-western Africa, California, southwestern Australia, central Chile, southwestern South Africa	dry, sunny, warm summers and mild, wetter winters; precipitation averages 15–20 in. (38–51 cm) annually; typical temperatures are 75°–80°F (24–27°C) on summer days; the average winter temperature is 50°F (10°C)	scrub woodland and grassland
Middle Latitudes	**HUMID SUBTROPICAL**	east coasts in middle latitudes; particularly southeastern United States, eastern Asia, central southern Europe, southeastern parts of South America, South Africa, and Australia	hot, humid summers and mild, humid winters; precipitation year-round; coastal areas are in the paths of hurricanes and typhoons; precipitation averages 40 in. (102 cm) annually; typical temperatures are 75°–90°F (24°–32°C) in summer and 45°–50°F (7°–10°C) in winter	mixed forest

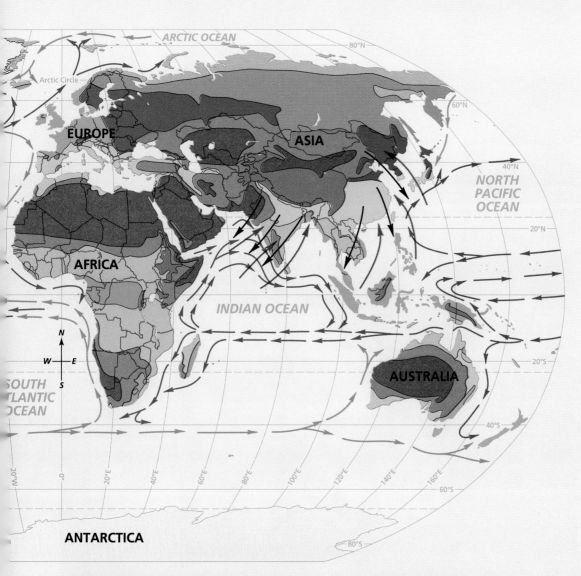

	Climate	Geographic Distribution	Major Weather Patterns	Vegetation
Middle Latitudes	**MARINE WEST COAST**	west coasts in upper-middle latitudes; particularly northwestern Europe and North America, southwestern South America, central southern South Africa, southeastern Australia, New Zealand	cloudy, mild summers and cool, rainy winters; strong ocean influence; precipitation averages 20–60 in. (51–152 cm) annually, with some coastal mountains receiving more than 200 in. (508 cm); average temperature in hottest month usually is between 60°F and 70°F (16°–21°C); average temperature in coolest month usually is above 32°F (0°C)	temperate evergreen forest
	HUMID CONTINENTAL	east coasts and interiors of upper-middle-latitude continents; particularly northeastern North America, northern and eastern Europe, northeastern Asia	four distinct seasons; long, cold winters and short, warm summers; precipitation amounts vary, usually 20–50 in. or more (51–127 cm) annually; average summer temperature is 75°F (24°C); average winter temperature is below freezing	mixed forest
High Latitudes	**SUBARCTIC**	higher latitudes of interior and east coasts of continents; particularly northern parts of North America, Europe, and Asia	extremes of temperature; long, cold winters and short, warm summers; low precipitation amounts all year; precipitation averages 5–15 in. (13–38 cm) in summer; temperatures in warmest month average 60°F (16°C), but can warm to 90°F (32°C); winter temperatures average below 0°F (–18°C)	northern evergreen forest
	TUNDRA	high-latitude coasts; particularly far northern parts of North America, Europe, and Asia, Antarctic Peninsula, subantarctic islands	cold all year; very long, cold winters and very short, cool summers; low precipitation amounts; precipitation average is 5–15 in. (13–38 cm) annually; warmest month averages 40°F (4°C); coolest month averages a little below 0°F (–18°C)	moss, lichens, low shrubs; permafrost bogs in summer
	ICE CAP	polar regions; particularly Antarctica, Greenland, Arctic Basin islands	freezing cold; snow and ice year-round; precipitation averages less than 10 in. (25 cm) annually; average temperatures in warmest month are not higher than freezing	no vegetation
	HIGHLAND	high mountain regions, particularly western parts of North and South America, eastern parts of Asia and Africa, southern and central Europe and Asia	greatly varied temperatures and precipitation amounts over short distances as elevation changes	forest to tundra vegetation, depending on altitude

The World's Basic Biomes

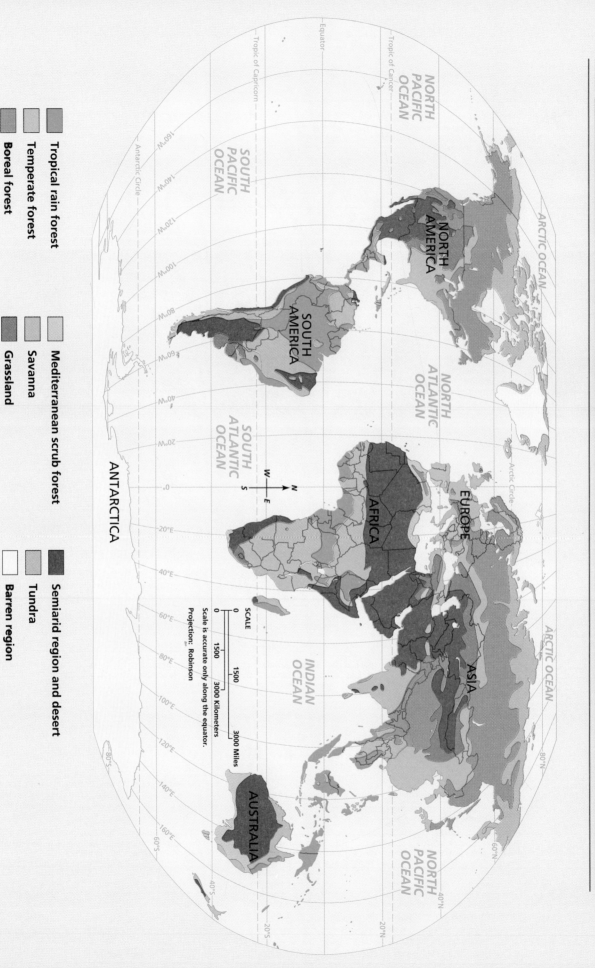

Legend:

- Tropical rain forest
- Temperate forest
- Boreal forest
- Mediterranean scrub forest
- Savanna
- Grassland
- Semiarid region and desert
- Tundra
- Barren region

SCALE

0   1500   3000 Kilometers

0   1500   3000 Miles

Scale is accurate only along the equator.

Projection: Robinson

UNITED STATES AND CANADA

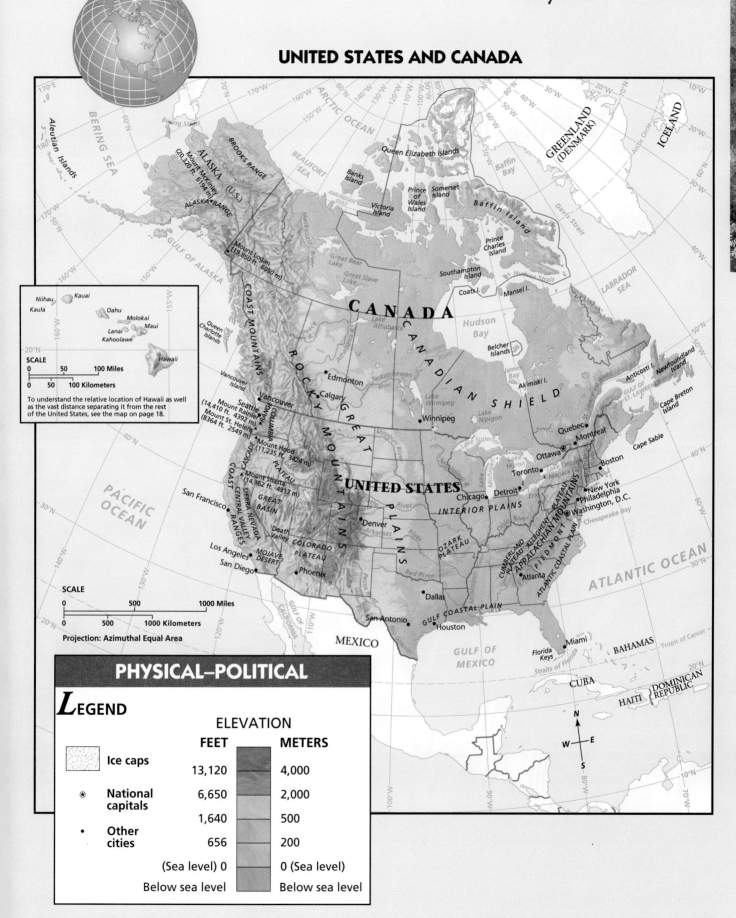

SCALE

Niihau · Kauai
Kaula
Oahu
Molokai · Maui
Lanai
Kahoolawe
Hawaii

20°N

SCALE
0   50   100 Miles
0   50   100 Kilometers

To understand the relative location of Hawaii as well as the vast distance separating it from the rest of the United States, see the map on page 18.

SCALE
0   500   1000 Miles
0   500   1000 Kilometers

Projection: Azimuthal Equal Area

PHYSICAL–POLITICAL

*L*EGEND

		ELEVATION	
		FEET	**METERS**
⬚	Ice caps	13,120	4,000
⊛	National capitals	6,650	2,000
•	Other cities	1,640	500
		656	200
		(Sea level) 0	0 (Sea level)
		Below sea level	Below sea level

41

Thematic Maps

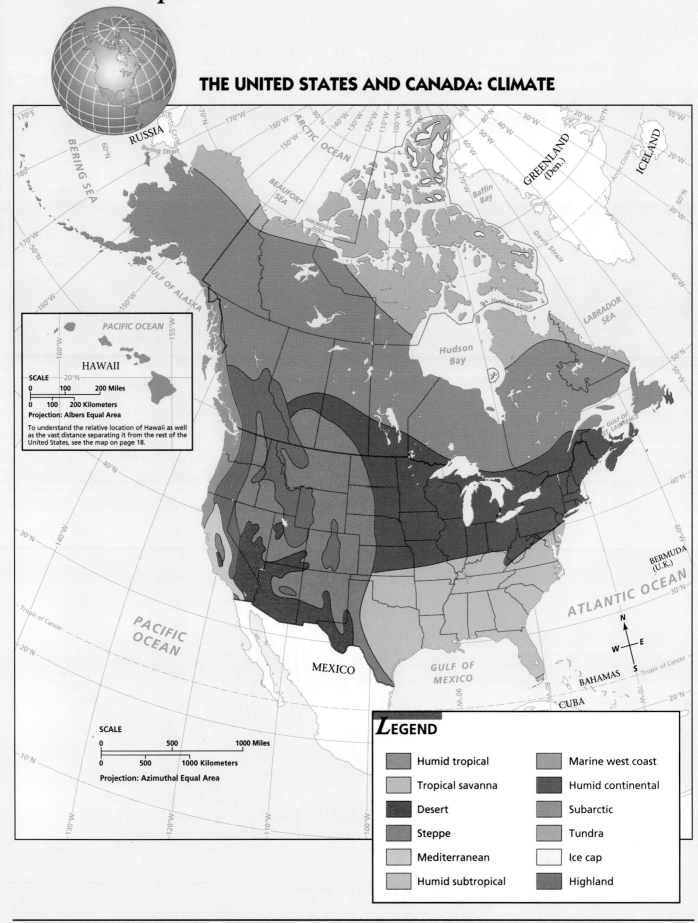

THE UNITED STATES AND CANADA: CLIMATE

RUSSIA

BERING SEA

Arctic Circle

Bering Strait

BEAUFORT SEA

ARCTIC OCEAN

AMUNDSEN GULF

GULF OF ALASKA

Baffin Bay

GREENLAND (Den.)

ICELAND

Davis Strait

Hudson Strait

LABRADOR SEA

Hudson Bay

GULF OF ST. LAWRENCE

HAWAII

PACIFIC OCEAN

SCALE

0   100   200 Miles

0   100   200 Kilometers

Projection: Albers Equal Area

To understand the relative location of Hawaii as well as the vast distance separating it from the rest of the United States, see the map on page 18.

PACIFIC OCEAN

Tropic of Cancer

MEXICO

GULF OF MEXICO

ATLANTIC OCEAN

BERMUDA (U.K.)

Tropic of Cancer

BAHAMAS

CUBA

N   W E   S

SCALE

0   500   1000 Miles

0   500   1000 Kilometers

Projection: Azimuthal Equal Area

LEGEND

▨ Humid tropical		▨ Marine west coast	
▨ Tropical savanna		▨ Humid continental	
▨ Desert		▨ Subarctic	
▨ Steppe		▨ Tundra	
▨ Mediterranean		▨ Ice cap	
▨ Humid subtropical		▨ Highland	

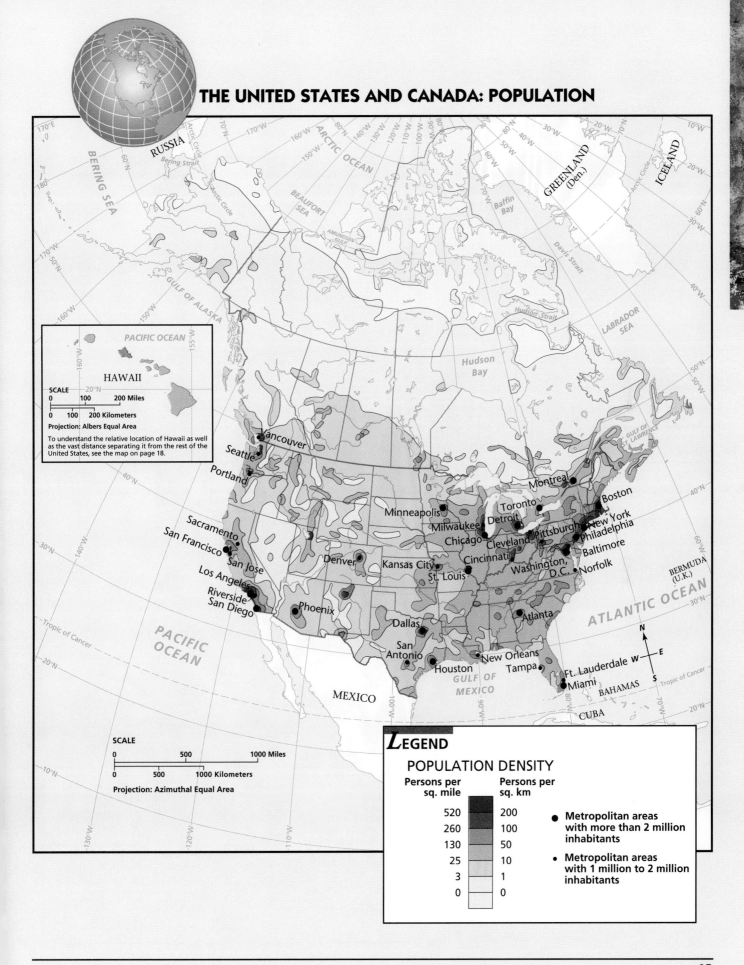

RUSSIA

BERING SEA

Arctic Circle
Bering Strait

ARCTIC OCEAN

BEAUFORT SEA

AMUNDSEN GULF

GULF OF ALASKA

GREENLAND (Den.)

Baffin Bay

Davis Strait

ICELAND

Arctic Circle

LABRADOR SEA

Hudson Strait

Hudson Bay

GULF OF ST. LAWRENCE

HAWAII

PACIFIC OCEAN

SCALE
0   100   200 Miles
0   100   200 Kilometers
Projection: Albers Equal Area

To understand the relative location of Hawaii as well as the vast distance separating it from the rest of the United States, see the map on page 18.

Vancouver
Seattle
Portland
Sacramento
San Francisco
San Jose
Los Angeles
Riverside
San Diego
Phoenix

Minneapolis
Milwaukee
Chicago
Denver
Kansas City
St. Louis

Montreal
Toronto
Detroit
Cleveland
Cincinnati
Pittsburgh
Washington, D.C.

Boston
New York
Philadelphia
Baltimore
Norfolk

BERMUDA (U.K.)

ATLANTIC OCEAN

Dallas
San Antonio
Houston
New Orleans
Tampa
Ft. Lauderdale
Miami
Atlanta

BAHAMAS
CUBA

PACIFIC OCEAN

Tropic of Cancer

MEXICO

GULF OF MEXICO

Tropic of Cancer

N
W   E
S

SCALE
0   500   1000 Miles
0   500   1000 Kilometers
Projection: Azimuthal Equal Area

LEGEND

POPULATION DENSITY

Persons per sq. mile	Persons per sq. km
520	200
260	100
130	50
25	10
3	1
0	0

● Metropolitan areas with more than 2 million inhabitants

● Metropolitan areas with 1 million to 2 million inhabitants

THE UNITED STATES AND CANADA: ECONOMY

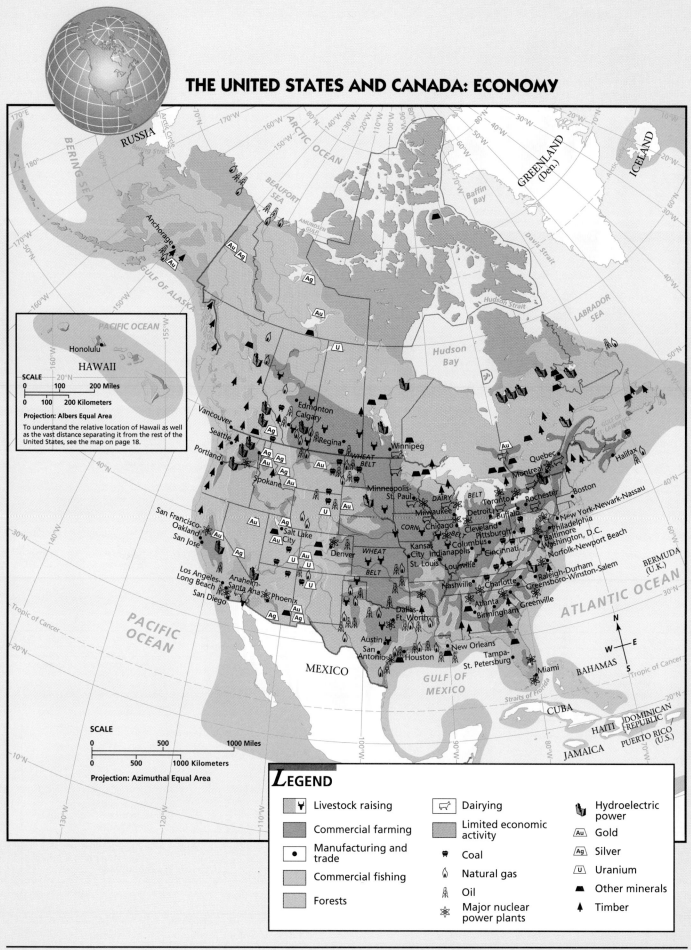

HAWAII

SCALE
0   100   200 Miles
0   100   200 Kilometers

Projection: Albers Equal Area

To understand the relative location of Hawaii as well as the vast distance separating it from the rest of the United States, see the map on page 18.

SCALE
0   500   1000 Miles
0   500   1000 Kilometers

Projection: Azimuthal Equal Area

LEGEND

Livestock raising	Dairying	Hydroelectric power
Commercial farming	Limited economic activity	Au Gold
Manufacturing and trade	Coal	Ag Silver
Commercial fishing	Natural gas	U Uranium
Forests	Oil	Other minerals
	Major nuclear power plants	Timber

MIDDLE AND SOUTH AMERICA

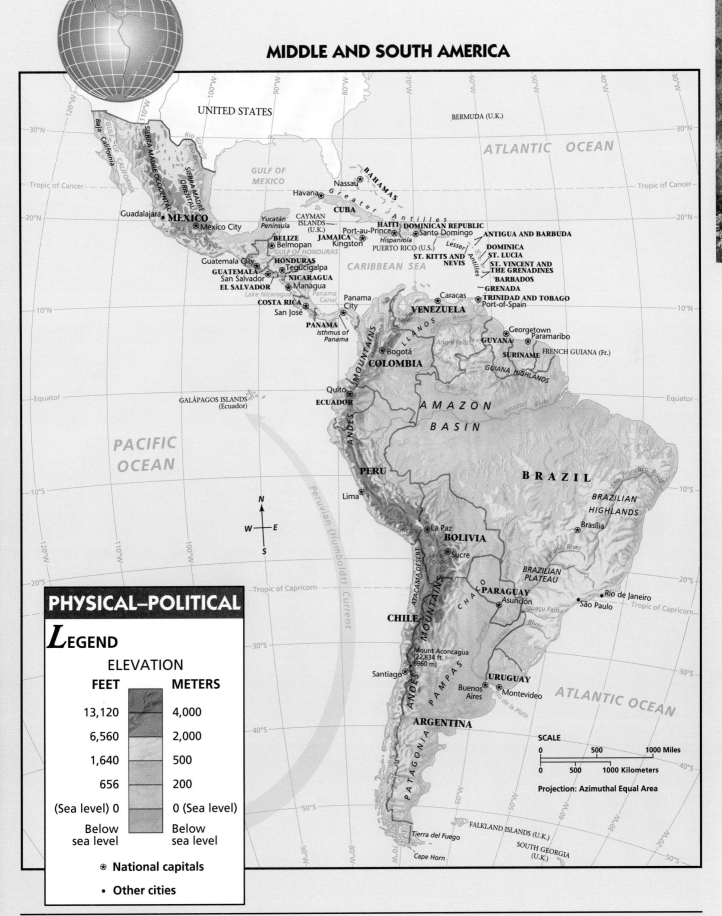

UNITED STATES

BERMUDA (U.K.)

ATLANTIC OCEAN

Tropic of Cancer

GULF OF CALIFORNIA

Baja California

SIERRA MADRE OCCIDENTAL

SIERRA MADRE ORIENTAL

Rio Grande

GULF OF MEXICO

Nassau

BAHAMAS

Havana

Greater Antilles

Guadalajara • MEXICO

• Mexico City

Yucatán Peninsula

CUBA

CAYMAN ISLANDS (U.K.)

HAITI

Port-au-Prince

DOMINICAN REPUBLIC

Santo Domingo

ANTIGUA AND BARBUDA

BELIZE

⊛ Belmopan

JAMAICA

Kingston

Hispaniola

PUERTO RICO (U.S.)

DOMINICA

ST. KITTS AND NEVIS

ST. LUCIA

GULF OF HONDURAS

Guatemala City

HONDURAS

⊛ Tegucigalpa

CARIBBEAN SEA

Lesser Antilles

ST. VINCENT AND THE GRENADINES

GUATEMALA

San Salvador

NICARAGUA

BARBADOS

EL SALVADOR

⊛ Managua

GRENADA

Lake Nicaragua

Panama Canal

COSTA RICA

Panama City

Caracas

TRINIDAD AND TOBAGO

Port-of-Spain

San José

PANAMA

Isthmus of Panama

VENEZUELA

LLANOS

Georgetown

Paramaribo

⊛ Bogotá

Angel Falls

Orinoco River

GUYANA

SURINAME

FRENCH GUIANA (Fr.)

COLOMBIA

GUIANA HIGHLANDS

Quito

ANDES MOUNTAINS

Rio Negro

Equator

GALÁPAGOS ISLANDS (Ecuador)

ECUADOR

AMAZON BASIN

Amazon River

PACIFIC OCEAN

PERU

BRAZIL

BRAZILIAN HIGHLANDS

São Francisco River

Lima

⊛ La Paz

⊛ Brasília

Peruvian (Humboldt) Current

ATACAMA DESERT

BOLIVIA

⊛ Sucre

Poopó

BRAZILIAN PLATEAU

Tropic of Capricorn

Rio de Janeiro

CHACO

PARAGUAY

⊛ Asunción

São Paulo

CHILE

ANDES MOUNTAINS

Iguaçu Falls

Paraná River

Mount Aconcagua (22,834 ft. 6960 m)

PAMPAS

URUGUAY

Santiago

Buenos Aires

⊛ Montevideo

Río de la Plata

ATLANTIC OCEAN

ARGENTINA

PATAGONIA

FALKLAND ISLANDS (U.K.)

Tierra del Fuego

SOUTH GEORGIA (U.K.)

Cape Horn

N
W · E
S

PHYSICAL–POLITICAL

*L*EGEND

ELEVATION

FEET	METERS
13,120	4,000
6,560	2,000
1,640	500
656	200
(Sea level) 0	0 (Sea level)
Below sea level	Below sea level

⊛ **National capitals**

• **Other cities**

SCALE

0 — 500 — 1000 Miles

0 — 500 — 1000 Kilometers

Projection: Azimuthal Equal Area

Thematic Maps

MIDDLE AND SOUTH AMERICA: CLIMATE

UNITED STATES

ATLANTIC OCEAN

GULF OF MEXICO

GULF OF CALIFORNIA

Tropic of Cancer

GULF OF HONDURAS

CARIBBEAN SEA

PACIFIC OCEAN

Equator

N
W · E
S

Rio de la Plata

ATLANTIC OCEAN

SCALE

0   500   1000 Miles

0   500   1000 Kilometers

Projection: Azimuthal Equal Area

*L*EGEND

▮ Humid tropical	▮ Humid subtropical
▮ Tropical savanna	▮ Marine west coast
▮ Desert	▮ Subarctic
▮ Steppe	▮ Highland
▮ Mediterranean	

MIDDLE AND SOUTH AMERICA: POPULATION

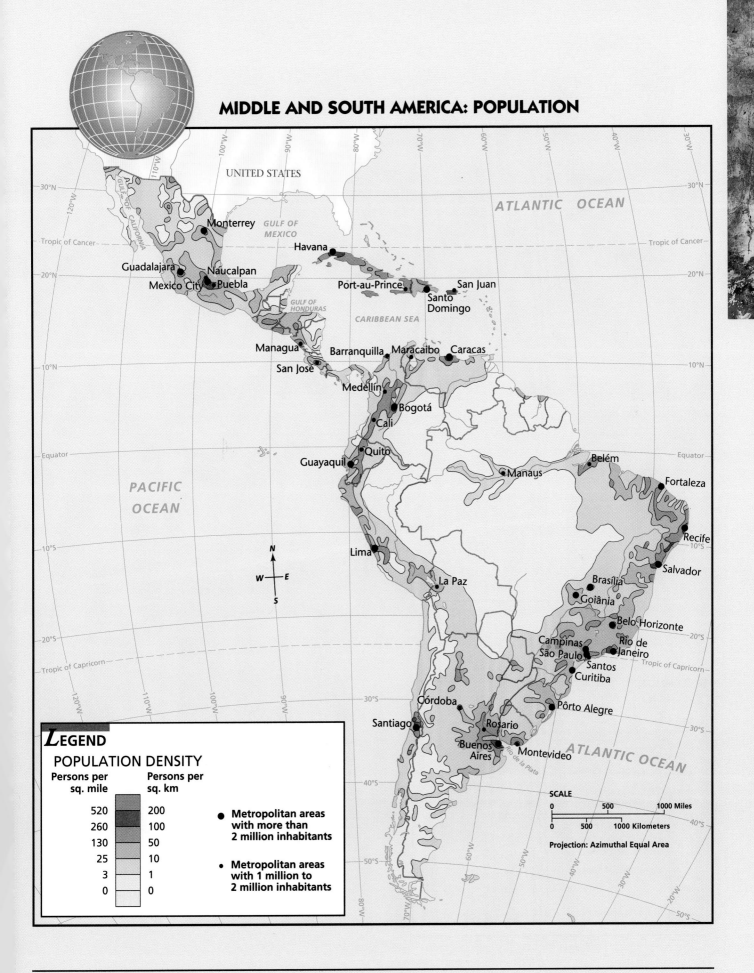

UNITED STATES

ATLANTIC OCEAN

GULF OF MEXICO

Tropic of Cancer

Monterrey

Havana

Guadalajara
Naucalpan
Mexico City
Puebla

Port-au-Prince
Santo Domingo
San Juan

GULF OF HONDURAS

Managua
San José

CARIBBEAN SEA

Barranquilla
Maracaibo
Caracas

Medellín
Bogotá
Cali

Quito
Guayaquil

Belém

Equator

Manaus

Fortaleza

PACIFIC OCEAN

Recife

Lima

La Paz

Salvador

Brasília
Goiânia

Belo Horizonte

Campinas
São Paulo
Santos
Curitiba

Rio de Janeiro

Tropic of Capricorn

Córdoba

Pôrto Alegre

Santiago

Rosario

Buenos Aires
Montevideo

Río de la Plata

ATLANTIC OCEAN

LEGEND

POPULATION DENSITY

Persons per sq. mile	Persons per sq. km
520	200
260	100
130	50
25	10
3	1
0	0

● Metropolitan areas with more than 2 million inhabitants

• Metropolitan areas with 1 million to 2 million inhabitants

SCALE

0   500   1000 Miles

0   500   1000 Kilometers

Projection: Azimuthal Equal Area

MIDDLE AND SOUTH AMERICA: ECONOMY

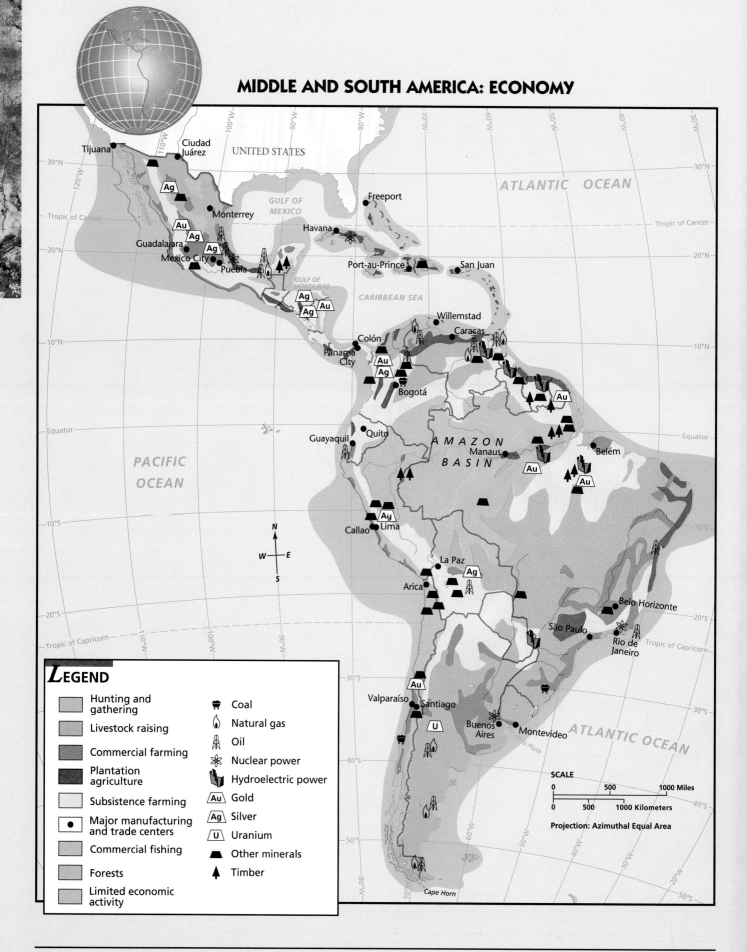

LEGEND

- Hunting and gathering
- Livestock raising
- Commercial farming
- Plantation agriculture
- Subsistence farming
- ● Major manufacturing and trade centers
- Commercial fishing
- Forests
- Limited economic activity

- 🛒 Coal
- 🜂 Natural gas
- Oil
- ✳ Nuclear power
- Hydroelectric power
- Au Gold
- Ag Silver
- U Uranium
- ▲ Other minerals
- ▲ Timber

SCALE
0 | 500 | 1000 Miles
0 | 500 | 1000 Kilometers

Projection: Azimuthal Equal Area

UNITED STATES
ATLANTIC OCEAN
Tijuana
Ciudad Juárez
Freeport
GULF OF MEXICO
Monterrey
Havana
Guadalajara
Mexico City
Puebla
Port-au-Prince
San Juan
GULF OF HONDURAS
CARIBBEAN SEA
Willemstad
Caracas
Colón
Panama City
Bogotá
Guayaquil
Quito
AMAZON BASIN
Manaus
Belém
PACIFIC OCEAN
Callao
Lima
La Paz
Arica
Belo Horizonte
São Paulo
Rio de Janeiro
Valparaíso
Santiago
Buenos Aires
Montevideo
ATLANTIC OCEAN
La Plata
Cape Horn

Tropic of Cancer
Equator
Tropic of Capricorn

AFRICA

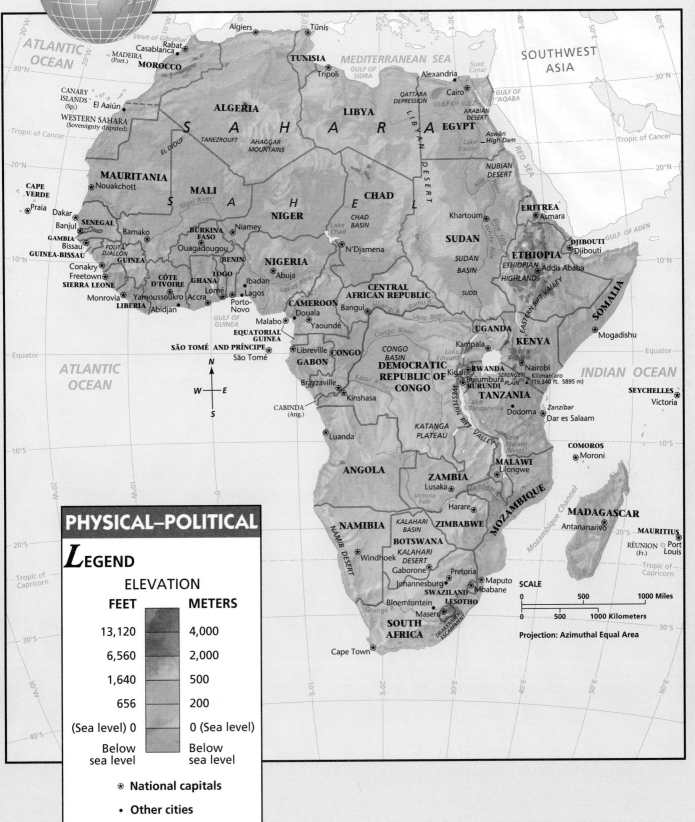

ATLANTIC OCEAN

Strait of Gibraltar

Algiers ⊛   Tūnis ⊛

MADEIRA (Port.)

Casablanca ●
Rabat ⊛
MOROCCO

TUNISIA
Tripoli ⊛

MEDITERRANEAN SEA
GULF OF SIDRA

Alexandria ●

SOUTHWEST ASIA

Suez Canal

CANARY ISLANDS (Sp.)
El Aaiún ●
WESTERN SAHARA (Sovereignty disputed)

ALGERIA

LIBYA

QATTARA DEPRESSION
Cairo ⊛
GULF OF SUEZ
GULF OF AQABA

EGYPT
ARABIAN DESERT

Aswān High Dam
Lake Nasser

RED SEA

S A H A R A

EL DJOUF   TANEZROUFT   AHAGGAR MOUNTAINS

LIBYAN DESERT

NUBIAN DESERT

MAURITANIA
Nouakchott ⊛

MALI

CHAD

ERITREA
Asmara ●

CAPE VERDE
● Praia
Dakar ●
Banjul ●
SENEGAL
GAMBIA
Bissau ●
GUINEA-BISSAU
Bamako ⊛
FOUTA DJALLON

S A H E L

BURKINA FASO
Ouagadougou ⊛
Niamey ⊛
NIGER
CHAD BASIN
Lake Chad
N'Djamena ⊛

Khartoum ⊛
SUDAN
SUDAN BASIN
Blue Nile
White Nile

DJIBOUTI ⊛ Djibouti
GULF OF ADEN

GUINEA
Conakry ●
Freetown ●
SIERRA LEONE
CÔTE D'IVOIRE
GHANA
TOGO
BENIN
Ibadan ●
NIGERIA
Abuja ⊛
Lomé Accra ⊛ Porto-Novo
Lagos ●
Yamoussoukro ⊛
Monrovia ●
LIBERIA
Abidjan ●
GULF OF GUINEA

CENTRAL AFRICAN REPUBLIC
Bangui ⊛

ETHIOPIA
ETHIOPIAN HIGHLANDS
Addis Ababa ●

SUDD

SOMALIA

CAMEROON
Douala ●
Yaoundé ⊛
Malabo ⊛
EQUATORIAL GUINEA
SÃO TOMÉ AND PRÍNCIPE
São Tomé ⊛
Libreville ⊛
GABON
CONGO
CONGO BASIN
Ubangi R.
Bomu R.
Uele River

UGANDA
Kampala ⊛
Lake Edward
Lake Victoria

KENYA
Nairobi ⊛
Mogadishu ●

INDIAN OCEAN

N
W ← → E
S

Brazzaville ⊛
Kinshasa ⊛
CABINDA (Ang.)
Kasai River
DEMOCRATIC REPUBLIC OF CONGO
Congo River
RWANDA
Kigali ⊛
BURUNDI
Bujumbura ⊛
SERENGETI PLAIN
▲ Kilimanjaro (19,340 ft. 5895 m)
WESTERN RIFT VALLEY
EASTERN RIFT VALLEY

SEYCHELLES
Victoria ⊛

Equator

ATLANTIC OCEAN

Luanda ●
KATANGA PLATEAU
TANZANIA
Dodoma ⊛
Zanzibar
Dar es Salaam ●
Lake Tanganyika

COMOROS
⊛ Moroni

ANGOLA
Lake Malawi (Nyasa)
Lusaka ⊛
Victoria Falls
Zambezi R.
ZAMBIA
MALAWI
Lilongwe ⊛

MADAGASCAR
Antananarivo ⊛

MAURITIUS
RÉUNION (Fr.)
Port Louis ⊛

NAMIBIA
KALAHARI BASIN
NAMIB DESERT
BOTSWANA
KALAHARI DESERT
Windhoek ⊛
Gaborone ⊛
ZIMBABWE
Harare ⊛
MOZAMBIQUE
Mozambique Channel

Pretoria ⊛
Johannesburg ●
Maputo ⊛
Mbabane ⊛
SWAZILAND
Bloemfontein ⊛
LESOTHO
Maseru ⊛
Orange R.
DRAKENSBERG ESCARPMENT
SOUTH AFRICA
Cape Town ●

Tropic of Cancer

Tropic of Capricorn

PHYSICAL–POLITICAL

*L*EGEND

ELEVATION

FEET	METERS
13,120	4,000
6,560	2,000
1,640	500
656	200
(Sea level) 0	0 (Sea level)
Below sea level	Below sea level

⊛ **National capitals**

● **Other cities**

SCALE

0   500   1000 Miles

0   500   1000 Kilometers

Projection: Azimuthal Equal Area

Thematic Maps

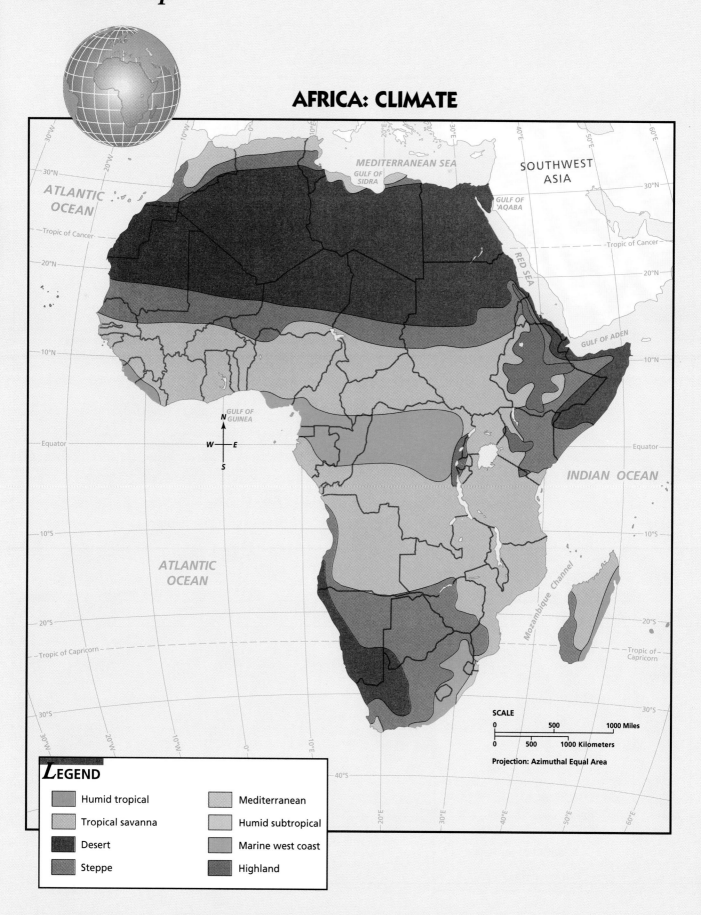

AFRICA: CLIMATE

MEDITERRANEAN SEA
GULF OF SIDRA

SOUTHWEST ASIA

GULF OF AQABA

ATLANTIC OCEAN

Tropic of Cancer

30°N

20°N

10°N

RED SEA

GULF OF ADEN

GULF OF GUINEA

N
W   E
S

Equator

ATLANTIC OCEAN

INDIAN OCEAN

Equator

Mozambique Channel

Tropic of Capricorn

Tropic of Capricorn

SCALE

0   500   1000 Miles

0   500   1000 Kilometers

Projection: Azimuthal Equal Area

LEGEND

- Humid tropical
- Tropical savanna
- Desert
- Steppe
- Mediterranean
- Humid subtropical
- Marine west coast
- Highland

AFRICA: POPULATION

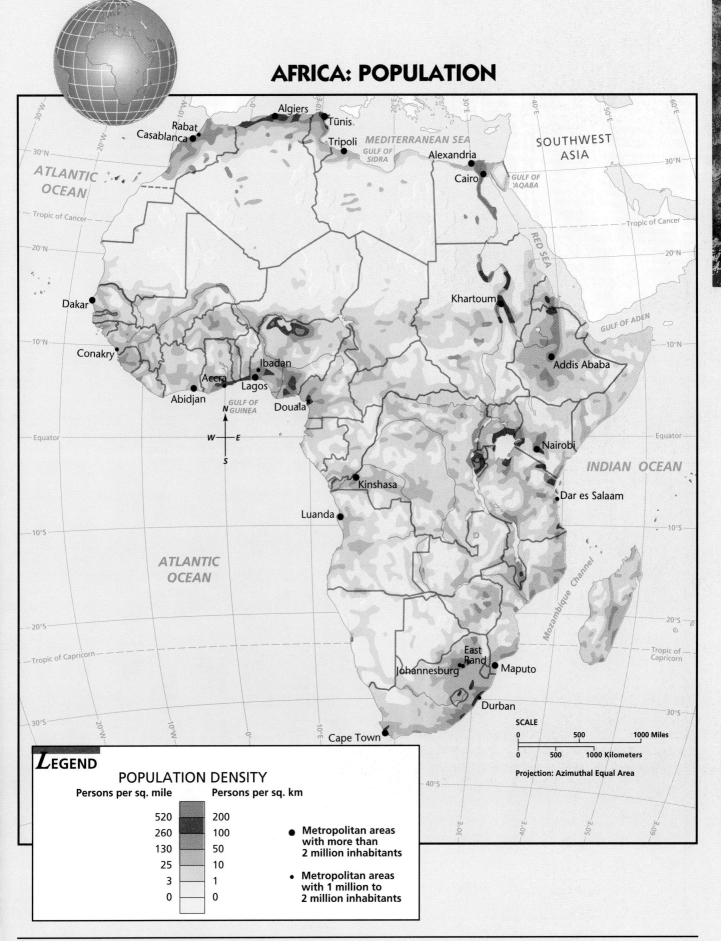

ATLANTIC OCEAN

MEDITERRANEAN SEA

SOUTHWEST ASIA

GULF OF SIDRA

GULF OF 'AQABA

RED SEA

GULF OF ADEN

Rabat
Casablanca
Algiers
Tūnis
Tripoli
Alexandria
Cairo
Khartoum
Dakar
Conakry
Ibadan
Accra
Lagos
Abidjan
Douala
Addis Ababa
GULF OF GUINEA
Kinshasa
Nairobi
Dar es Salaam
Luanda
INDIAN OCEAN
ATLANTIC OCEAN
Mozambique Channel
East Rand
Johannesburg
Maputo
Durban
Cape Town

Tropic of Cancer
Equator
Tropic of Capricorn

N
W   E
S

SCALE

0   500   1000 Miles

0   500   1000 Kilometers

Projection: Azimuthal Equal Area

LEGEND

POPULATION DENSITY

Persons per sq. mile	Persons per sq. km
520	200
260	100
130	50
25	10
3	1
0	0

● Metropolitan areas with more than 2 million inhabitants

• Metropolitan areas with 1 million to 2 million inhabitants

AFRICA: ECONOMY

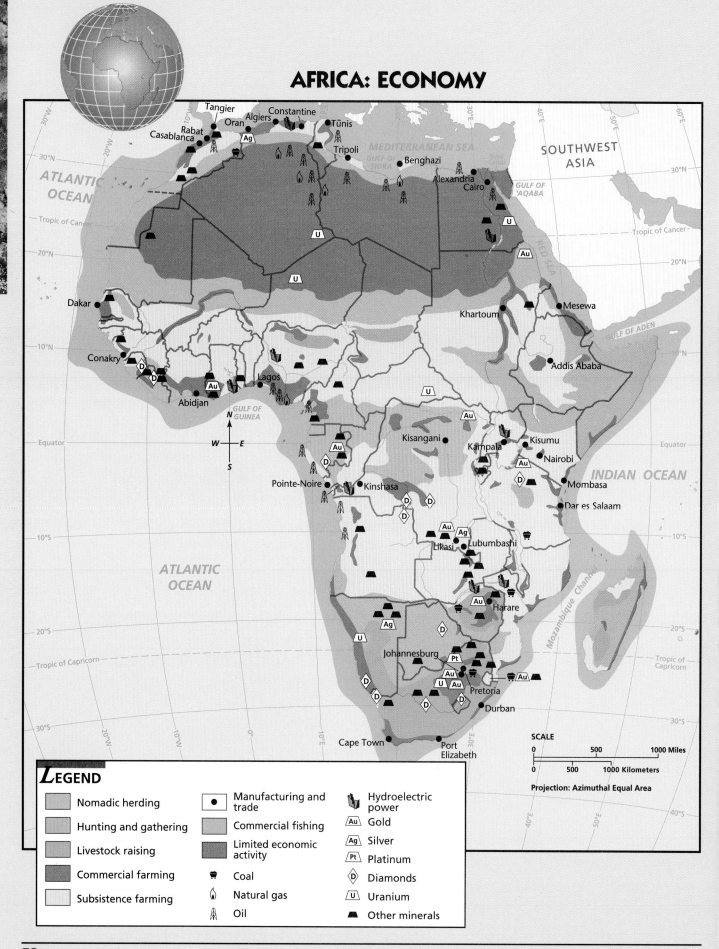

LEGEND

- Nomadic herding
- Hunting and gathering
- Livestock raising
- Commercial farming
- Subsistence farming
- Manufacturing and trade
- Commercial fishing
- Limited economic activity
- Coal
- Natural gas
- Oil
- Hydroelectric power
- Au Gold
- Ag Silver
- Pt Platinum
- Diamonds
- U Uranium
- Other minerals

SCALE

0   500   1000 Miles

0   500   1000 Kilometers

Projection: Azimuthal Equal Area

EUROPE

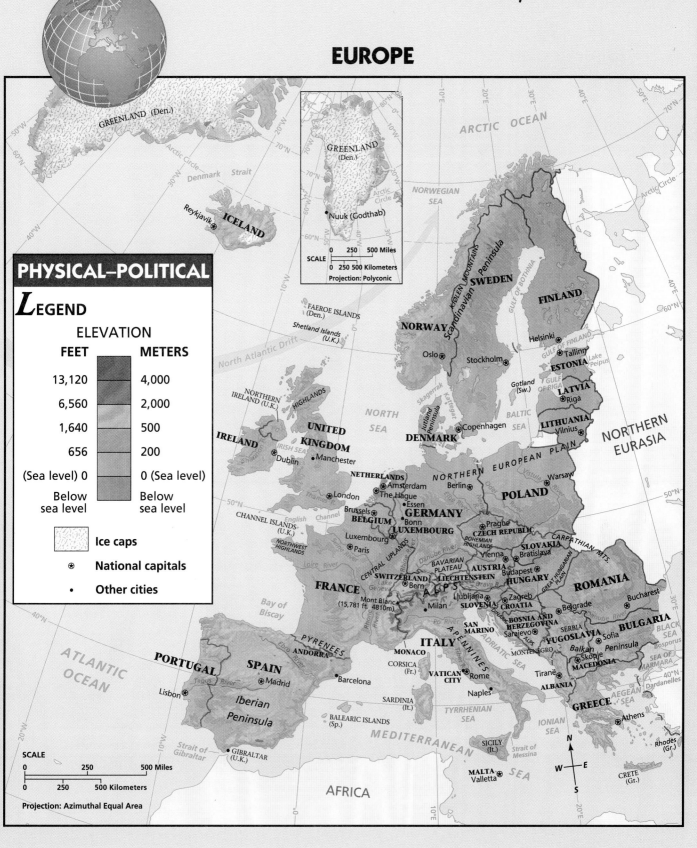

PHYSICAL–POLITICAL

*L*EGEND

ELEVATION

FEET	METERS
13,120	4,000
6,560	2,000
1,640	500
656	200
(Sea level) 0	0 (Sea level)
Below sea level	Below sea level

Ice caps

⊛ National capitals

• Other cities

GREENLAND (Den.)

GREENLAND (Den.)

Nuuk (Godthab)

SCALE
0   250   500 Miles
0 250 500 Kilometers
Projection: Polyconic

ARCTIC OCEAN

NORWEGIAN SEA

Arctic Circle

Denmark Strait

Reykjavik ⊛ ICELAND

FAEROE ISLANDS (Den.)

Shetland Islands (U.K.)

North Atlantic Drift

KJÖLEN MOUNTAINS
Scandinavian Peninsula
SWEDEN
FINLAND
NORWAY
Helsinki •
Oslo ⊛
Stockholm ⊛
GULF OF BOTHNIA
GULF OF FINLAND
Tallinn ⊛
ESTONIA
Lake Peipus
Gotland (Sw.)
GULF OF RIGA
LATVIA
Riga ⊛
LITHUANIA
Vilnius ⊛
NORTHERN EURASIA

NORTHERN IRELAND (U.K.)
HIGHLANDS
UNITED KINGDOM
IRELAND
IRISH SEA
Shannon
Dublin ⊛ • Manchester
London ⊛
NORTH SEA
Skagerrak
Kattegat
Jutland Peninsula
DENMARK
Copenhagen ⊛
BALTIC SEA
NORTHERN EUROPEAN PLAIN
Warsaw ⊛
POLAND
Vistula River
Berlin ⊛
Oder River
50°N

CHANNEL ISLANDS (U.K.)
English Channel
NETHERLANDS
Amsterdam ⊛
The Hague •
Brussels ⊛
BELGIUM
Essen •
Bonn
GERMANY
LUXEMBOURG
Luxembourg ⊛
Prague ⊛
CZECH REPUBLIC
BOHEMIAN HIGHLANDS
CARPATHIAN MTS.

NORTHWEST HIGHLANDS
Paris ⊛
Loire River
CENTRAL UPLANDS
Danube River
BAVARIAN PLATEAU
Vienna ⊛
SLOVAKIA
Bratislava ⊛
GREAT HUNGARIAN PLAIN

FRANCE
Bay of Biscay
Rhône River
SWITZERLAND
Geneva
Bern ⊛
LIECHTENSTEIN
Milan •
AUSTRIA
Budapest ⊛
HUNGARY
Ljubljana ⊛
SLOVENIA
Zagreb ⊛
CROATIA
Drava
ROMANIA
Belgrade ⊛
Bucharest ⊛
Danube River

Mont Blanc (15,781 ft. 4810m)
A L P S
APENNINES
SAN MARINO
BOSNIA AND HERZEGOVINA
Sarajevo ⊛
SERBIA
YUGOSLAVIA
Sofia ⊛
BULGARIA
BLACK SEA
Bosporus

PYRENEES
ANDORRA
ITALY
MONACO
CORSICA (Fr.)
VATICAN CITY
Rome ⊛
Tiber R.
ADRIATIC SEA
MONTENEGRO
Skopje •
MACEDONIA
Balkan Peninsula
SEA OF MARMARA
Dardanelles

ATLANTIC OCEAN
PORTUGAL
SPAIN
Ebro River
Madrid ⊛
Barcelona •
Iberian Peninsula
Lisbon ⊛
Tagus River
BALEARIC ISLANDS (Sp.)
SARDINIA (It.)
TYRRHENIAN SEA
Naples •
Tirane ⊛
ALBANIA
GREECE
Athens ⊛
AEGEAN SEA
IONIAN SEA
Rhodes (Gr.)

Strait of Gibraltar
GIBRALTAR (U.K.)
MEDITERRANEAN SEA
SICILY (It.)
Strait of Messina
MALTA
Valletta •
CRETE (Gr.)

N
W   E
S

SCALE
0   250   500 Miles
0   250   500 Kilometers
Projection: Azimuthal Equal Area

AFRICA

Thematic Maps

EUROPE

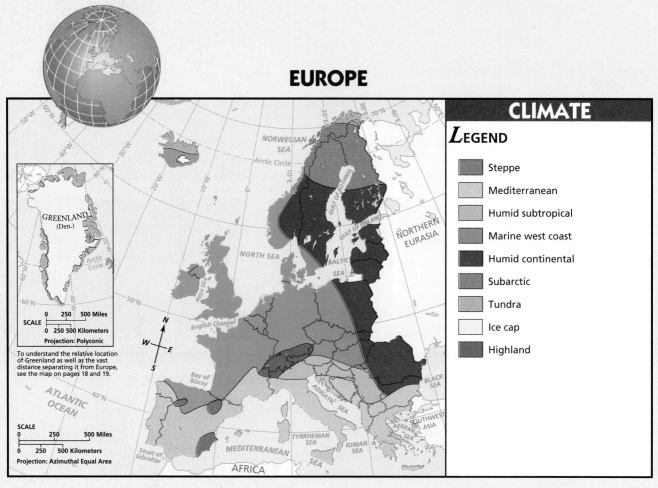

CLIMATE

LEGEND

- Steppe
- Mediterranean
- Humid subtropical
- Marine west coast
- Humid continental
- Subarctic
- Tundra
- Ice cap
- Highland

GREENLAND
(Den.)

SCALE
0   250   500 Miles
0 250 500 Kilometers
Projection: Polyconic

To understand the relative location of Greenland as well as the vast distance separating it from Europe, see the map on pages 18 and 19.

SCALE
0   250   500 Miles
0   250   500 Kilometers
Projection: Azimuthal Equal Area

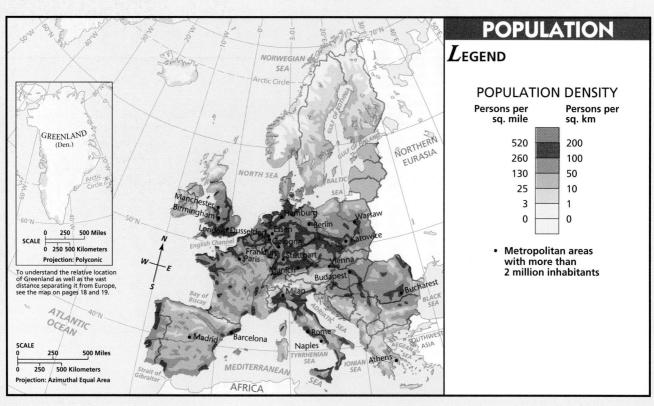

POPULATION

LEGEND

POPULATION DENSITY

Persons per sq. mile	Persons per sq. km
520	200
260	100
130	50
25	10
3	1
0	0

- Metropolitan areas with more than 2 million inhabitants

GREENLAND
(Den.)

SCALE
0   250   500 Miles
0 250 500 Kilometers
Projection: Polyconic

To understand the relative location of Greenland as well as the vast distance separating it from Europe, see the map on pages 18 and 19.

SCALE
0   250   500 Miles
0   250   500 Kilometers
Projection: Azimuthal Equal Area

EUROPE

ECONOMY

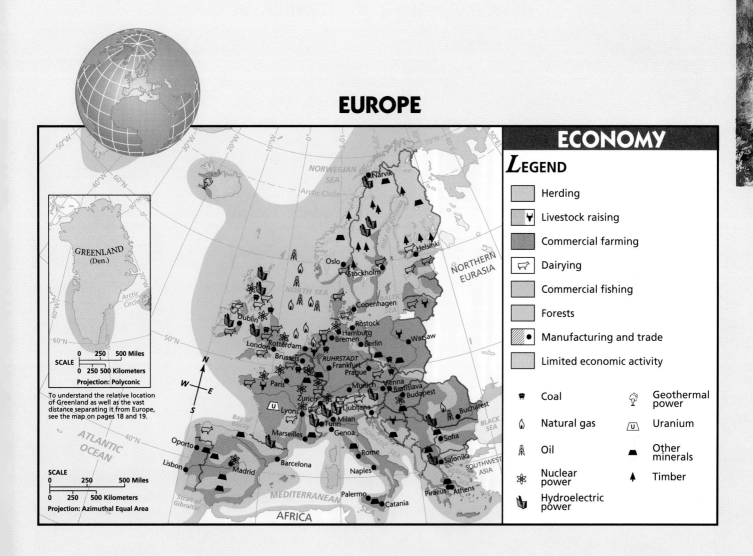

LEGEND

- Herding
- Livestock raising
- Commercial farming
- Dairying
- Commercial fishing
- Forests
- Manufacturing and trade
- Limited economic activity

- Coal
- Natural gas
- Oil
- Nuclear power
- Hydroelectric power

- Geothermal power
- Uranium
- Other minerals
- Timber

GREENLAND
(Den.)

SCALE
0   250   500 Miles
0 250 500 Kilometers
Projection: Polyconic

To understand the relative location of Greenland as well as the vast distance separating it from Europe, see the map on pages 18 and 19.

SCALE
0   250   500 Miles
0   250   500 Kilometers
Projection: Azimuthal Equal Area

ATLANTIC OCEAN

NORWEGIAN SEA
Arctic Circle
NORTH SEA
NORTHERN EURASIA

Narvik
Oslo
Stockholm
Helsinki
Copenhagen
Dublin
Rostock
Hamburg
Bremen
Berlin
Warsaw
London
Rotterdam
Brussels
RUHRSTADT
Frankfurt
Prague
Paris
Munich
Vienna
Bratislava
Budapest
Zurich
Lyons
Ljubljana
Bucharest
Milan
Turin
Genoa
Marseilles
Sofia
Rome
Salonika
Oporto
Barcelona
Naples
Lisbon
Madrid
Palermo
Piraeus
Athens
Catania

Bay of Biscay
MEDITERRANEAN SEA
Strait of Gibraltar
AFRICA
BLACK SEA
SOUTHWEST ASIA

Physical–Political

RUSSIA AND NORTHERN EURASIA

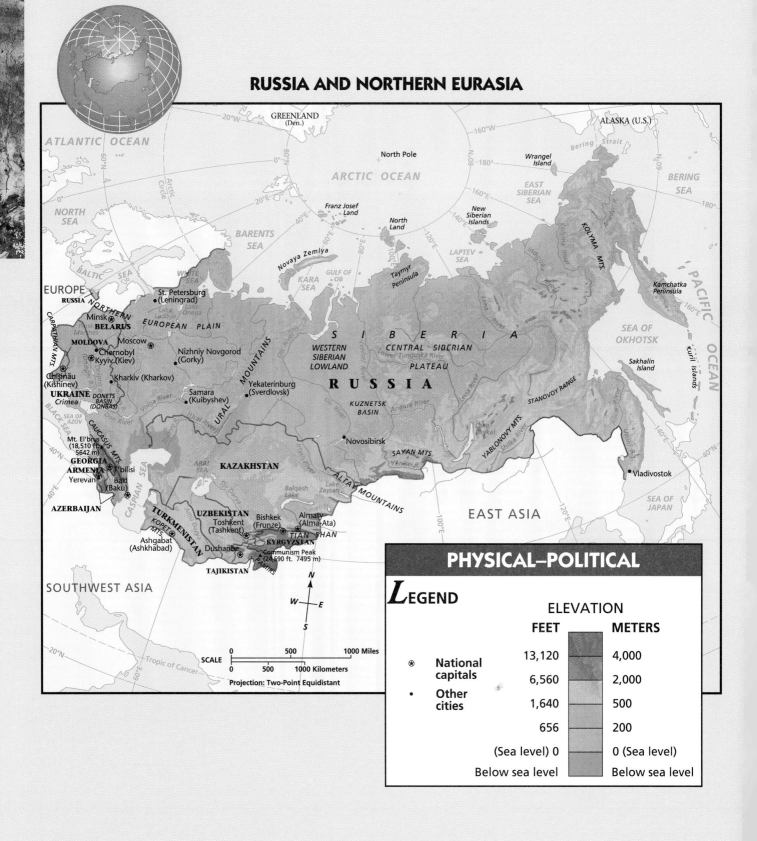

GREENLAND (Den.)

ALASKA (U.S.)

ATLANTIC OCEAN

North Pole

ARCTIC OCEAN

Bering Strait

Wrangel Island

EAST SIBERIAN SEA

BERING SEA

NORTH SEA

BARENTS SEA

Franz Josef Land

North Land

New Siberian Islands

LAPTEV SEA

KOLYMA MTS.

Novaya Zemlya

KARA SEA

Taymyr Peninsula

GULF OF OB

Kamchatka Peninsula

BALTIC SEA

WHITE SEA

Lake Onega

St. Petersburg (Leningrad)

SEA OF OKHOTSK

Kuril Islands

EUROPE

RUSSIA

NORTHERN

EUROPEAN PLAIN

SIBERIA

Sakhalin Island

Minsk

BELARUS

MOLDOVA

Moscow

Nizhniy Novgorod (Gorky)

Chernobyl

Kyyiv (Kiev)

WESTERN SIBERIAN LOWLAND

CENTRAL SIBERIAN PLATEAU

Lower Tunguska River

RUSSIA

CARPATHIAN MTS.

Kharkiv (Kharkov)

Yekaterinburg (Sverdlovsk)

Chişinău (Kishinev)

Samara (Kuibyshev)

UKRAINE

DONETS BASIN (DONBAS)

Crimea

KUZNETSK BASIN

Angara River

STANOVOY RANGE

SEA OF AZOV

Volga River

URAL MOUNTAINS

Ob River

BLACK SEA

Don River

Ural River

Novosibirsk

YABLONOVY MTS.

Shilka River

Vladivostok

SEA OF JAPAN

Mt. El'brus (18,510 ft. 5642 m)

CAUCASUS MTS.

SAYAN MTS.

Yenisey R.

GEORGIA

ARMENIA

T'bilisi

Baki (Baku)

ALTAY MOUNTAINS

EAST ASIA

Yerevan

CASPIAN SEA

ARAL SEA

KAZAKHSTAN

AZERBAIJAN

Balqash Lake

Lake Zaysan

TURKMENISTAN

KOPET MTS.

UZBEKISTAN

Toshkent (Tashkent)

Bishkek (Frunze)

Almaty (Alma-Ata)

Amu Darya

Syr Darya

TIAN SHAN

Ashgabat (Ashkhabad)

Dushanbe

KYRGYZSTAN

Communism Peak (24,590 ft. 7495 m)

PAMIRS

TAJIKISTAN

SOUTHWEST ASIA

Tropic of Cancer

N W E S

SCALE
0   500   1000 Miles
0 500 1000 Kilometers

Projection: Two-Point Equidistant

PHYSICAL–POLITICAL

*L*EGEND

⊛ National capitals

• Other cities

ELEVATION

FEET	METERS
13,120	4,000
6,560	2,000
1,640	500
656	200
(Sea level) 0	0 (Sea level)
Below sea level	Below sea level

RUSSIA AND NORTHERN EURASIA

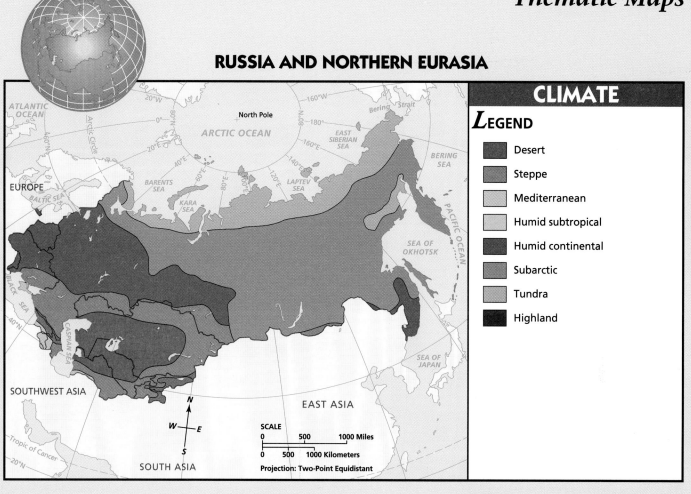

CLIMATE

LEGEND

- Desert
- Steppe
- Mediterranean
- Humid subtropical
- Humid continental
- Subarctic
- Tundra
- Highland

SCALE
0   500   1000 Miles
0   500   1000 Kilometers
Projection: Two-Point Equidistant

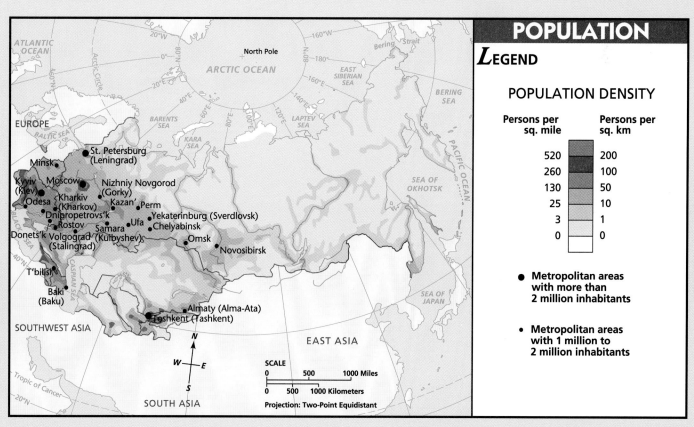

POPULATION

LEGEND

POPULATION DENSITY

Persons per sq. mile	Persons per sq. km
520	200
260	100
130	50
25	10
3	1
0	0

● Metropolitan areas with more than 2 million inhabitants

• Metropolitan areas with 1 million to 2 million inhabitants

SCALE
0   500   1000 Miles
0   500   1000 Kilometers
Projection: Two-Point Equidistant

RUSSIA AND NORTHERN EURASIA

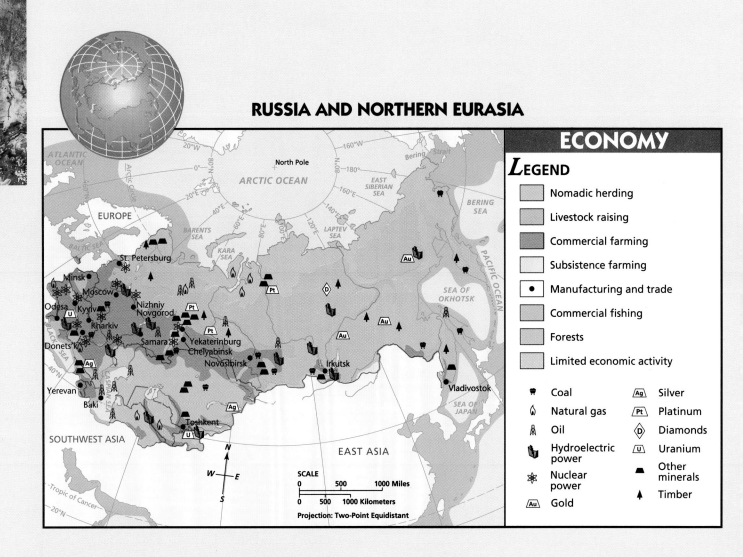

ECONOMY

LEGEND

- Nomadic herding
- Livestock raising
- Commercial farming
- Subsistence farming
- Manufacturing and trade
- Commercial fishing
- Forests
- Limited economic activity

- Coal
- Natural gas
- Oil
- Hydroelectric power
- Nuclear power
- Au Gold
- Ag Silver
- Pt Platinum
- D Diamonds
- U Uranium
- Other minerals
- Timber

SCALE
0   500   1000 Miles
0   500   1000 Kilometers
Projection: Two-Point Equidistant

SOUTHWEST ASIA

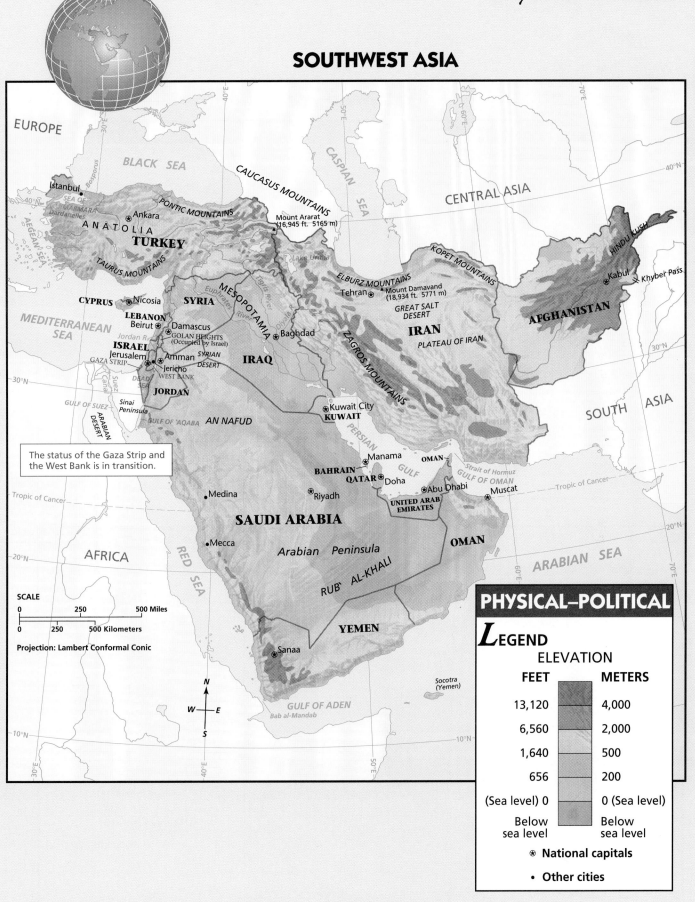

EUROPE

BLACK SEA

CAUCASUS MOUNTAINS

CASPIAN SEA

CENTRAL ASIA

Istanbul
SEA OF MARMARA
Dardanelles
Bosporus
Ankara
PONTIC MOUNTAINS
ANATOLIA
TURKEY
AEGEAN SEA
TAURUS MOUNTAINS

Mount Ararat
(16,945 ft. 5165 m)
Lake Urmia

KOPET MOUNTAINS

HINDU KUSH

Kabul
Khyber Pass

ELBURZ MOUNTAINS
Tehran
Mount Damavand
(18,934 ft. 5771 m)
GREAT SALT DESERT

AFGHANISTAN

CYPRUS
Nicosia
SYRIA
MESOPOTAMIA
Euphrates River
Tigris River

LEBANON
Beirut
Damascus
GOLAN HEIGHTS
(Occupied by Israel)
Baghdad
Diyala
ZAGROS MOUNTAINS

IRAN
PLATEAU OF IRAN

MEDITERRANEAN
SEA

Jordan R.
ISRAEL
Jerusalem
GAZA STRIP
Amman
Jericho
WEST BANK
DEAD SEA
SYRIAN
DESERT
IRAQ

SOUTH ASIA

30°N

JORDAN

Sinai
Peninsula
GULF OF SUEZ
Suez Canal
GULF OF 'AQABA
ARABIAN
DESERT
AN NAFUD

Kuwait City
KUWAIT

PERSIAN GULF

The status of the Gaza Strip and
the West Bank is in transition.

Manama
BAHRAIN
QATAR
Doha
OMAN
Abu Dhabi
GULF OF OMAN
Strait of Hormuz
Muscat

Tropic of Cancer

Medina
Riyadh

UNITED ARAB
EMIRATES

Tropic of Cancer

AFRICA

RED SEA

Mecca

SAUDI ARABIA

Arabian   Peninsula

RUB' AL-KHALI

OMAN

ARABIAN SEA

20°N

SCALE
0   250   500 Miles
0   250   500 Kilometers

Projection: Lambert Conformal Conic

YEMEN

Sanaa

Socotra
(Yemen)

N
W   E
S

GULF OF ADEN
Bab al-Mandab

PHYSICAL–POLITICAL

𝐿EGEND
ELEVATION

FEET		METERS
13,120		4,000
6,560		2,000
1,640		500
656		200
(Sea level) 0		0 (Sea level)
Below sea level		Below sea level

⊛ **National capitals**

• **Other cities**

Thematic Maps

SOUTHWEST ASIA

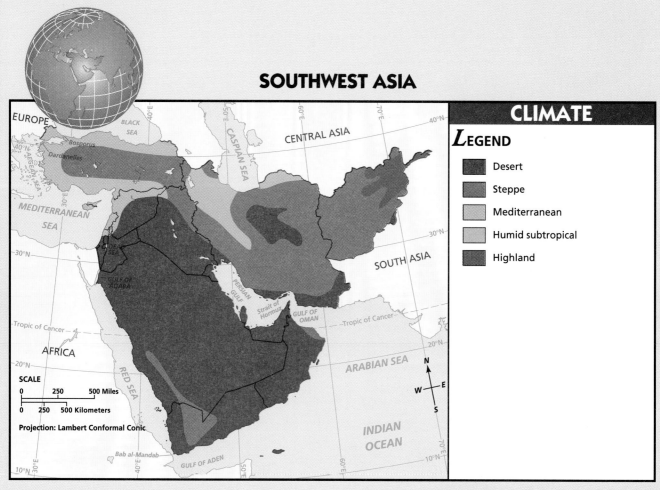

CLIMATE

LEGEND

- Desert
- Steppe
- Mediterranean
- Humid subtropical
- Highland

EUROPE • BLACK SEA • CENTRAL ASIA • Bosporus • Dardanelles • CASPIAN SEA • MEDITERRANEAN SEA • GULF OF AQABA • RED SEA • PERSIAN GULF • Strait of Hormuz • GULF OF OMAN • SOUTH ASIA • Tropic of Cancer • AFRICA • ARABIAN SEA • INDIAN OCEAN • Bab al-Mandab • GULF OF ADEN

SCALE
0   250   500 Miles
0   250   500 Kilometers
Projection: Lambert Conformal Conic

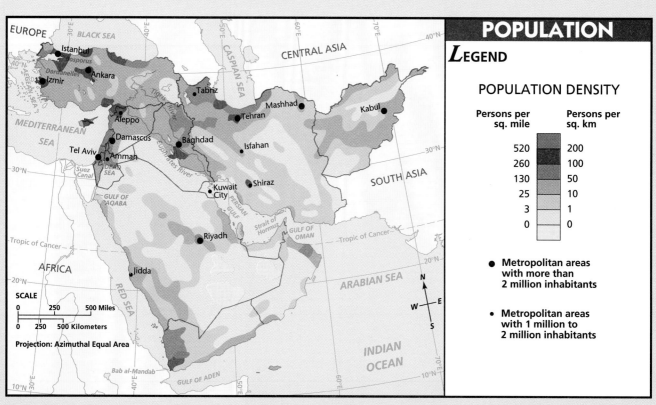

POPULATION

LEGEND

POPULATION DENSITY

Persons per sq. mile	Persons per sq. km
520	200
260	100
130	50
25	10
3	1
0	0

- ● Metropolitan areas with more than 2 million inhabitants
- • Metropolitan areas with 1 million to 2 million inhabitants

EUROPE • BLACK SEA • CENTRAL ASIA • Istanbul • Ankara • Izmir • Dardanelles • Bosporus • AEGEAN SEA • Tabriz • Mashhad • Tehran • Kabul • Aleppo • Tigris River • Damascus • Baghdad • Isfahan • Tel Aviv • Amman • DEAD SEA • Euphrates River • MEDITERRANEAN SEA • Suez Canal • GULF OF AQABA • Kuwait City • Shiraz • PERSIAN GULF • Strait of Hormuz • GULF OF OMAN • SOUTH ASIA • Riyadh • Tropic of Cancer • AFRICA • Jidda • RED SEA • ARABIAN SEA • INDIAN OCEAN • Bab al-Mandab • GULF OF ADEN

SCALE
0   250   500 Miles
0   250   500 Kilometers
Projection: Azimuthal Equal Area

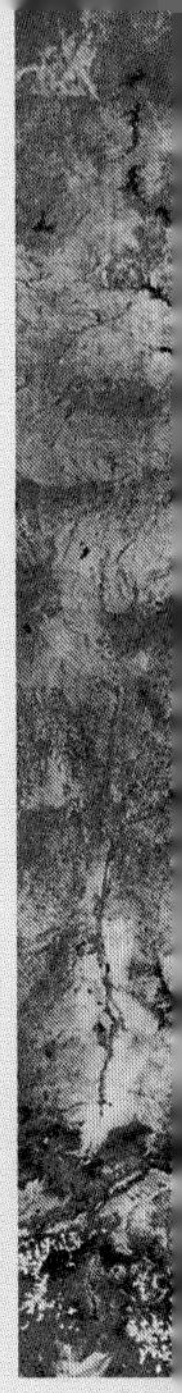

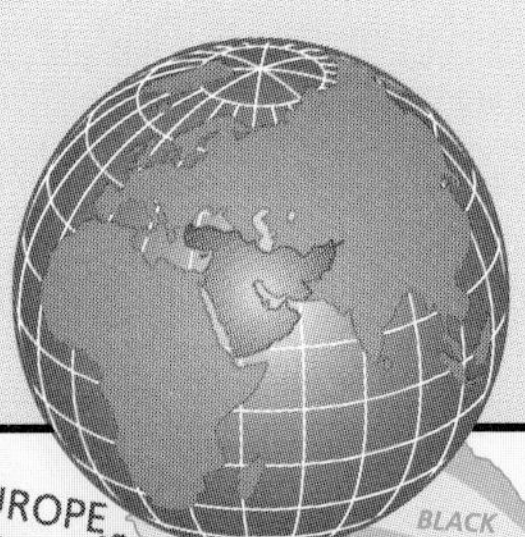

SOUTHWEST ASIA

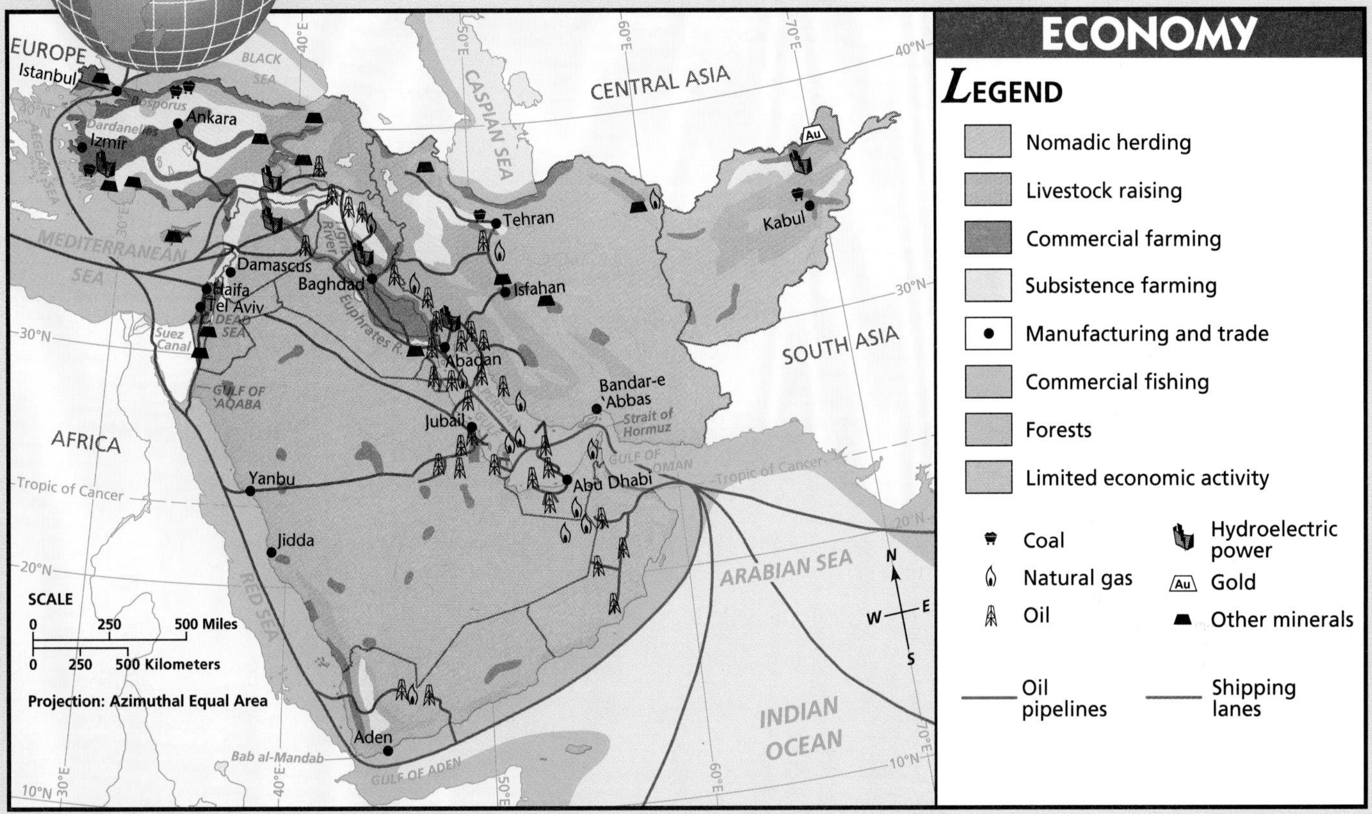
ECONOMY
LEGEND
Nomadic herding
Livestock raising
Commercial farming
Subsistence farming
Manufacturing and trade
Commercial fishing
Forests
Limited economic activity
Coal
Natural gas
Oil
Hydroelectric power
Gold
Other minerals
Oil pipelines
Shipping lanes
EUROPE
Istanbul
BLACK SEA
Bosporus
Ankara
Dardanelles
Izmir
AEGEAN SEA
MEDITERRANEAN SEA
CASPIAN SEA
CENTRAL ASIA
Tehran
Isfahan
Kabul
Damascus
Baghdad
Haifa
Tel Aviv
DEAD SEA
Suez Canal
Euphrates R.
Abadan
Bandar-e `Abbas
Strait of Hormuz
SOUTH ASIA
GULF OF AQABA
Jubail
Abu Dhabi
GULF OF OMAN
AFRICA
Tropic of Cancer
Yanbu
Jidda
RED SEA
ARABIAN SEA
INDIAN OCEAN
Aden
Bab al-Mandab
GULF OF ADEN
SCALE
0 250 500 Miles
0 250 500 Kilometers
Projection: Azimuthal Equal Area
N
S
E
W
40°N
30°N
20°N
10°N
30°E
40°E
50°E
60°E
70°E
Au

Physical–Political

EAST AND SOUTHEAST ASIA

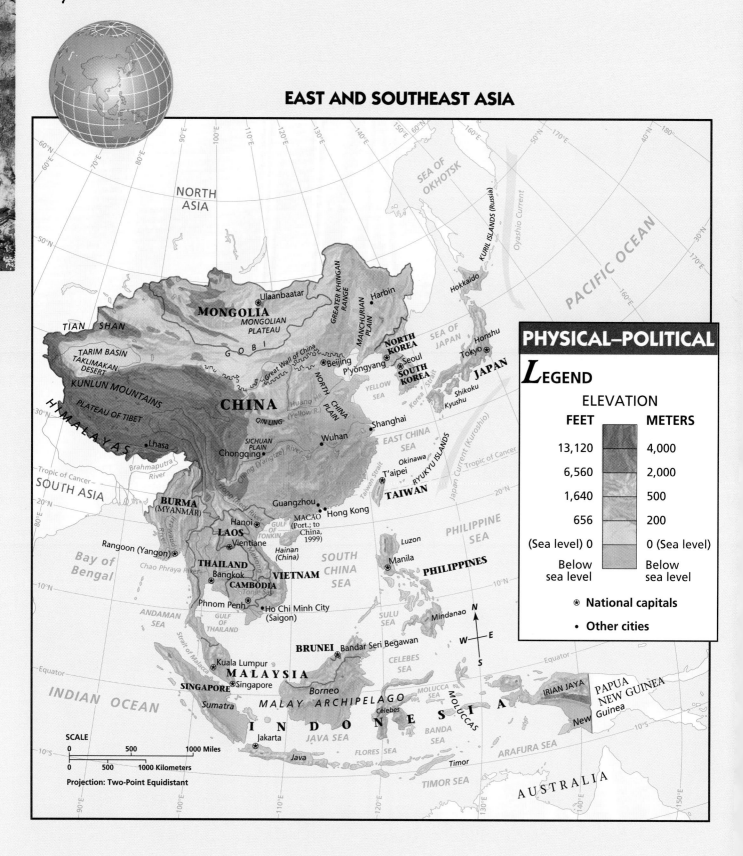

NORTH
ASIA

SEA OF
OKHOTSK

KURIL ISLANDS (Russia)

Oyashio Current

PACIFIC OCEAN

Ulaanbaatar

MONGOLIA
MONGOLIAN
PLATEAU

GREATER KHINGAN
RANGE

Harbin

MANCHURIAN
PLAIN

Hokkaido

TIAN SHAN

GOBI

NORTH
KOREA

SEA OF
JAPAN

Honshu

Tokyo

JAPAN

TARIM BASIN
TAKLIMAKAN
DESERT

Great Wall of China

Beijing

P'yŏngyang

Seoul

SOUTH
KOREA

Shikoku

Kyushu

KUNLUN MOUNTAINS

NORTH CHINA PLAIN

YELLOW
SEA

Korea Strait

PLATEAU OF TIBET

CHINA

Huang He
(Yellow R.)

QIN LING

Shanghai

Wuhan

EAST CHINA
SEA

HIMALAYAS

Lhasa

SICHUAN
PLAIN

Chongqing

Chang (Yangtze) River

Okinawa

Tropic of Cancer

RYUKYU ISLANDS

Japan Current (Kuroshio)

Brahmaputra
River

T'aipei

TAIWAN

SOUTH ASIA

Tropic of Cancer

BURMA
(MYANMAR)

Guangzhou

MACAO
(Port.; to
China,
1999)

Hong Kong

Hanoi

GULF
OF
TONKIN

PHILIPPINE
SEA

Rangoon (Yangon)

LAOS

Vientiane

Hainan
(China)

Luzon

SOUTH
CHINA
SEA

Manila

PHILIPPINES

Bay of
Bengal

Chao Phraya River

THAILAND

Bangkok

VIETNAM

CAMBODIA

Tonle Sap

Phnom Penh

Ho Chi Minh City
(Saigon)

ANDAMAN
SEA

GULF
OF
THAILAND

SULU
SEA

Mindanao

N

W E

S

BRUNEI

Bandar Seri Begawan

CELEBES
SEA

Kuala Lumpur

MALAYSIA

MOLUCCA
SEA

Equator

IRIAN JAYA

PAPUA
NEW GUINEA

SINGAPORE

Singapore

Borneo

MALAY ARCHIPELAGO

Célebes

MOLUCCAS

INDONESIA

New Guinea

INDIAN OCEAN

Sumatra

Jakarta

JAVA SEA

BANDA
SEA

Java

FLORES SEA

Timor

ARAFURA SEA

Equator

TIMOR SEA

AUSTRALIA

Strait of Malacca

PHYSICAL–POLITICAL

LEGEND

ELEVATION

FEET		METERS
13,120		4,000
6,560		2,000
1,640		500
656		200
(Sea level) 0		0 (Sea level)
Below sea level		Below sea level

⊛ National capitals

• Other cities

SCALE

0   500   1000 Miles

0   500   1000 Kilometers

Projection: Two-Point Equidistant

Thematic Maps

EAST AND SOUTHEAST ASIA

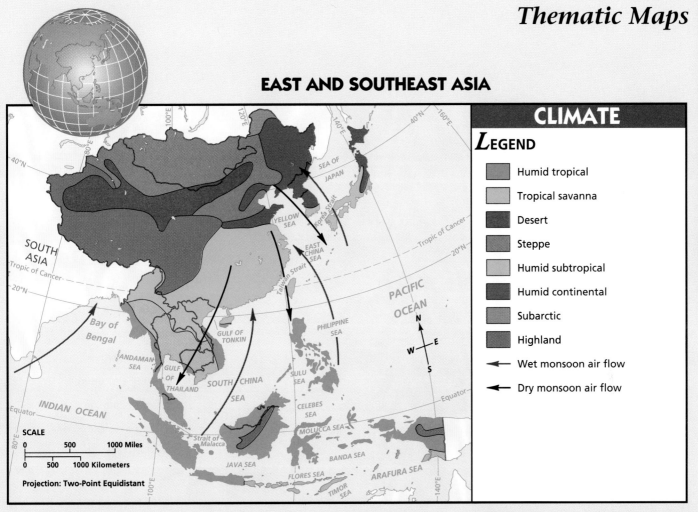

CLIMATE

LEGEND

- Humid tropical
- Tropical savanna
- Desert
- Steppe
- Humid subtropical
- Humid continental
- Subarctic
- Highland
- ← Wet monsoon air flow
- ← Dry monsoon air flow

SCALE
0   500   1000 Miles
0   500   1000 Kilometers

Projection: Two-Point Equidistant

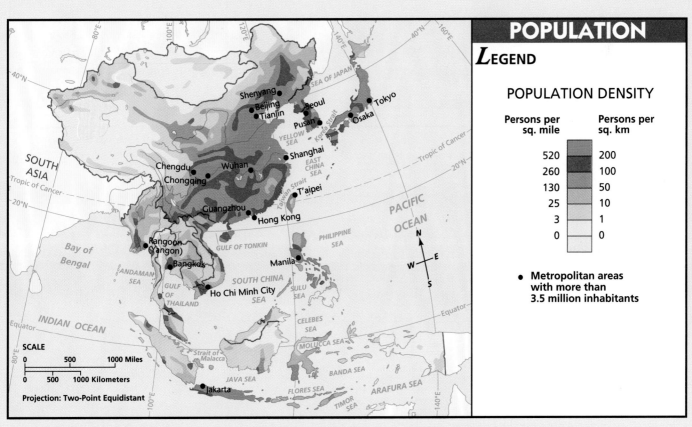

POPULATION

LEGEND

POPULATION DENSITY

Persons per sq. mile	Persons per sq. km
520	200
260	100
130	50
25	10
3	1
0	0

● Metropolitan areas with more than 3.5 million inhabitants

SCALE
0   500   1000 Miles
0   500   1000 Kilometers

Projection: Two-Point Equidistant

EAST AND SOUTHEAST ASIA

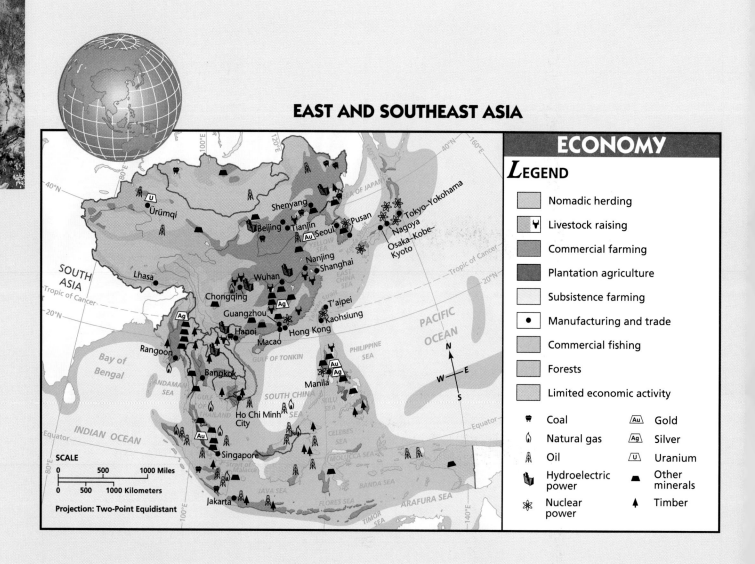

ECONOMY

LEGEND

- Nomadic herding
- Livestock raising
- Commercial farming
- Plantation agriculture
- Subsistence farming
- • Manufacturing and trade
- Commercial fishing
- Forests
- Limited economic activity

Coal		Au	Gold
Natural gas		Ag	Silver
Oil		U	Uranium
Hydroelectric power			Other minerals
Nuclear power			Timber

SCALE

0   500   1000 Miles

0   500   1000 Kilometers

Projection: Two-Point Equidistant

SOUTH ASIA

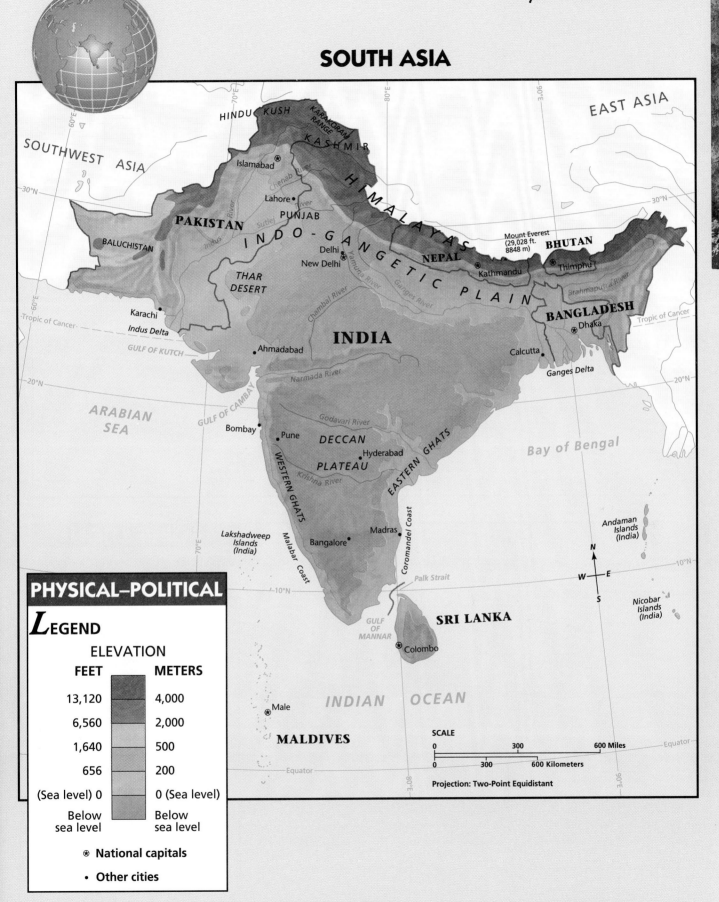

PHYSICAL–POLITICAL

LEGEND

ELEVATION

FEET	METERS
13,120	4,000
6,560	2,000
1,640	500
656	200
(Sea level) 0	0 (Sea level)
Below sea level	Below sea level

⊛ **National capitals**

• **Other cities**

SCALE

Projection: Two-Point Equidistant

Thematic Maps

SOUTH ASIA

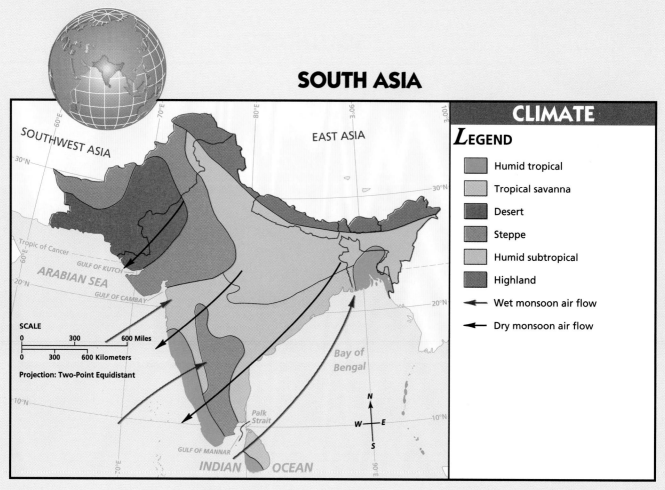

CLIMATE

LEGEND

- Humid tropical
- Tropical savanna
- Desert
- Steppe
- Humid subtropical
- Highland
- ← Wet monsoon air flow
- ← Dry monsoon air flow

SOUTHWEST ASIA

EAST ASIA

30°N
30°N
Tropic of Cancer
GULF OF KUTCH
ARABIAN SEA
20°N
20°N
GULF OF CAMBAY

SCALE
0   300   600 Miles
0   300   600 Kilometers
Projection: Two-Point Equidistant

10°N

Bay of Bengal

Palk Strait

N
W   E
S

10°N

GULF OF MANNAR
INDIAN OCEAN

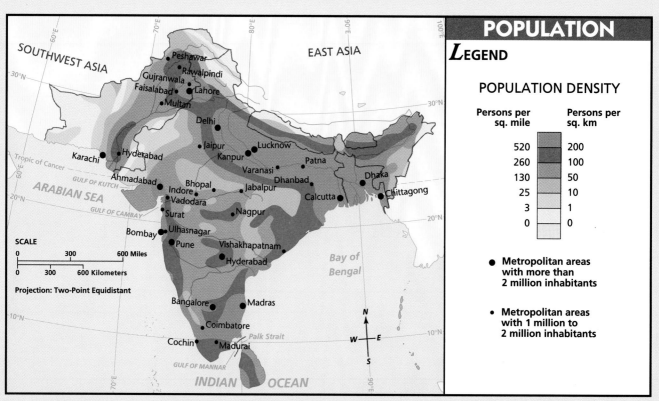

POPULATION

LEGEND

POPULATION DENSITY

Persons per sq. mile	Persons per sq. km
520	200
260	100
130	50
25	10
3	1
0	0

● Metropolitan areas with more than 2 million inhabitants

● Metropolitan areas with 1 million to 2 million inhabitants

SOUTHWEST ASIA

EAST ASIA

Peshawar
Rawalpindi
Gujranwala
Faisalabad   Lahore
Multan
Delhi
30°N
Jaipur   Lucknow
Karachi   Hyderabad   Kanpur   Patna
Tropic of Cancer   Varanasi
Ahmadabad   Dhanbad   Dhaka
GULF OF KUTCH   Bhopal   Jabalpur
Indore   Calcutta   Chittagong
Vadodara
20°N   Surat
GULF OF CAMBAY
Bombay   Ulhasnagar
Pune   Vishakhapatnam
Hyderabad

ARABIAN SEA

Bay of Bengal

SCALE
0   300   600 Miles
0   300   600 Kilometers
Projection: Two-Point Equidistant

Bangalore   Madras

10°N
Coimbatore
Palk Strait
Cochin   Madurai

N
W   E
S

10°N

GULF OF MANNAR
INDIAN OCEAN

SOUTH ASIA

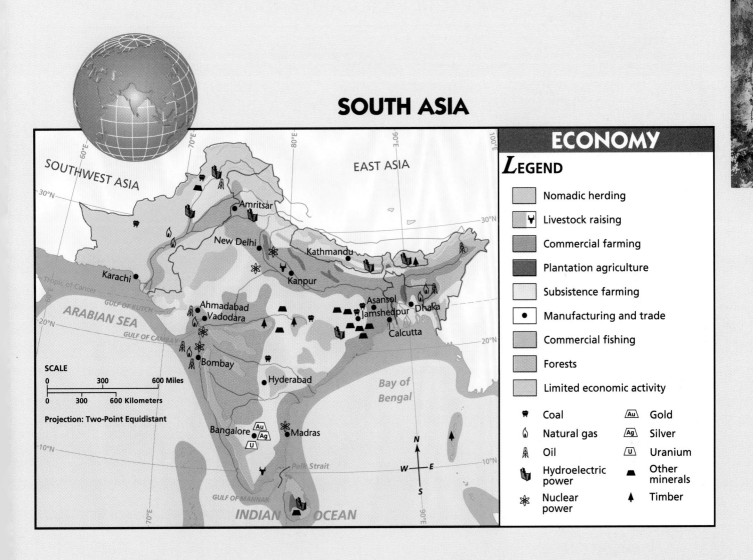

LEGEND

- Nomadic herding
- Livestock raising
- Commercial farming
- Plantation agriculture
- Subsistence farming
- • Manufacturing and trade
- Commercial fishing
- Forests
- Limited economic activity

Coal		Au	Gold
Natural gas		Ag	Silver
Oil		U	Uranium
Hydroelectric power		Other minerals
Nuclear power		Timber

SOUTHWEST ASIA

EAST ASIA

30°N

Amritsar

New Delhi

Kathmandu

Karachi

Kanpur

ARABIAN SEA

Tropic of Cancer

GULF OF KUTCH

Ahmadabad
Vadodara

Asansol
Jamshedpur

Dhaka

20°N

GULF OF CAMBAY

Calcutta

Bombay

Hyderabad

Bay of Bengal

SCALE

0	300	600 Miles
0	300	600 Kilometers

Projection: Two-Point Equidistant

Bangalore Au / Ag / U

Madras

10°N

Palk Strait

N
W E
S

10°N

GULF OF MANNAR

INDIAN OCEAN

Physical–Political

THE PACIFIC WORLD AND ANTARCTICA

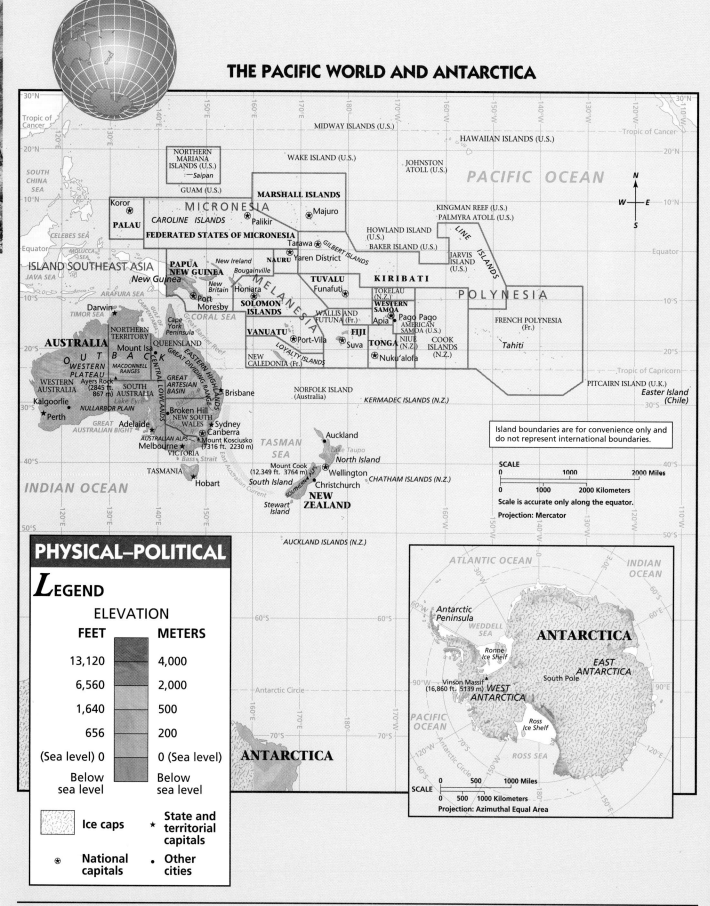

Tropic of Cancer

MIDWAY ISLANDS (U.S.)

HAWAIIAN ISLANDS (U.S.)

Tropic of Cancer

WAKE ISLAND (U.S.)

JOHNSTON ATOLL (U.S.)

PACIFIC OCEAN

NORTHERN MARIANA ISLANDS (U.S.)
Saipan

SOUTH CHINA SEA

GUAM (U.S.)

Koror

PALAU

MICRONESIA

CAROLINE ISLANDS

Palikir

FEDERATED STATES OF MICRONESIA

MARSHALL ISLANDS

Majuro

KINGMAN REEF (U.S.)
PALMYRA ATOLL (U.S.)

HOWLAND ISLAND (U.S.)

BAKER ISLAND (U.S.)

JARVIS ISLAND (U.S.)

LINE ISLANDS

POLYNESIA

CELEBES SEA

Equator

ISLAND SOUTHEAST ASIA

MOLUCCA SEA

JAVA SEA

Tarawa

GILBERT ISLANDS

NAURU Yaren District

Equator

PAPUA NEW GUINEA

New Ireland

New Guinea

Bougainville

New Britain Honiara

Port Moresby

SOLOMON ISLANDS

MELANESIA

ARAFURA SEA

TUVALU

Funafuti

KIRIBATI

TOKELAU (N.Z.)

WESTERN SAMOA

WALLIS AND FUTUNA (Fr.) Apia

Pago Pago

AMERICAN SAMOA (U.S.)

FRENCH POLYNESIA (Fr.)

Darwin

TIMOR SEA

NORTHERN TERRITORY

Cape York Peninsula

CORAL SEA

VANUATU

Port-Vila

FIJI

Suva

TONGA

NIUE (N.Z.)

COOK ISLANDS (N.Z.)

Tahiti

AUSTRALIA

OUTBACK

WESTERN PLATEAU

MACDONNELL RANGES

Ayers Rock (2845 ft. 867 m)

QUEENSLAND

GREAT DIVIDING RANGE

EASTERN HIGHLANDS

CENTRAL LOWLANDS

GREAT ARTESIAN BASIN

NEW CALEDONIA (Fr.)

LOYALTY ISLANDS

Nuku'alofa

Tropic of Capricorn

PITCAIRN ISLAND (U.K.)

Easter Island (Chile)

WESTERN AUSTRALIA

Kalgoorlie

SOUTH AUSTRALIA

Lake Eyre

Brisbane

NORFOLK ISLAND (Australia)

KERMADEC ISLANDS (N.Z.)

Island boundaries are for convenience only and do not represent international boundaries.

Perth

NULLARBOR PLAIN

GREAT AUSTRALIAN BIGHT

Adelaide

Broken Hill

NEW SOUTH WALES

Sydney

Canberra

Auckland

Lake Taupo

North Island

SCALE
0   1000   2000 Miles
0   1000   2000 Kilometers
Scale is accurate only along the equator.
Projection: Mercator

Melbourne

VICTORIA

AUSTRALIAN ALPS

Mount Kosciusko (7316 ft. 2230 m)

Bass Strait

TASMAN SEA

TASMANIA

Mount Cook (12,349 ft. 3764 m)

South Island

SOUTHERN ALPS

Wellington

Christchurch

CHATHAM ISLANDS (N.Z.)

INDIAN OCEAN

Hobart

Stewart Island

NEW ZEALAND

AUCKLAND ISLANDS (N.Z.)

PHYSICAL–POLITICAL

Legend

ELEVATION

FEET	METERS
13,120	4,000
6,560	2,000
1,640	500
656	200
(Sea level) 0	0 (Sea level)
Below sea level	Below sea level

Ice caps

★ State and territorial capitals

⊛ National capitals

• Other cities

ATLANTIC OCEAN

WEDDELL SEA

Antarctic Peninsula

Ronne Ice Shelf

Vinson Massif (16,860 ft. 5139 m)

WEST ANTARCTICA

INDIAN OCEAN

ANTARCTICA

EAST ANTARCTICA

South Pole

Ross Ice Shelf

PACIFIC OCEAN

ROSS SEA

SCALE
0   500   1000 Miles
0   500   1000 Kilometers
Projection: Azimuthal Equal Area

Antarctic Circle

ANTARCTICA

THE PACIFIC WORLD AND ANTARCTICA

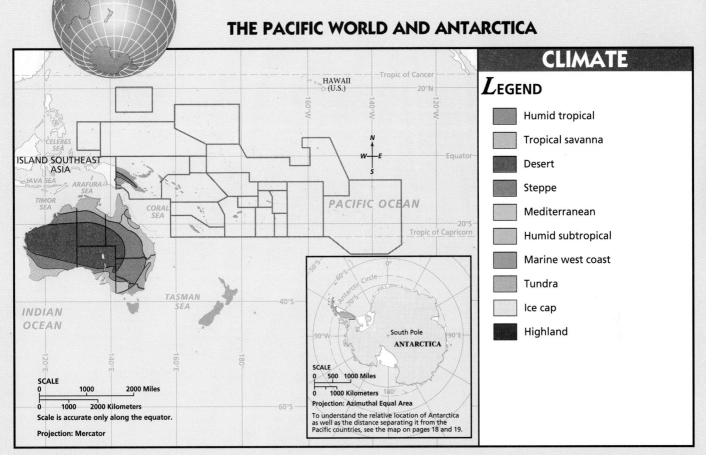

CLIMATE

*L*EGEND

- Humid tropical
- Tropical savanna
- Desert
- Steppe
- Mediterranean
- Humid subtropical
- Marine west coast
- Tundra
- Ice cap
- Highland

SCALE
0   1000   2000 Miles
0   1000   2000 Kilometers
Scale is accurate only along the equator.

Projection: Mercator

SCALE
0   500   1000 Miles
0   1000 Kilometers
Projection: Azimuthal Equal Area

To understand the relative location of Antarctica as well as the distance separating it from the Pacific countries, see the map on pages 18 and 19.

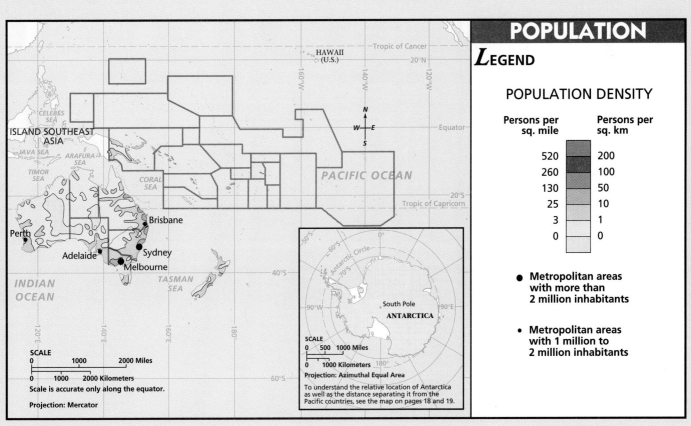

POPULATION

*L*EGEND

POPULATION DENSITY

Persons per sq. mile	Persons per sq. km
520	200
260	100
130	50
25	10
3	1
0	0

- ● Metropolitan areas with more than 2 million inhabitants
- ● Metropolitan areas with 1 million to 2 million inhabitants

SCALE
0   1000   2000 Miles
0   1000   2000 Kilometers
Scale is accurate only along the equator.

Projection: Mercator

SCALE
0   500   1000 Miles
0   1000 Kilometers
Projection: Azimuthal Equal Area

To understand the relative location of Antarctica as well as the distance separating it from the Pacific countries, see the map on pages 18 and 19.

THE PACIFIC WORLD AND ANTARCTICA

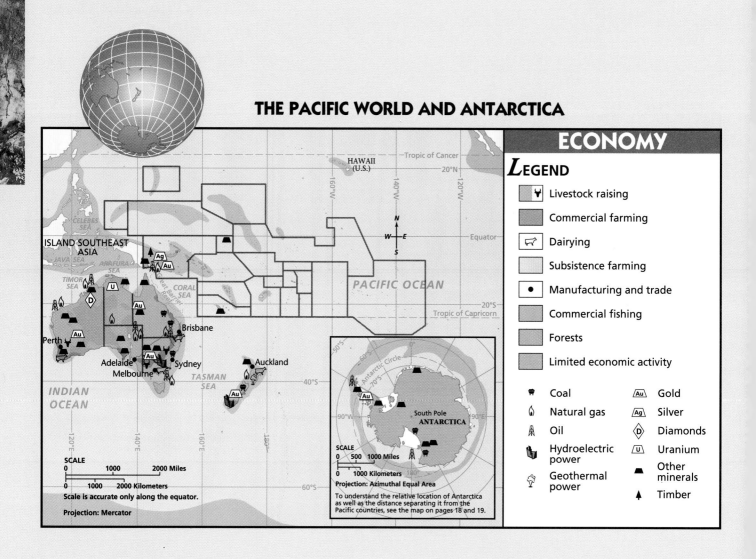

ECONOMY

LEGEND

- Livestock raising
- Commercial farming
- Dairying
- Subsistence farming
- Manufacturing and trade
- Commercial fishing
- Forests
- Limited economic activity

Coal		Au	Gold
Natural gas		Ag	Silver
Oil		D	Diamonds
Hydroelectric power		U	Uranium
Geothermal power		Other minerals	
		Timber	

Map labels:

HAWAII (U.S.)

Tropic of Cancer
20°N
160°W
140°W
120°W

ISLAND SOUTHEAST ASIA

CELEBES SEA
JAVA SEA
TIMOR SEA
ARAFURA SEA
CORAL SEA
Great Barrier Reef

Equator

PACIFIC OCEAN

20°S
Tropic of Capricorn

Perth
Adelaide
Melbourne
Sydney
Brisbane
Auckland

INDIAN OCEAN

TASMAN SEA

40°S

120°E
140°E
160°E
180°

60°S

SCALE
```
0        1000        2000 Miles
0    1000     2000 Kilometers
```
Scale is accurate only along the equator.

Projection: Mercator

Inset map (Antarctica):

50°S
60°S
Antarctic Circle
70°S
90°W
90°E
South Pole
ANTARCTICA
180°

SCALE
```
0    500   1000 Miles
0        1000 Kilometers
```
Projection: Azimuthal Equal Area

To understand the relative location of Antarctica as well as the distance separating it from the Pacific countries, see the map on pages 18 and 19.

WORLD HISTORY

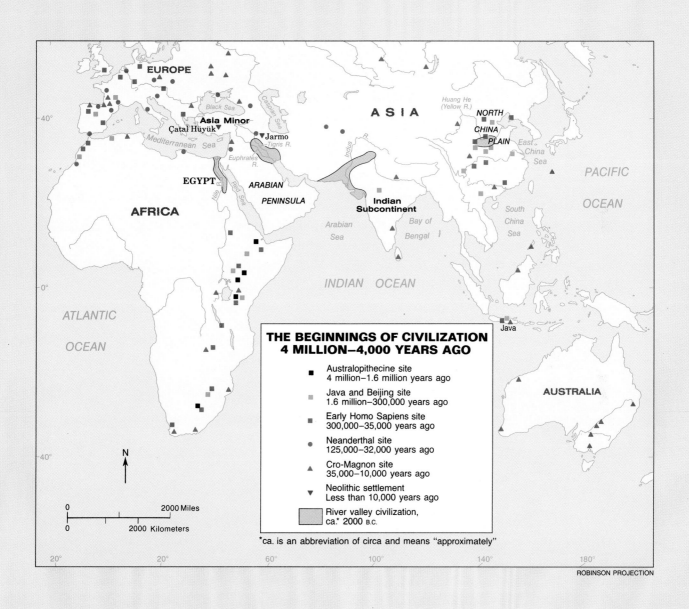

**THE BEGINNINGS OF CIVILIZATION
4 MILLION–4,000 YEARS AGO**

- ■ Australopithecine site
  4 million–1.6 million years ago
- ■ Java and Beijing site
  1.6 million–300,000 years ago
- ■ Early Homo Sapiens site
  300,000–35,000 years ago
- ● Neanderthal site
  125,000–32,000 years ago
- ▲ Cro-Magnon site
  35,000–10,000 years ago
- ▼ Neolithic settlement
  Less than 10,000 years ago
- ▨ River valley civilization,
  ca.* 2000 B.C.

*ca. is an abbreviation of circa and means "approximately"

ROBINSON PROJECTION

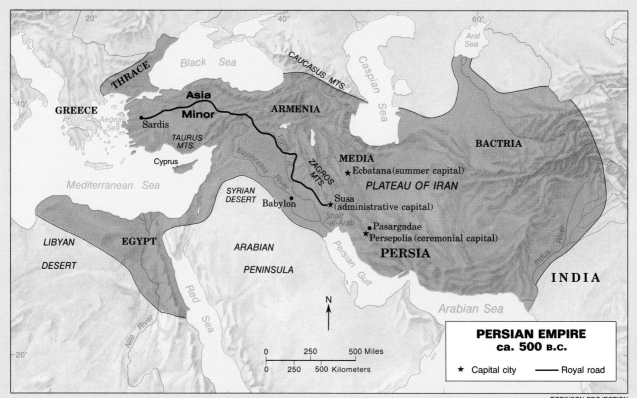

**PERSIAN EMPIRE
ca. 500 B.C.**

★ Capital city   —— Royal road

ROBINSON PROJECTION

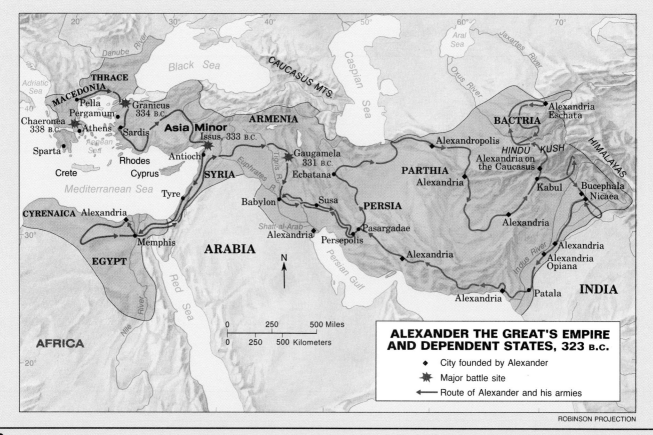

**ALEXANDER THE GREAT'S EMPIRE
AND DEPENDENT STATES, 323 B.C.**

◆ City founded by Alexander

✦ Major battle site

◄—— Route of Alexander and his armies

ROBINSON PROJECTION

Qin and Han Dynasties, 221 B.C.–A.D. 220

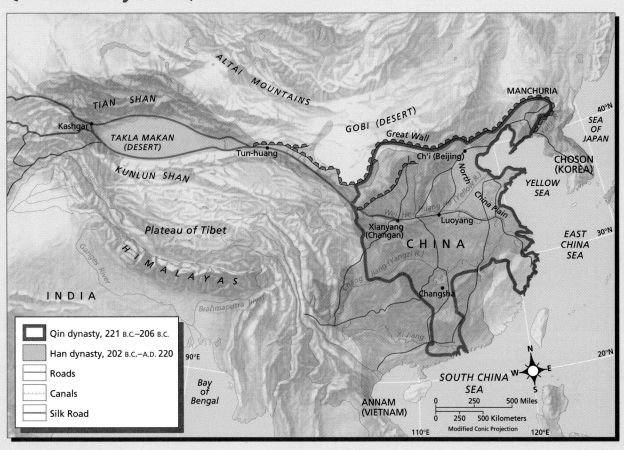

Legend:
- Qin dynasty, 221 B.C.–206 B.C.
- Han dynasty, 202 B.C.–A.D. 220
- Roads
- Canals
- Silk Road

Map labels:
ALTAI MOUNTAINS
TIAN SHAN
Kashgar
TAKLA MAKAN (DESERT)
Tun-huang
KUNLUN SHAN
Plateau of Tibet
HIMALAYAS
INDIA
Ganges River
Brahmaputra River
Bay of Bengal
GOBI (DESERT)
Great Wall
MANCHURIA
Ch'i (Beijing)
North River
Yellow R.
Wei He / Huang He (Yellow R.)
CHINA
Xianyang (Changan)
Luoyang
Chang Jiang (Yangzi R.)
Changsha
Xi Jiang
CHOSON (KOREA)
YELLOW SEA
EAST CHINA SEA
SEA OF JAPAN
SOUTH CHINA SEA
ANNAM (VIETNAM)
40°N
30°N
20°N
90°E
110°E
120°E
0 250 500 Miles
0 250 500 Kilometers
Modified Conic Projection

THE HEIGHT OF THE ROMAN EMPIRE
A.D. 117

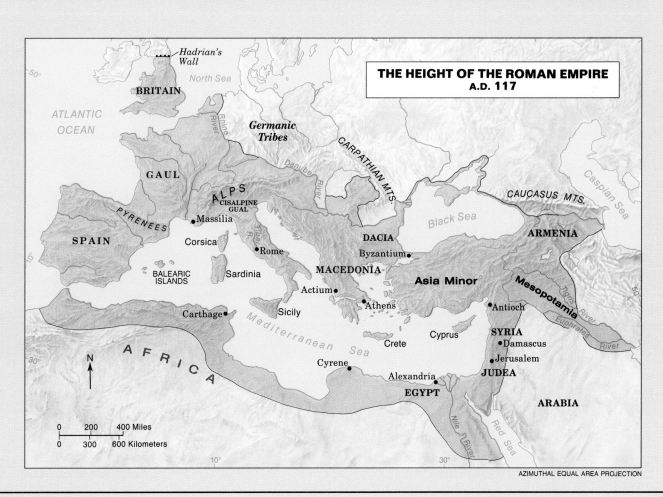

Map labels:
Hadrian's Wall
North Sea
BRITAIN
ATLANTIC OCEAN
GAUL
Rhine River
Germanic Tribes
CARPATHIAN MTS.
CAUCASUS MTS.
Caspian Sea
SPAIN
PYRENEES
ALPS
CISALPINE GUAL
Massilia
Corsica
Rome
Tiber R.
BALEARIC ISLANDS
Sardinia
Danube River
DACIA
Byzantium
Black Sea
ARMENIA
MACEDONIA
Asia Minor
Mesopotamia
Tigris River
Euphrates River
Actium
Athens
Antioch
Carthage
Sicily
Mediterranean Sea
Crete
Cyprus
SYRIA
Damascus
Jerusalem
JUDEA
Cyrene
Alexandria
EGYPT
Nile River
Red Sea
ARABIA
AFRICA
50°
40°
30°
10°
30°
50°
N
0 200 400 Miles
0 300 600 Kilometers
AZIMUTHAL EQUAL AREA PROJECTION

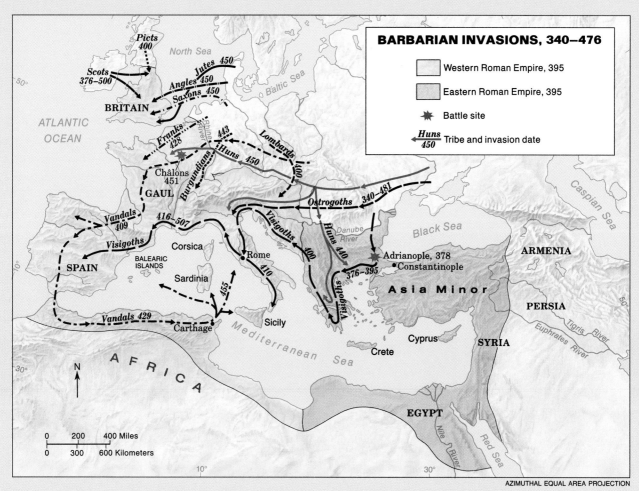

BARBARIAN INVASIONS, 340–476

Western Roman Empire, 395

Eastern Roman Empire, 395

★ Battle site

← Huns / 450   Tribe and invasion date

Picts 400

Scots 376–500

Angles 450   *Jutes 450*

Saxons 450

BRITAIN

Franks 428

Lombards 400

443

Huns 450

Châlons 451

Burgundians

GAUL

Vandals 409

416–507

Visigoths

SPAIN

Corsica

Ostrogoths 340–481

★ Chalons 451

Visigoths 400

Rome

410

Huns 440

Danube River

Adrianople, 378

• Constantinople

ARMENIA

PERSIA

BALEARIC ISLANDS

Sardinia

455

Visigoths 376–395

Rome

Sicily

Vandals 429

Carthage

Mediterranean Sea

Crete

Cyprus

SYRIA

Asia Minor

Caspian Sea

Tigris River

Euphrates River

AFRICA

EGYPT

Nile River

Red Sea

ATLANTIC OCEAN

North Sea

Baltic Sea

Black Sea

50°

10°

30°

10°

30°

50°

0   200   400 Miles
0   300   600 Kilometers

N

AZIMUTHAL EQUAL AREA PROJECTION

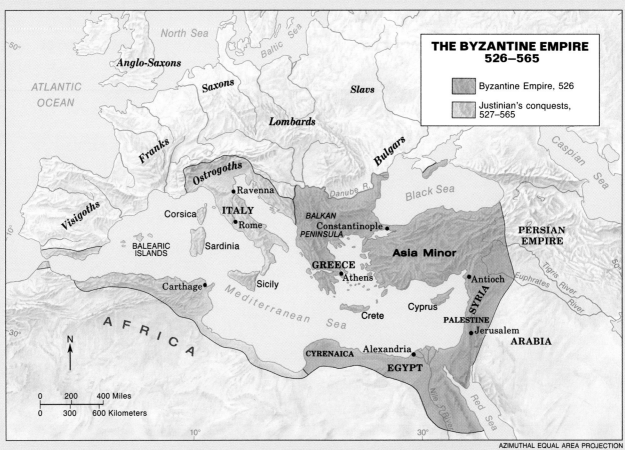

THE BYZANTINE EMPIRE 526–565

Byzantine Empire, 526

Justinian's conquests, 527–565

Anglo-Saxons

Saxons

Slavs

Lombards

Bulgars

Franks

Ostrogoths

• Ravenna

ITALY

• Rome

Visigoths

Corsica

BALEARIC ISLANDS

Sardinia

Sicily

Carthage •

Danube R.

BALKAN PENINSULA

Constantinople •

GREECE

• Athens

Crete

Asia Minor

PERSIAN EMPIRE

Cyprus

• Antioch

SYRIA

PALESTINE

• Jerusalem

ARABIA

CYRENAICA

Alexandria •

EGYPT

Mediterranean Sea

AFRICA

ATLANTIC OCEAN

North Sea

Baltic Sea

Black Sea

Caspian Sea

Tigris River

Euphrates River

Nile River

Red Sea

50°

10°

30°

10°

30°

50°

0   200   400 Miles
0   300   600 Kilometers

N

AZIMUTHAL EQUAL AREA PROJECTION

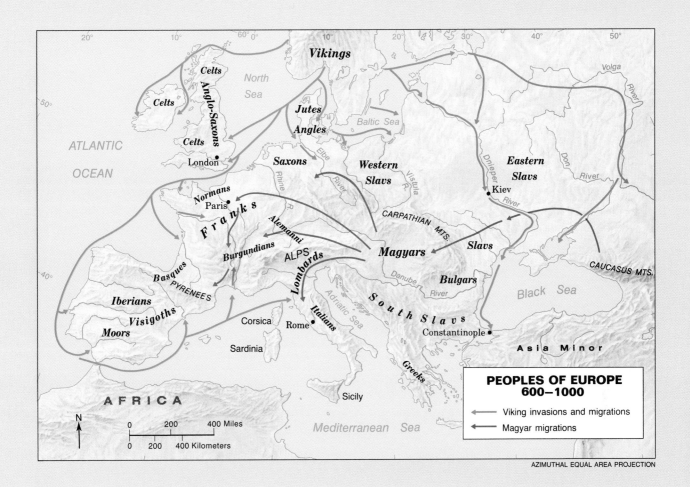

PEOPLES OF EUROPE 600–1000

← Viking invasions and migrations

← Magyar migrations

Vikings

Celts

Celts

Anglo-Saxons

Celts

London

Jutes

Angles

Saxons

Western Slavs

Normans

Paris

Franks

Alemanni

Burgundians

ALPS

Lombards

Basques

PYRENEES

Iberians

Visigoths

Moors

Corsica

Sardinia

Rome

Italians

Magyars

Bulgars

South Slavs

Greeks

Sicily

Constantinople

Eastern Slavs

Kiev

Slavs

CARPATHIAN MTS.

CAUCASUS MTS.

Danube River

Black Sea

Asia Minor

North Sea

Baltic Sea

ATLANTIC OCEAN

AFRICA

Mediterranean Sea

Volga River

Don River

Dnieper River

Vistula R.

Elbe River

Rhine R.

Adriatic Sea

N

0   200   400 Miles

0   200   400 Kilometers

AZIMUTHAL EQUAL AREA PROJECTION

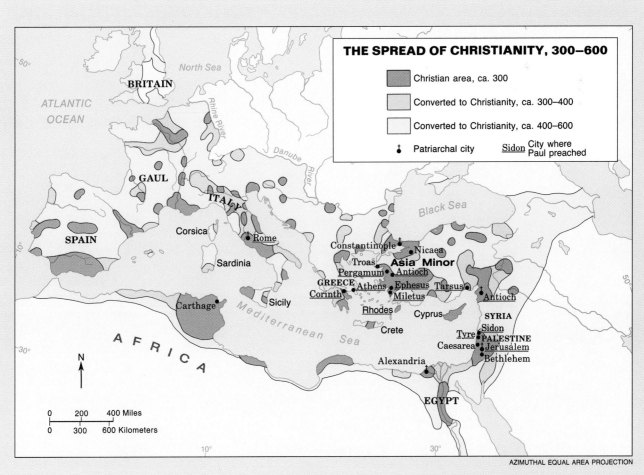

THE SPREAD OF CHRISTIANITY, 300–600

Christian area, ca. 300

Converted to Christianity, ca. 300–400

Converted to Christianity, ca. 400–600

† Patriarchal city

Sidon — City where Paul preached

BRITAIN

GAUL

ITALY

SPAIN

Corsica

Rome

Sardinia

Carthage

Sicily

Constantinople

Nicaea

Troas

Pergamum

Antioch

GREECE

Athens

Ephesus

Tarsus

Corinth

Miletus

Rhodes

Cyprus

Antioch

Crete

SYRIA

Tyre

Sidon

PALESTINE

Caesarea

Jerusalem

Bethlehem

Alexandria

EGYPT

Asia Minor

Black Sea

North Sea

ATLANTIC OCEAN

AFRICA

Mediterranean Sea

Rhine River

Danube River

N

0   200   400 Miles

0   300   600 Kilometers

AZIMUTHAL EQUAL AREA PROJECTION

Religions in Asia, c. 750–1450

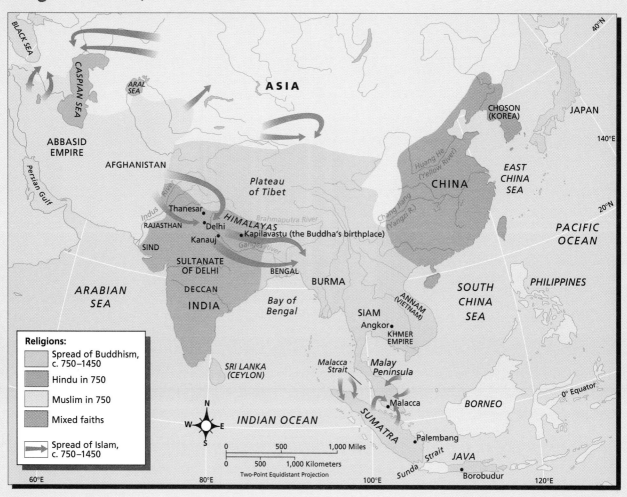

Religions:
- Spread of Buddhism, c. 750–1450
- Hindu in 750
- Muslim in 750
- Mixed faiths
- ← Spread of Islam, c. 750–1450

BLACK SEA
CASPIAN SEA
ARAL SEA
ASIA
CHOSON (KOREA)
JAPAN
140°E
40°N
ABBASID EMPIRE
Persian Gulf
AFGHANISTAN
Plateau of Tibet
CHINA
Huang He (Yellow River)
EAST CHINA SEA
20°N
Indus River
Thanesar
RAJASTHAN
Delhi
Kanauj
SIND
HIMALAYAS
Brahmaputra River
Kapilavastu (the Buddha's birthplace)
Ganges River
Chang Jiang (Yangzi R.)
PACIFIC OCEAN
SULTANATE OF DELHI
DECCAN
INDIA
BENGAL
BURMA
SOUTH CHINA SEA
PHILIPPINES
ARABIAN SEA
Bay of Bengal
SIAM
Angkor
KHMER EMPIRE
ANNAM (VIETNAM)
SRI LANKA (CEYLON)
Malacca Strait
Malay Peninsula
BORNEO
0° Equator
INDIAN OCEAN
SUMATRA
Malacca
Palembang
Sunda Strait
JAVA
Borobudur
120°E
100°E
80°E
60°E

0   500   1,000 Miles
0   500   1,000 Kilometers
Two-Point Equidistant Projection

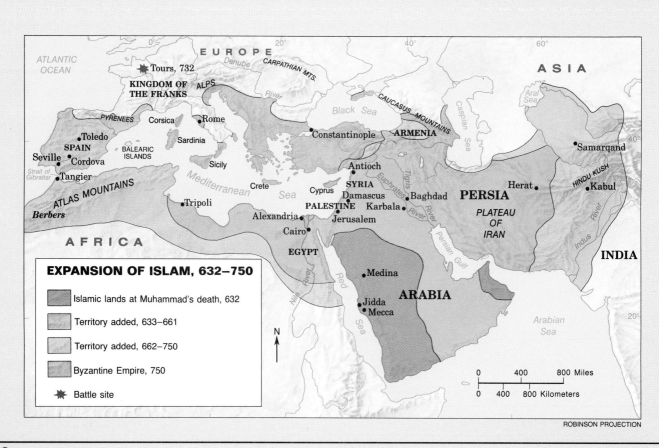

EXPANSION OF ISLAM, 632–750

- Islamic lands at Muhammad's death, 632
- Territory added, 633–661
- Territory added, 662–750
- Byzantine Empire, 750
- ★ Battle site

ATLANTIC OCEAN
EUROPE
Danube
CARPATHIAN MTS.
ASIA
★ Tours, 732
KINGDOM OF THE FRANKS
ALPS
River
Black Sea
CAUCASUS MOUNTAINS
Aral Sea
Caspian Sea
PYRENEES
Corsica
Rome
Constantinople
ARMENIA
Samarqand
Toledo
SPAIN
Sardinia
BALEARIC ISLANDS
Antioch
Euphrates
Tigris
PERSIA
Herat
HINDU KUSH
Seville
Cordova
Strait of Gibraltar
Tangier
Sicily
Crete
Cyprus
SYRIA
Damascus
Baghdad
Kabul
ATLAS MOUNTAINS
Mediterranean
Sea
PALESTINE
Karbala
River
PLATEAU OF IRAN
Indus River
Berbers
Tripoli
Alexandria
Jerusalem
Cairo
Persian Gulf
INDIA
AFRICA
EGYPT
Medina
Nile River
Red Sea
ARABIA
Jidda
Mecca
Arabian Sea
20°

0   400   800 Miles
0   400   800 Kilometers

ROBINSON PROJECTION

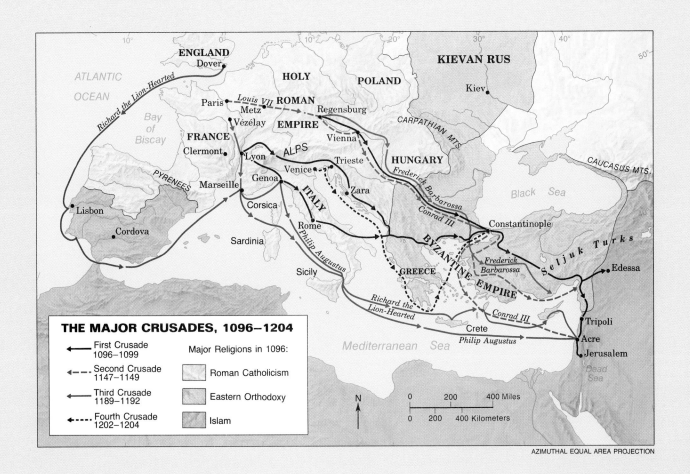

THE MAJOR CRUSADES, 1096–1204

→ First Crusade
1096–1099

⤍ Second Crusade
1147–1149

← Third Crusade
1189–1192

⤏ Fourth Crusade
1202–1204

Major Religions in 1096:

Roman Catholicism

Eastern Orthodoxy

Islam

0   200   400 Miles

0   200   400 Kilometers

AZIMUTHAL EQUAL AREA PROJECTION

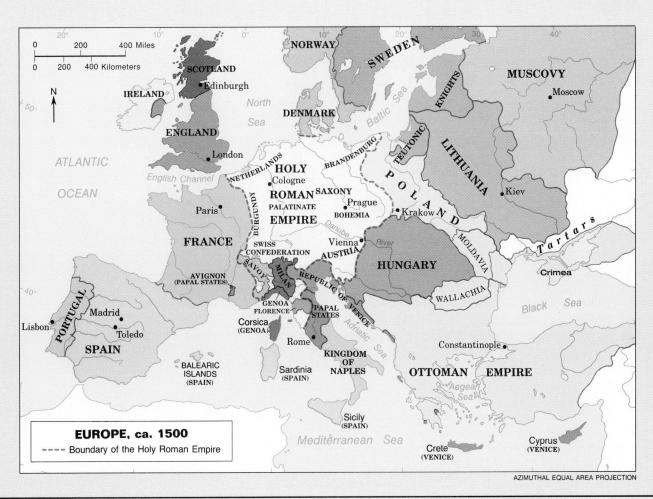

0   200   400 Miles

0   200   400 Kilometers

EUROPE, ca. 1500

--- Boundary of the Holy Roman Empire

AZIMUTHAL EQUAL AREA PROJECTION

EUROPEAN RELIGIONS, 1600

- Lutheran
- Calvinist
- Anglican
- Roman Catholic with Protestant minorities
- Roman Catholic
- Orthodox
- Muslim

ICELAND

ATLANTIC OCEAN

SWEDEN

NORWAY

RUSSIA

SCOTLAND
• Edinburgh

DENMARK
Copenhagen •

COURLAND

IRELAND • Dublin

North Sea

Baltic Sea

PRUSSIA

POLAND AND LITHUANIA

Warsaw •

ENGLAND
• London

NETHERLANDS

SPANISH NETHERLANDS

English Channel

HOLY

POMERANIA
MECKLENBURG
BRANDENBURG

HESSE

SAXONY

• Wittenburg

Worms • Paris

ROMAN

PALATINATE

ANSBACH

BOHEMIA

• Prague

Nantes •

WÜRTTEMBERG

FRANCE

Zurich •

EMPIRE

SWITZERLAND

BAVARIA

AUSTRIA

TRANSYLVANIA

HUNGARY

La Rochelle •

Geneva •

Milan •

TIROL

• Trent

VENICE

PORTUGAL

• Madrid

SPAIN

Lisbon •

Corsica

PAPAL

STATES

Rome •

Sardinia

NAPLES

• Naples

Adriatic Sea

Black Sea

OTTOMAN EMPIRE

Mediterranean Sea

Sicily

AFRICA

0   250   500 Miles
0   250   500 Kilometers

N

AZIMUTHAL EQUAL AREA PROJECTION

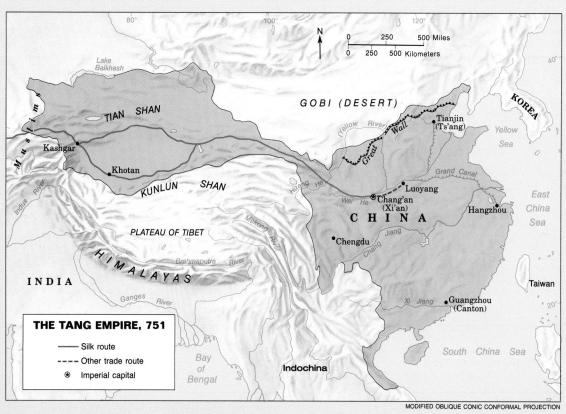

THE TANG EMPIRE, 751

- —— Silk route
- ---- Other trade route
- ⊛ Imperial capital

Lake Balkhash

TIAN SHAN

Muslims

Kashgar

Khotan

KUNLUN SHAN

PLATEAU OF TIBET

HIMALAYAS

Indus River

INDIA

Ganges River

Brahmaputra River

Mekong River

Bay of Bengal

GOBI (DESERT)

Yellow River

Great Wall

Tianjin (Ts'ang) •

KOREA

Yellow Sea

Grand Canal

Huang He

Wei He

⊛ Chang'an (Xi'an)

• Luoyang

CHINA

• Chengdu

Chang Jiang

Hangzhou •

East China Sea

Taiwan

Xi Jiang

Guangzhou (Canton) •

South China Sea

Indochina

0   250   500 Miles
0   250   500 Kilometers

N

MODIFIED OBLIQUE CONIC CONFORMAL PROJECTION

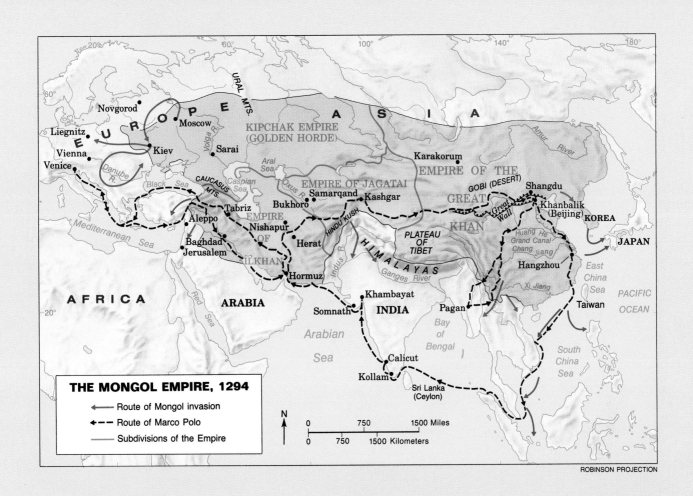

THE MONGOL EMPIRE, 1294

← Route of Mongol invasion

←--- Route of Marco Polo

— Subdivisions of the Empire

N

| 0 | 750 | 1500 Miles |
| 0 | 750 | 1500 Kilometers |

ROBINSON PROJECTION

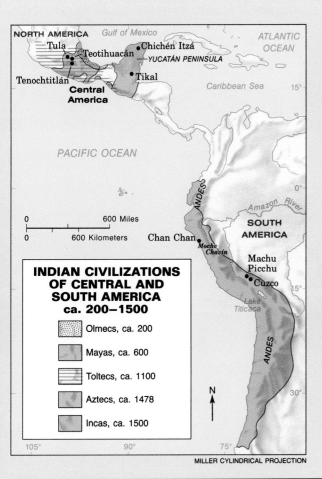

INDIAN CIVILIZATIONS OF CENTRAL AND SOUTH AMERICA ca. 200–1500

- Olmecs, ca. 200
- Mayas, ca. 600
- Toltecs, ca. 1100
- Aztecs, ca. 1478
- Incas, ca. 1500

| 0 | 600 Miles |
| 0 | 600 Kilometers |

N

MILLER CYLINDRICAL PROJECTION

Early African Kingdoms

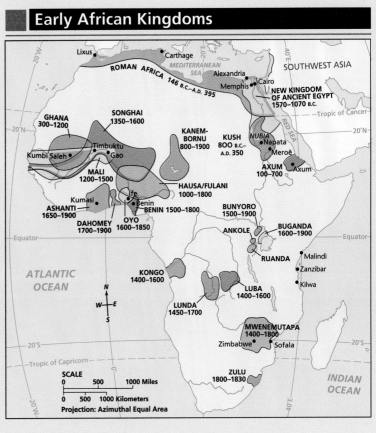

Lixus

Carthage

MEDITERRANEAN SEA

SOUTHWEST ASIA

ROMAN AFRICA 146 B.C.–A.D. 395

Alexandria

Memphis   Cairo

NEW KINGDOM OF ANCIENT EGYPT 1570–1070 B.C.

Tropic of Cancer

GHANA 300–1200

SONGHAI 1350–1600

KANEM-BORNU 800–1900

KUSH 800 B.C.–A.D. 350

NUBIA
Napata

20°N

Timbuktu
Gao

Meroë

Kumbi Saleh

AXUM 100–700   Axum

MALI 1200–1500

HAUSA/FULANI 1000–1800

Kumasi   Ife
Benin

ASHANTI 1650–1900   BENIN 1500–1800

BUNYORO 1500–1900

DAHOMEY 1700–1900   OYO 1600–1850

BUGANDA 1600–1900

ANKOLE

Equator

RUANDA   Malindi

KONGO 1400–1600

Zanzibar

LUBA 1400–1600   Kilwa

ATLANTIC OCEAN

LUNDA 1450–1700

N
W   E
S

MWENEMUTAPA 1400–1800

20°S

Zimbabwe   Sofala

INDIAN OCEAN

Tropic of Capricorn

SCALE

| 0 | 500 | 1000 Miles |
| 0 | 500 | 1000 Kilometers |

Projection: Azimuthal Equal Area

ZULU 1800–1830

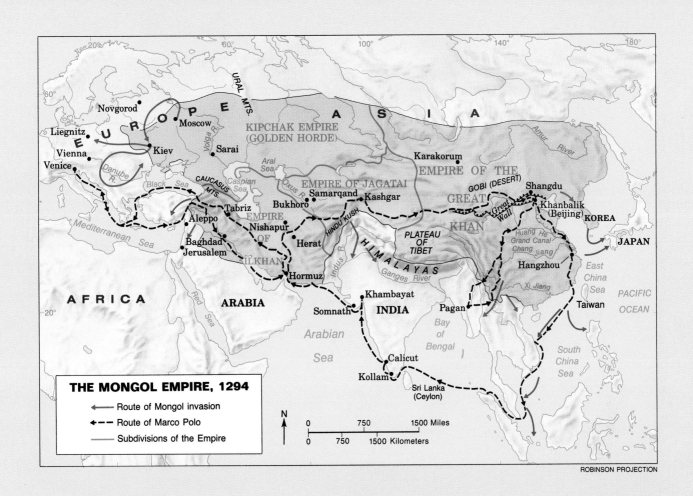

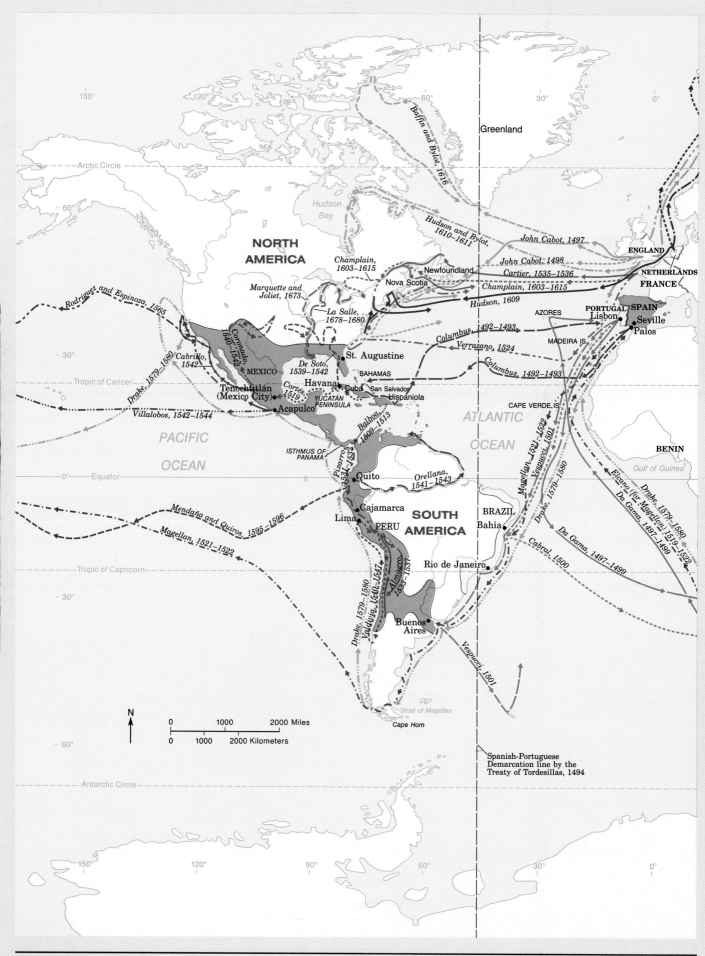

NORTH AMERICA

Greenland

Baffin and Bylot, 1616

Hudson Bay

Champlain, 1603–1615

Hudson and Bylot, 1610–1611

Newfoundland

Nova Scotia

John Cabot, 1497

ENGLAND

John Cabot, 1498

NETHERLANDS

Cartier, 1535–1536

FRANCE

Champlain, 1603–1615

Marquette and Joliet, 1673

La Salle, 1678–1680

Hudson, 1609

Rodriguez and Espinoza, 1565

Coronado, 1540–1542

Cabrillo, 1542

De Soto, 1539–1542

St. Augustine

Columbus, 1492–1493

Verrazano, 1524

PORTUGAL Lisbon

SPAIN

Seville

Palos

AZORES

MADEIRA IS.

MEXICO

Cortés 1519

Havana

BAHAMAS

Cuba San Salvador

Hispaniola

Columbus, 1492–1493

Drake, 1579–1580

Tropic of Cancer

Tenochtitlán (Mexico City)

Acapulco

YUCATÁN PENINSULA

ATLANTIC OCEAN

CAPE VERDE IS.

Villalobos, 1542–1544

Balboa, 1509–1513

BENIN

Gulf of Guinea

PACIFIC OCEAN

ISTHMUS OF PANAMA

Pizarro, 1531–1532

Quito

Orellana, 1541–1543

Magellan, 1521–1522

Vespucci 1501

Drake, 1579–1580

Elcano (for Magellan), 1519–1522

Da Gama, 1497–1499

Equator

Cajamarca

SOUTH AMERICA

BRAZIL

Bahia

Da Gama, 1497–1499

Lima

PERU

Mendaña and Quiros, 1595–1596

Cabral, 1500

Magellan, 1521–1522

Rio de Janeiro

Tropic of Capricorn

Almagro 1535–1537

Valdivia, 1540–1547

Drake, 1579–1580

Buenos Aires

Vespucci, 1501

Strait of Magellan

Cape Horn

Arctic Circle

Antarctic Circle

N

0   1000   2000 Miles

0   1000   2000 Kilometers

Spanish-Portuguese Demarcation line by the Treaty of Tordesillas, 1494

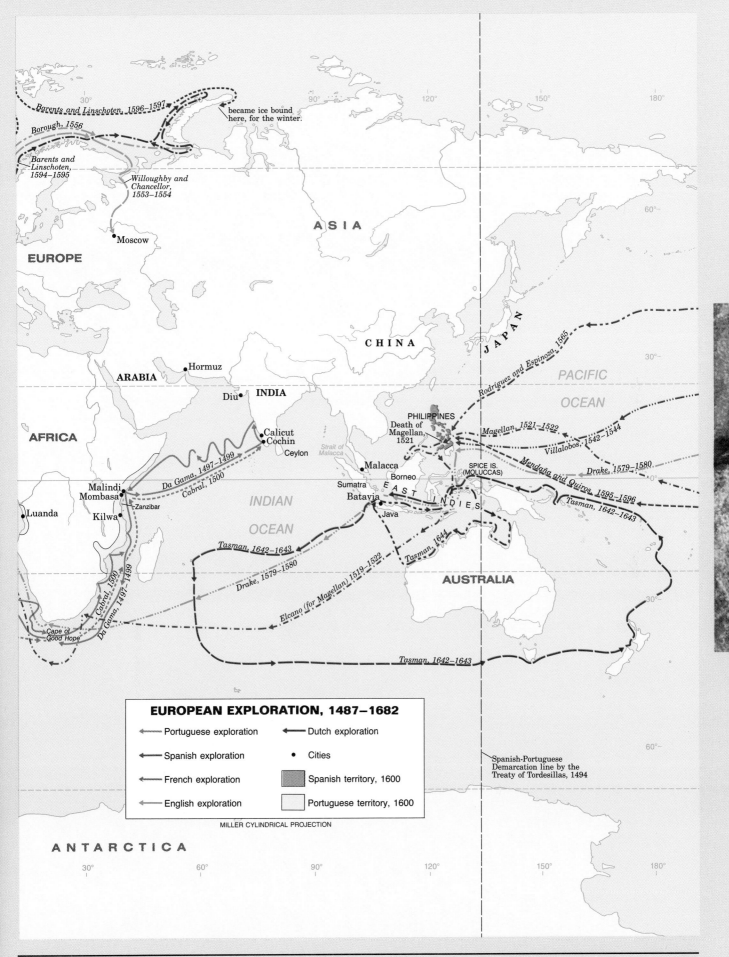

Barents and Linschoten, 1596–1597

became ice bound here, for the winter.

Borough, 1556

Barents and Linschoten, 1594–1595

Willoughby and Chancellor, 1553–1554

• Moscow

EUROPE

ASIA

CHINA

JAPAN

PACIFIC OCEAN

Rodríguez and Espinoza, 1565

ARABIA

• Hormuz

Diu • **INDIA**

AFRICA

Calicut
Cochin

Ceylon

Strait of Malacca

PHILIPPINES
Death of Magellan, 1521

Magellan, 1521–1522

Villalobos, 1542–1544

Da Gama, 1497–1499
Cabral, 1500

Malindi •
Mombasa •
Zanzibar

Malacca

Borneo

Sumatra

**SPICE IS.
(MOLUCCAS)**

Mendaña and Quiros, 1595–1596

Drake, 1579–1580

Batavia

Java

E A S T   I N D I E S

Tasman, 1642–1643

Luanda •

Kilwa •

INDIAN OCEAN

Tasman, 1642–1643

Drake, 1579–1580

Tasman, 1644

Da Gama, 1497–1499
Cabral, 1500

Elcano (for Magellan) 1519–1522

AUSTRALIA

Cape of Good Hope

Tasman, 1642–1643

EUROPEAN EXPLORATION, 1487–1682

⟵ Portuguese exploration   ⟵ Dutch exploration

⟵ Spanish exploration   • Cities

⟵ French exploration   ▨ Spanish territory, 1600

⟵ English exploration   ▢ Portuguese territory, 1600

Spanish-Portuguese Demarcation line by the Treaty of Tordesillas, 1494

MILLER CYLINDRICAL PROJECTION

ANTARCTICA

30°   60°   90°   120°   150°   180°

Greenland

Hudson Bay

NORTH AMERICA

R O C K Y M T S

NEW FRANCE

Montréal
Québec
Albany
Boston
New York
Philadelphia

NEWFOUNDLAND

NOVA SCOTIA

LOUISIANA

Charleston
FLORIDA

MEXICO

Mexico City

Havana
Cuba
Jamaica
BELIZE
Hispaniola
Guadeloupe
Martinique
Barbados
Curaçao

Panamá

GUIANA

SOUTH AMERICA

Lima
PERU

A N D E S

Bahia

PAMPAS

Strait of Magellan

Cape Horn

ATLANTIC OCEAN

PACIFIC OCEAN

ATLANTIC OCEAN

ICELAND (DENMARK)

North Sea

DENMARK
ENGLAND
NETHERLANDS
FRANCE

PORTUGAL **SPAIN**
Lisbon Seville
Ceuta
Melilla

AZORES

MADEIRA IS.

CANARY IS.

CAPE VERDE IS.

St. Louis
Gambia

TASO

Elmina

N

| 0 | 1000 | 2000 Miles |
| 0 | 1000 | 2000 Kilometers |

82

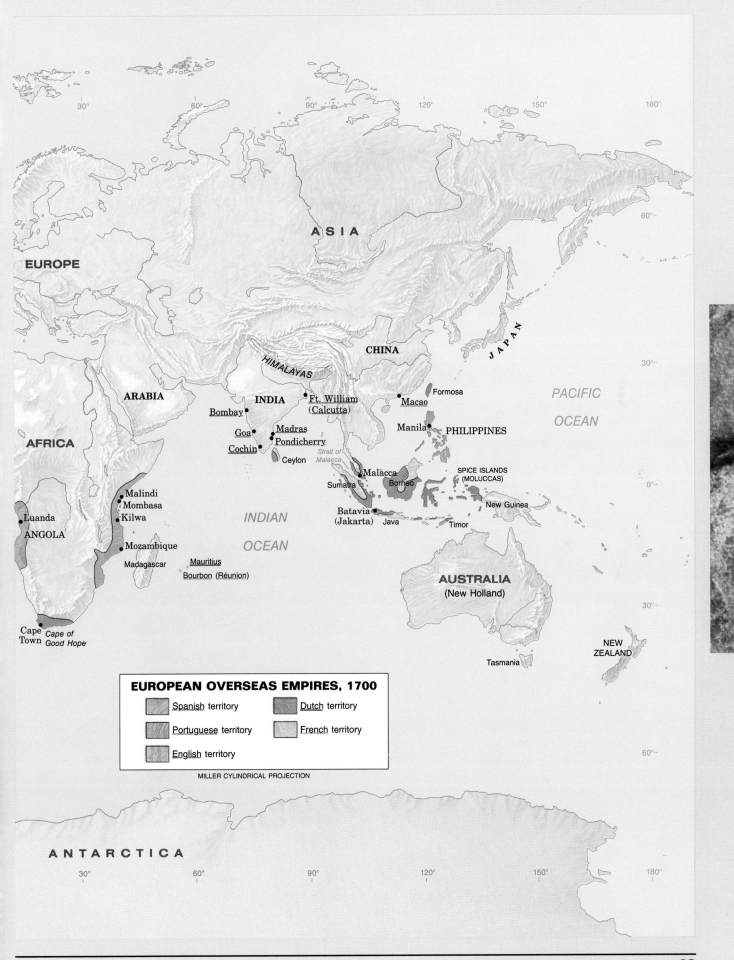

EUROPE

ASIA

AFRICA

ARABIA

INDIA

HIMALAYAS

CHINA

JAPAN

Ft. William
(Calcutta)

Bombay

Goa

Madras
Pondicherry

Cochin

Ceylon

Macao

Formosa

Manila

PHILIPPINES

PACIFIC

OCEAN

Strait of
Malacca

Malacca

Sumatra

Borneo

SPICE ISLANDS
(MOLUCCAS)

INDIAN

OCEAN

Malindi
Mombasa
Kilwa

Luanda
ANGOLA

Mozambique

Madagascar

Mauritius
Bourbon (Réunion)

Batavia
(Jakarta)

Java

Timor

New Guinea

AUSTRALIA
(New Holland)

Cape
Town

Cape of
Good Hope

Tasmania

NEW
ZEALAND

EUROPEAN OVERSEAS EMPIRES, 1700

Spanish territory

Dutch territory

Portuguese territory

French territory

English territory

MILLER CYLINDRICAL PROJECTION

ANTARCTICA

EUROPE AFTER THE TREATY OF WESTPHALIA, 1648

- ▢ Possessions of the Spanish Hapsburgs
- ▨ Possessions of the Austrian Hapsburgs
- ▨ Possessions of the Hohenzollerns

RUSSIA

Moscow

SWEDEN

Stockholm

KINGDOM OF DENMARK AND NORWAY

Baltic Sea

EAST PRUSSIA

POMERANIA

POLAND

Warsaw

Berlin

BRANDENBURG-PRUSSIA

SAXONY

SCOTLAND

North Sea

IRELAND

ENGLAND

London

UNITED NETHERLANDS

SPANISH NETHERLANDS

HOLY ROMAN EMPIRE

BOHEMIA

Prague

ATLANTIC OCEAN

English Channel

Rhine

Paris

ALSACE

BAVARIA

Vienna

Buda Pest

HUNGARY

FRANCHE COMTÉ

AUSTRIA

Bay of Biscay

FRANCE

SWITZERLAND

SAVOY

PIEDMONT

MILAN

REPUBLIC OF VENICE

Danube River

Black Sea

Avignon

TUSCANY

GENOA

PAPAL STATES

Adriatic Sea

OTTOMAN

Constantinople

40°

Corsica

Rome

PORTUGAL

Madrid

SPAIN

NAPLES

EMPIRE

Aegean Sea

30°

BALEARIC ISLANDS

Sardinia

Mediterranean Sea

Sicily

N

Crete

AFRICA

10°   0°   10°   20°

| 0 | 150 | 300 Miles |
| 0 | 150 | 300 Kilometers |

AZIMUTHAL EQUAL AREA PROJECTION

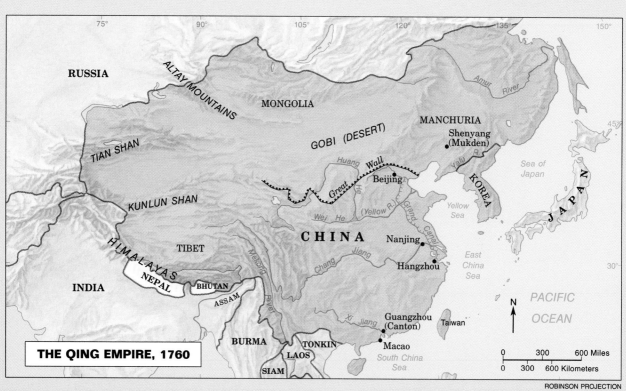

THE QING EMPIRE, 1760

75°   90°   105°   120°   135°   150°

RUSSIA

ALTAY MOUNTAINS

MONGOLIA

MANCHURIA

Shenyang (Mukden)

Amur River

TIAN SHAN

GOBI (DESERT)

Huang He

Great Wall

Beijing

Yalu R.

Sea of Japan

45°

KUNLUN SHAN

Wei He

(Yellow) R.

Grand Canal

Yellow Sea

KOREA

JAPAN

HIMALAYAS

TIBET

CHINA

Nanjing

Chang Jiang

Hangzhou

East China Sea

30°

INDIA

NEPAL

BHUTAN

ASSAM

Mekong River

Xi Jiang

Guangzhou (Canton)

Taiwan

PACIFIC OCEAN

BURMA

TONKIN

LAOS

Macao

South China Sea

N

SIAM

| 0 | 300 | 600 Miles |
| 0 | 300 | 600 Kilometers |

ROBINSON PROJECTION

84

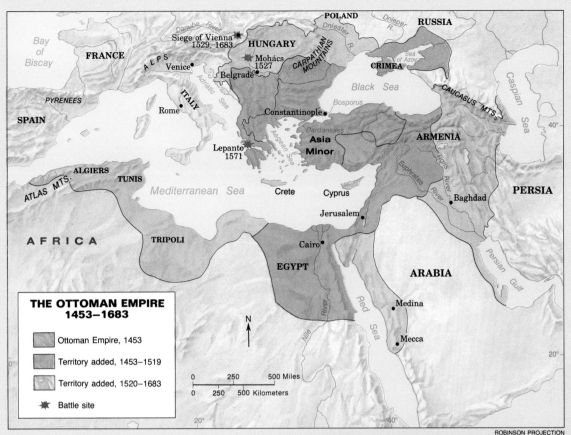

THE OTTOMAN EMPIRE
1453–1683

Bay of Biscay

FRANCE

SPAIN

PYRENEES

ALPS

Venice

ITALY

Rome

Adriatic Sea

Danube River

Siege of Vienna 1529, 1683

HUNGARY

Mohács 1527

Belgrade

CARPATHIAN MOUNTAINS

POLAND

Dniester R.

Dnieper R.

RUSSIA

CRIMEA

Sea of Azov

Black Sea

Bosporus

Constantinople

Dardanelles

Aegean Sea

Lepanto 1571

Asia Minor

CAUCASUS MTS.

Caspian Sea

ARMENIA

Tigris River

Euphrates River

PERSIA

40°

ATLAS MTS.

ALGIERS

TUNIS

Mediterranean Sea

Crete

Cyprus

Baghdad

Jerusalem

Persian Gulf

AFRICA

TRIPOLI

Cairo

EGYPT

Nile River

Red Sea

ARABIA

Medina

Mecca

20°

Ottoman Empire, 1453

Territory added, 1453–1519

Territory added, 1520–1683

★ Battle site

N

| 0 | 250 | 500 Miles |
| 0 | 250 | 500 Kilometers |

20° 40°

ROBINSON PROJECTION

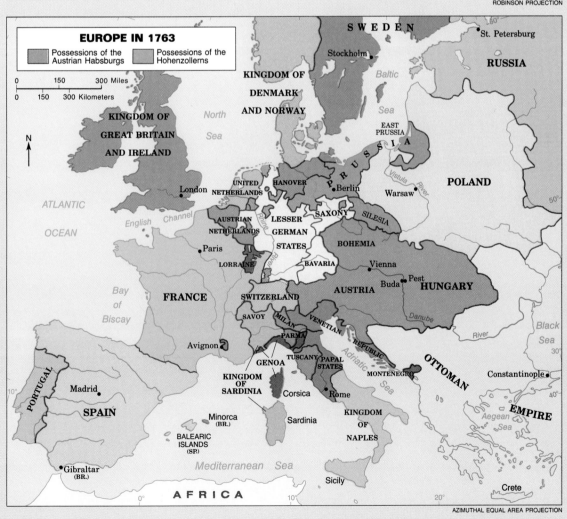

EUROPE IN 1763

Possessions of the Austrian Habsburgs

Possessions of the Hohenzollerns

| 0 | 150 | 300 Miles |
| 0 | 150 | 300 Kilometers |

N

SWEDEN

Stockholm

St. Petersburg

60°

KINGDOM OF DENMARK AND NORWAY

Baltic Sea

RUSSIA

KINGDOM OF GREAT BRITAIN AND IRELAND

North Sea

EAST PRUSSIA

P R U S S I A

POLAND

London

ATLANTIC OCEAN

English Channel

UNITED NETHERLANDS

HANOVER

Berlin

Vistula River

Warsaw

50°

Rhine River

AUSTRIAN NETHERLANDS

LESSER GERMAN STATES

SAXONY

SILESIA

Paris

LORRAINE

BAVARIA

BOHEMIA

Vienna

FRANCE

SWITZERLAND

AUSTRIA

Buda Pest

HUNGARY

Bay of Biscay

SAVOY

MILAN

PARMA

VENETIAN

Danube

Black Sea

Avignon

GENOA

TUSCANY

PAPAL STATES

REPUBLIC

MONTENEGRO

Adriatic Sea

OTTOMAN

Constantinople

40°

PORTUGAL

Madrid

SPAIN

KINGDOM OF SARDINIA

Corsica

Rome

Sardinia

KINGDOM OF NAPLES

EMPIRE

Aegean Sea

30°

Minorca (BR.)

BALEARIC ISLANDS (SP.)

Mediterranean Sea

Sicily

Crete

Gibraltar (BR.)

0° 10° 20°

AFRICA

AZIMUTHAL EQUAL AREA PROJECTION

NAPOLEONIC EUROPE, 1805–1815

- Empire of the French, 1812
- States controlled by Napoleon, 1812
- States allied with Napoleon, 1812
- States allied against Napoleon, 1812
- Neutral states, 1812
- ★ Battle site

GREAT BRITAIN

ATLANTIC OCEAN

London

English Channel

N

Waterloo 1815

Paris

150   300 Miles

150   300 Kilometers

EMPIRE OF THE FRENCH

SWITZERLAND

KINGDOM OF ITALY

PORTUGAL

Lisbon

Madrid

SPAIN

Strait of Gibraltar

Trafalgar 1805

GIBRALTAR (BR.)

North Sea

KINGDOM OF DENMARK AND NORWAY

SWEDEN

Baltic Sea

Rhine River

KINGDOM OF WESTPHALIA

Berlin

Leipzig 1813

SAXONY

CONFEDERATION OF THE RHINE

Vienna

ILLYRIAN PROVINCES

Venice

Danube

BALEARIC ISLANDS

Corsica

Elba

Rome

KINGDOM OF SARDINIA

KINGDOM OF NAPLES

Mediterranean Sea

AFRICA

MALTA (BR.)

St. Petersburg

Borodino 1812

Moscow

Route of the Grand Army 1812

Niemen River

PRUSSIA

RUSSIAN EMPIRE

GRAND DUCHY OF WARSAW

Austerlitz 1805

AUSTRIAN EMPIRE

Black Sea

OTTOMAN

MONTENEGRO

Corfu

IONIAN ISLANDS (British)

KINGDOM OF SICILY

Adriatic Sea

Constantinople

EMPIRE

ASIA

Aegean Sea

Crete

AZIMUTHAL EQUAL AREA PROJECTION

EUROPE AFTER THE CONGRESS OF VIENNA, 1815

——— Boundary of the German Confederation

St. Petersburg
Moscow

KINGDOM OF
SWEDEN AND NORWAY
Stockholm

North Sea
DENMARK
Baltic Sea
Copenhagen

RUSSIAN EMPIRE

Niemen River

UNITED KINGDOM
OF
GREAT BRITAIN
AND
IRELAND
London

ATLANTIC OCEAN

English Channel

Amsterdam
Berlin
NETHER-LANDS
GERMAN
LESSER
GERMAN
CONFEDERATION
STATES
LUX.
Vienna
AUSTRIAN EMPIRE

P R U S S I A
Rhine River

N

Paris

FRANCE

SWITZERLAND

0   150   300 Miles
0   150   300 Kilometers

PIEDMONT
Turin
PARMA
MODENA
LUCA
TUSCANY
PAPAL
STATES
Danube River

Black Sea

OTTOMAN

Constantinople

EMPIRE

Asia Minor

Adriatic Sea

PORTUGAL
Lisbon
Madrid
SPAIN

KINGDOM OF SARDINIA
Corsica (FR.)
Rome
Naples
Sardinia

BALEARIC ISLANDS (SP.)

KINGDOM
OF THE
TWO SICILIES
Sicily

IONIAN ISLANDS (BR.)

Aegean Sea

Crete

Mediterranean Sea

GIBRALTAR (BR.)

A F R I C A

50°
40°
30°
10°
0°   10°   20°

AZIMUTHAL EQUAL AREA PROJECTION

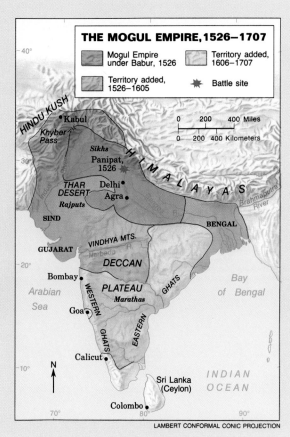

THE MOGUL EMPIRE, 1526–1707

Mogul Empire under Babur, 1526
Territory added, 1526–1605
Territory added, 1606–1707
★ Battle site

40°

HINDU KUSH
Kabul
Khyber Pass
Sikhs
Panipat, 1526
THAR DESERT
Delhi
Agra
Rajputs
SIND
GUJARAT
VINDHYA MTS.
Narbada R.
DECCAN
PLATEAU
Marathas
Bombay
Goa
WESTERN GHATS
EASTERN GHATS
Calicut

H I M A L A Y A S
Brahmaputra River
BENGAL

30°
20°
10°

Arabian Sea
Bay of Bengal

INDIAN OCEAN

Sri Lanka (Ceylon)
Colombo

0   200   400 Miles
0   200   400 Kilometers

70°   80°   90°

LAMBERT CONFORMAL CONIC PROJECTION

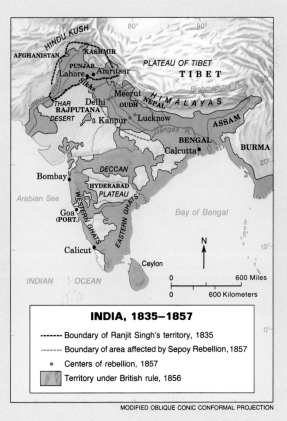

70°   80°   90°
HINDU KUSH
AFGHANISTAN
KASHMIR
PUNJAB
Lahore
Amritsar
Sikhs
Meerut
Delhi
THAR
RAJPUTANA
DESERT
OUDH
NEPAL
Kanpur
Lucknow

PLATEAU OF TIBET
T I B E T
Brahmaputra R.
H I M A L A Y A S
ASSAM
BENGAL
Calcutta
BURMA

Ganges R.

Bombay
DECCAN
HYDERABAD PLATEAU
Goa (PORT.)
WESTERN GHATS
EASTERN GHATS
Calicut

Arabian Sea

Bay of Bengal

Ceylon

INDIAN OCEAN

N

0   600 Miles
0   600 Kilometers

30°
20°
10°
0°

INDIA, 1835–1857

------- Boundary of Ranjit Singh's territory, 1835
------- Boundary of area affected by Sepoy Rebellion, 1857
• Centers of rebellion, 1857
Territory under British rule, 1856

MODIFIED OBLIQUE CONIC CONFORMAL PROJECTION

DISPUTED TERRITORY
(SPAIN VS. RUSSIA)

SPANISH LOUISIANA

UNITED STATES

ATLANTIC

OCEAN

45°

30°

• Monterrey

VICEROYALTY OF NEW SPAIN

Rio Grande

Missouri River

Mississippi River

EAST FLORIDA

WEST FLORIDA

Monterrey •

Guadalajara •

México •

Mérida •
Veracruz •

Gulf of Mexico

Havana •

BAHAMAS
(BR.)

CAPTAINCY-GENERAL OF CUBA

Cuba

Jamaica

Hispañiola

Haiti

Puerto Rico

Santo Domingo

W E S T

I N D I E S

BRITISH HONDURAS

CAPTAINCY-GENERAL OF GUATEMALA

Caribbean Sea

PACIFIC

OCEAN

Cartagena

Caracas •

Cumaná

CAPTAINCY-GENERAL OF VENEZUELA

GUIANAS

ISTHMUS OF PANAMA

Bogotá •

Popayán •
Quito •

Guayaquil •

VICEROYALTY OF NEW GRANADA

Amazon River

0°

Trujillo •

A
N
D
E
S

Lima •

Cuzco •

Arequipa •

La Paz •

B R A Z I L

BRAZILIAN HIGHLANDS

15°

N
↑

0   500   1000 Miles
0   500   1000 Kilometers

VICEROYALTY OF PERU

Salta •

Tucumán •

VICEROYALTY OF RÍO DE LA PLATA

Asunción •

Corrientes •

Santiago •

Concepción •

A
N
D
E
S

Buenos Aires •

PAMPAS

Montevideo •

Río de la Plata

30°

LATIN AMERICA, 1790

  Spanish territory

  Portuguese territory

  British territory

  French territory

  Dutch territory

45°

Strait of Magellan

FALKLAND ISLANDS
(ISLAS MALVINAS)

Cape Horn

120°   105°   90°   75°   60°   45°

MILLER CYLINDRICAL PROJECTION

OREGON COUNTRY
(disputed: U.S. vs. Britain)

UNITED STATES

MÉXICO, 1821

Colorado River
Missouri River
Mississippi River
Rio Grande

ATLANTIC
OCEAN

Gulf of
Mexico

México•
•Veracruz

BAHAMAS
(BR.)

CUBA
(SP.)

HAITI, 1803 PUERTO RICO
(SP.)

BRITISH
HONDURAS
(BR.)

JAMAICA
(BR.)

W E S T

I N D I E S

Caribbean
Sea

Guatemala City•

MOSQUITO
COAST
(BR.)

**UNITED
PROVINCES
OF
CENTRAL
AMERICA
1823**

ISTHMUS OF
PANAMA

Caracas•

TRINIDAD
(BR.)

G U I A N A S
(BR.)
(NETH.) (FR.)

**GREAT COLOMBIA
1819–1830**

Bogotá•

DISPUTED
TERRITORY

PACIFIC

OCEAN

•Quito

Amazon River

N

PERU, 1821

EMPIRE OF BRAZIL, 1822

Lima•

Salvador•

•La Paz

BOLIVIA, 1825

Chuquisaca•
(Sucre)

**PARAGUAY
1811**

São Paulo•

•Rio de Janeiro

0   500   1000 Miles
0   500   1000 Kilometers

Asunción•

Paraná River

**NEW NATIONS IN
LATIN AMERICA, 1828**

**URUGUAY
1828**

Santiago•

Buenos Aires•

•Montevideo

**CHILE
1817**

**UNITED
PROVINCES
OF
LA PLATA, 1816
(ARGENTINA)**

Río de
la Plata

Strait of
Magellan

FALKLAND ISLANDS
(ISLAS MALVINAS)

Cape Horn

MILLER CYLINDRICAL PROJECTION

45°
30°
15°
0°
15°
30°
45°

120°   105°   90°   75°   60°   45°

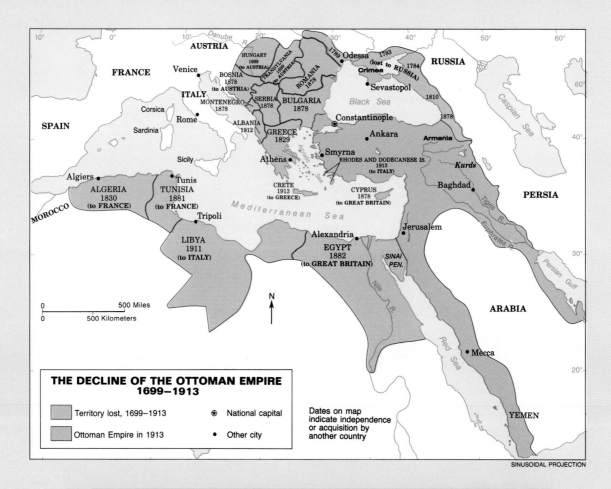

THE DECLINE OF THE OTTOMAN EMPIRE
1699–1913

Territory lost, 1699–1913

Ottoman Empire in 1913

⊛ National capital

• Other city

Dates on map indicate independence or acquisition by another country

SINUSOIDAL PROJECTION

Map labels:
AUSTRIA
FRANCE
Venice
HUNGARY 1699 (to AUSTRIA)
TRANSYLVANIA 1699
BOSNIA 1878 (to AUSTRIA)
ITALY
MONTENEGRO 1878
SERBIA 1878
ROMANIA 1878
1788 Odessa
1783
Crimea (lost to RUSSIA) 1784
RUSSIA
Corsica
Rome
BULGARIA 1878
Black Sea
Sevastopol
1810
SPAIN
Sardinia
ALBANIA 1912
GREECE 1829
Constantinople
Ankara
1878
Armenia
Caspian Sea
Sicily
Athens
Smyrna
RHODES AND DODECANESE IS. 1913 (to ITALY)
Kurds
Algiers
Tunis
CRETE 1913 (to GREECE)
CYPRUS 1878 (to GREAT BRITAIN)
Baghdad
PERSIA
ALGERIA 1830 (to FRANCE)
TUNISIA 1881 (to FRANCE)
Mediterranean Sea
MOROCCO
Tripoli
Alexandria
Jerusalem
Tigris R.
Euphrates R.
LIBYA 1911 (to ITALY)
EGYPT 1882 (to GREAT BRITAIN)
SINAI PEN.
Nile R.
Persian Gulf
N
ARABIA
Red Sea
Mecca
YEMEN

0 500 Miles
0 500 Kilometers

Colonialism and Independence in Africa

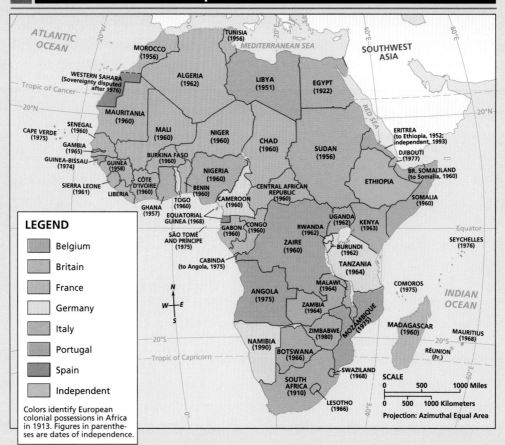

Map labels:
ATLANTIC OCEAN
TUNISIA (1956)
MEDITERRANEAN SEA
SOUTHWEST ASIA
MOROCCO (1956)
WESTERN SAHARA (Sovereignty disputed after 1976)
ALGERIA (1962)
LIBYA (1951)
EGYPT (1922)
Tropic of Cancer
MAURITANIA (1960)
SENEGAL (1960)
CAPE VERDE (1975)
20°N
MALI (1960)
NIGER (1960)
CHAD (1960)
SUDAN (1956)
ERITREA (to Ethiopia, 1952; independent, 1993)
DJIBOUTI (1977)
GAMBIA (1965)
GUINEA-BISSAU (1974)
BURKINA FASO (1960)
GUINEA (1958)
SIERRA LEONE (1961)
CÔTE D'IVOIRE (1960)
LIBERIA
NIGERIA (1960)
BENIN (1960)
TOGO (1960)
GHANA (1957)
CENTRAL AFRICAN REPUBLIC (1960)
CAMEROON (1960)
ETHIOPIA
BR. SOMALILAND (to Somalia, 1960)
SOMALIA (1960)
EQUATORIAL GUINEA (1968)
SÃO TOMÉ AND PRÍNCIPE (1975)
GABON (1960)
CONGO (1960)
RWANDA (1962)
UGANDA (1962)
KENYA (1963)
CABINDA (to Angola, 1975)
ZAIRE (1960)
BURUNDI (1962)
TANZANIA (1964)
SEYCHELLES (1976)
Equator
MALAWI (1964)
COMOROS (1975)
INDIAN OCEAN
ANGOLA (1975)
ZAMBIA (1964)
MOZAMBIQUE (1975)
MADAGASCAR (1960)
MAURITIUS (1968)
NAMIBIA (1990)
ZIMBABWE (1980)
20°S
RÉUNION (Fr.)
Tropic of Capricorn
BOTSWANA (1966)
SWAZILAND (1968)
SOUTH AFRICA (1910)
LESOTHO (1966)
RED SEA

N
W E
S

LEGEND

Belgium

Britain

France

Germany

Italy

Portugal

Spain

Independent

Colors identify European colonial possessions in Africa in 1913. Figures in parentheses are dates of independence.

SCALE
0 500 1000 Miles
0 500 1000 Kilometers
Projection: Azimuthal Equal Area

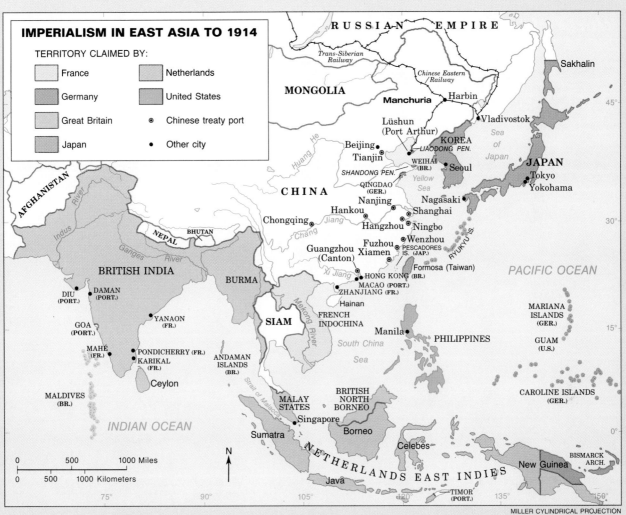

IMPERIALISM IN EAST ASIA TO 1914

TERRITORY CLAIMED BY:

- France
- Germany
- Great Britain
- Japan
- Netherlands
- United States
- ⊙ Chinese treaty port
- • Other city

RUSSIAN EMPIRE

Trans-Siberian Railway

MONGOLIA

Manchuria

Chinese Eastern Railway

Harbin

Sakhalin

Lüshun (Port Arthur)

Vladivostok

Sea of Japan

KOREA
LIAODONG PEN.

Beijing

Tianjin

WEIHAI (BR.)

Seoul

JAPAN

Tokyo

Yokohama

SHANDONG PEN.

QINGDAO (GER.)

Yellow Sea

Nagasaki

CHINA

Nanjing

Shanghai

Huang He

Hankou

Chongqing

Hangzhou

Ningbo

Jiang

Chang

Wenzhou

Fuzhou

RYUKYU IS.

AFGHANISTAN

Indus River

Ganges River

NEPAL

BHUTAN

Guangzhou (Canton)

Xiamen

PESCADORES IS. (JAP.)

PACIFIC OCEAN

BRITISH INDIA

BURMA

Xi Jiang

HONG KONG (BR.)

MACAO (PORT.)

ZHANJIANG (FR.)

Formosa (Taiwan)

MARIANA ISLANDS (GER.)

DIU (PORT.)

DAMAN (PORT.)

Hainan

FRENCH INDOCHINA

Manila

PHILIPPINES

GUAM (U.S.)

GOA (PORT.)

YANAON (FR.)

SIAM

MAHÉ (FR.)

PONDICHERRY (FR.)

KARIKAL (FR.)

Ceylon

ANDAMAN ISLANDS (BR.)

Mekong River

South China Sea

CAROLINE ISLANDS (GER.)

MALDIVES (BR.)

Strait of Malacca

INDIAN OCEAN

MALAY STATES

Singapore

BRITISH NORTH BORNEO

Sumatra

Borneo

Celebes

BISMARCK ARCH.

New Guinea

Java

NETHERLANDS EAST INDIES

TIMOR (PORT.)

Scale
0 — 500 — 1000 Miles
0 — 500 — 1000 Kilometers

75° · 90° · 105° · 120° · 135° · 150°

30° · 15° · 0°

MILLER CYLINDRICAL PROJECTION

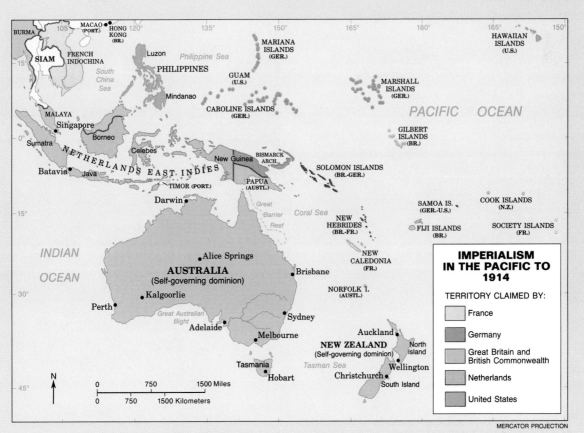

IMPERIALISM IN THE PACIFIC TO 1914

TERRITORY CLAIMED BY:

- France
- Germany
- Great Britain and British Commonwealth
- Netherlands
- United States

BURMA

MACAO (PORT.)

HONG KONG (BR.)

HAWAIIAN ISLANDS (U.S.)

SIAM

FRENCH INDOCHINA

Luzon

MARIANA ISLANDS (GER.)

South China Sea

Philippine Sea

PHILIPPINES

GUAM (U.S.)

MARSHALL ISLANDS (GER.)

Mindanao

CAROLINE ISLANDS (GER.)

PACIFIC OCEAN

MALAYA

Singapore

Borneo

GILBERT ISLANDS (BR.)

Sumatra

Celebes

NETHERLANDS EAST INDIES

BISMARCK ARCH.

New Guinea

SOLOMON ISLANDS (BR.-GER.)

Batavia

Java

TIMOR (PORT.)

PAPUA (AUSTL.)

Darwin

Great Barrier Reef

Coral Sea

NEW HEBRIDES (BR.-FR.)

SAMOA IS. (GER.-U.S.)

COOK ISLANDS (N.Z.)

FIJI ISLANDS (BR.)

SOCIETY ISLANDS (FR.)

INDIAN OCEAN

Alice Springs

AUSTRALIA (Self-governing dominion)

Brisbane

NEW CALEDONIA (FR.)

NORFOLK I. (AUSTL.)

Perth

Kalgoorlie

Great Australian Bight

Sydney

Auckland

Adelaide

Melbourne

NEW ZEALAND (Self-governing dominion)

North Island

Tasmania

Hobart

Tasman Sea

Christchurch

Wellington

South Island

Scale
0 — 750 — 1500 Miles
0 — 750 — 1500 Kilometers

105° · 120° · 135° · 150° · 165° · 180° · 150°

15° · 15° · 30° · 45°

MERCATOR PROJECTION

World War I, 1914–1917

The British blockade succeeds in disrupting German supply lines. As a result, food riots break out in 56 German cities.

The British withdraw from Gallipoli, ending any hope of sending supplies to Russia.

0   200   400 Miles
0   200   400 Kilometers
Azimuthal Equal-Area Projection

60°N
20°W   10°W   0°   10°E
50°N
40°N

ATLANTIC OCEAN
FAEROE IS. (Danish)
SHETLAND IS.
ORKNEY IS.
NORWAY
SWEDEN
FINLAND
BALTIC SEA
Petrograd
RUSSIA
GREAT BRITAIN
NORTH SEA
DENMARK
Berlin
EASTERN FRONT Nov. 1915
Lusitania sunk May 1915
London BELGIUM
NETHERLANDS
GERMANY
English Channel
Ypres Oct.–Nov. 1914 Apr.–May 1915
LUXEMBOURG
ALSACE-LORRAINE
Somme July–Nov. 1916
Paris
WESTERN FRONT
Battle of the Marne Sept. 1914
Verdun Feb.–July 1916
Vienna
AUSTRIA-HUNGARY
Budapest
Bay of Biscay
FRANCE
SWITZERLAND
Caporetto Oct.–Dec. 1917
ADRIATIC SEA
BOSNIA and HERZEGOVINA
Sarajevo
SERBIA
ROMANIA
BLACK SEA
Bosporus
BLACK SEA
PORTUGAL
SPAIN
ITALY
Rome
MONTENEGRO
ALBANIA
Balkans
BULGARIA
Constantinople
OTTOMAN EMPIRE
Dardanelles
Gallipoli April 1915–Jan. 1916
GREECE
MEDITERRANEAN SEA

Legend

- Allied Powers, 1916
- Central Powers, 1916
- Neutral countries
- → Allied forces
- → Central Powers forces
- ⌇ British naval blockade
- Farthest Russian advance (1914)
- Farthest advance of Central Powers
- Trench line, Western Front
- ✱ Battle
- ▽ Food riots
- ⫽ German submarine activity

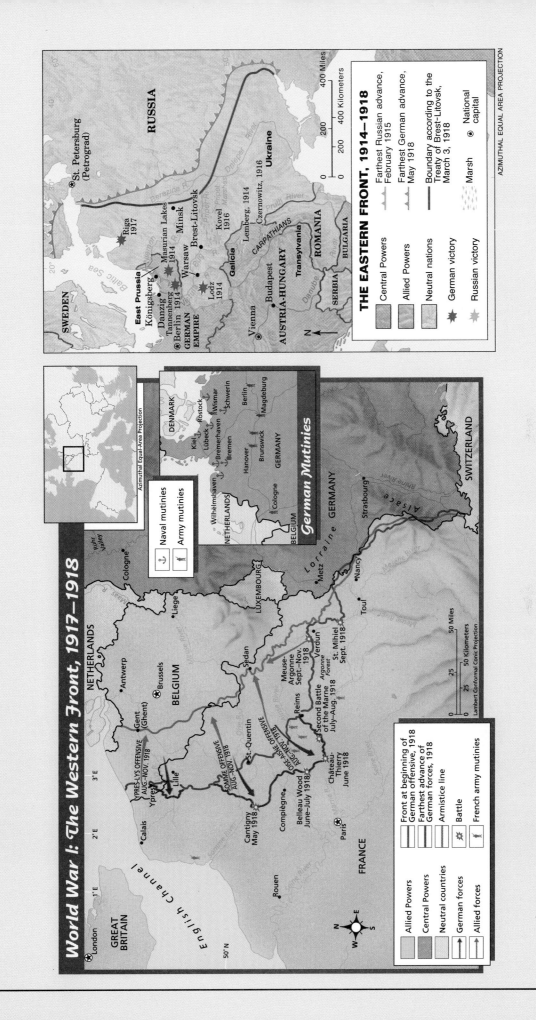

World War I: The Western Front, 1917–1918

Allied Powers
Central Powers
Neutral countries
German forces
Allied forces

Front at beginning of German offensive, 1918
Farthest advance of German forces, 1918
Armistice line
Battle
French army mutinies

GREAT BRITAIN
London
English Channel
Calais
Rouen
Compiègne
Paris
FRANCE

50°N
1°E   2°E   3°E

NETHERLANDS
Antwerp
Brussels
BELGIUM
Gent (Ghent)
Ypres
Lille
Liege
LUXEMBOURG
Cologne
Ruhr Valley
Sedan
St.-Quentin
Cantigny May 1918
Belleau Wood June–July 1918
Château-Thierry June 1918
Reims
Second Battle of the Marne July–Aug. 1918
Verdun
St. Mihiel Sept. 1918
Meuse-Argonne Sept.–Nov. 1918
Argonne Forest
Metz
Nancy
Toul
Strasbourg
Alsace
Lorraine
GERMANY
SWITZERLAND

YPRES-LYS OFFENSIVE AUG.–NOV. 1918
SOMME OFFENSIVE AUG.–NOV. 1918
OISE-AISNE OFFENSIVE AUG.–NOV. 1918
AUG.–NOV. 1918

0   25   50 Miles
0   25   50 Kilometers
Lambert Conformal Conic Projection

Azimuthal Equal-Area Projection

German Mutinies

Naval mutinies
Army mutinies

DENMARK
Kiel
Rostock
Wismar
Lübeck
Bremerhaven
Schwerin
Wilhelmshaven
Bremen
Hanover
Brunswick
Berlin
Magdeburg
Cologne
GERMANY
NETHERLANDS
BELGIUM

THE EASTERN FRONT, 1914–1918

Central Powers
Allied Powers
Neutral nations
German victory
Russian victory

Farthest Russian advance, February 1915
Farthest German advance, May 1918
Boundary according to the Treaty of Brest-Litovsk, March 3, 1918
Marsh
National capital

N

0   200   400 Miles
0   200   400 Kilometers

SWEDEN
Baltic Sea
St. Petersburg (Petrograd)
RUSSIA
Riga 1917
Masurian Lakes 1914
East Prussia
Königsberg
Danzig
Tannenberg 1914
Berlin
GERMAN EMPIRE
Minsk
Warsaw
Lodz 1914
Brest-Litovsk
Kovel 1916
Lemberg, 1914
Czernowitz, 1916
Galicia
Ukraine
CARPATHIANS
Vienna
Budapest
AUSTRIA-HUNGARY
Transylvania
ROMANIA
SERBIA
BULGARIA
Berezina R.
Dnieper River
Pripet River
Pruth River
Danube River

AZIMUTHAL EQUAL AREA PROJECTION

Europe and the Middle East After World War I

Legend:
- Lost by Germany
- Lost by Bulgaria
- Lost by Austria-Hungary
- Lost by Russia
- Lost by Ottoman empire
- British mandate
- French mandate
- Occupied by Allies

In 1922 the Bolsheviks were firmly in control of Russia, and they organized the Union of Soviet Socialist Republics.

ARCTIC OCEAN
NORTH AMERICA
EUROPE
ASIA
PACIFIC OCEAN
ATLANTIC OCEAN
AFRICA
PACIFIC OCEAN
Equator
SOUTH AMERICA
INDIAN OCEAN
AUSTRALIA
PACIFIC OCEAN
ANTARCTICA
Robinson Projection

ATLANTIC OCEAN

FINLAND
NORWAY
SWEDEN
ESTONIA
LATVIA
LITHUANIA
DENMARK
BALTIC SEA
IRISH FREE STATE
GREAT BRITAIN
NORTH SEA
NETHERLANDS
BELGIUM
GERMANY
Rhineland
Saar
Free City of Danzig
East Prussia
POLAND
LUXEMBOURG
Alsace-Lorraine
FRANCE
CZECHOSLOVAKIA
UNION OF SOVIET SOCIALIST REPUBLICS
SWITZERLAND
AUSTRIA
HUNGARY
ROMANIA
Danube R.
YUGOSLAVIA
BLACK SEA
SPAIN
CORSICA (French)
ITALY
Adriatic Sea
BULGARIA
ALBANIA
TURKEY
SARDINIA (Italian)
GREECE
LATAKIA
SYRIA
SICILY (Italian)
MEDITERRANEAN SEA
DODECANESE ISLANDS (Italian)
CRETE (Greek)
CYPRUS (British)
LEBANON
IRAQ
ALGERIA (French)
TUNISIA (French)
PALESTINE
TRANSJORDAN
NEJD
LIBYA (Italian)
EGYPT (British)
HEJAZ

0   250   500 Miles
0   250   500 Kilometers
Azimuthal Equal-Area Projection

10° W   0°   10° E   20° E   30° E   40° E
60° N
50° N

MAJOR BATTLES

1 — Britain, Aug.–Oct. 1940
2 — Leningrad, Sept. 1941–Jan. 1944
3 — El Alamein, Oct.–Nov. 1942
4 — Stalingrad, Nov. 1942–Feb. 1943
5 — Anzio, Jan.–Mar. 1944
6 — D-Day, June 6, 1944
7 — Minsk, June–Aug. 1944
8 — Battle of the Bulge, Dec. 1944
9 — Warsaw, Aug. 1944–Jan. 1945
10 — Berlin, Apr.–May, 1945

WORLD WAR II IN EUROPE AND NORTH AFRICA, 1939–1945

- Allied countries
- Axis countries
- Axis-controlled territory at its greatest extent, 1942
- Neutral countries
- Major battle
- Allied advance
- National capital
- Axis advance
- Other city

AZIMUTHAL EQUAL AREA PROJECTION

ATLANTIC OCEAN

North Sea

IRELAND

GREAT BRITAIN

London

English Channel

Antwerp

NETH.
BEL.
LUX.

Paris

FRANCE

Vichy

VICHY FRANCE 1940–1942

PORTUGAL

Lisbon

Madrid

SPAIN

SP. MOR.

MOROCCO (FR.)

Oran

Algiers

ALGERIA (FR.)

TUNISIA (FR.)

Tunis

Malta

LIBYA (IT.)

Corsica

Sardinia

Rome

Naples

ITALY

ALBANIA

Sicily

Mediterranean Sea

NORWAY

Narvik

Oslo

SWEDEN

Stockholm

DENMARK

Hamburg

Berlin

GERMANY

Torgau

Remagen

Prague

SWITZ.

Vienna

Budapest

HUNGARY

SLOVAKIA

YUGOSLAVIA

Danube R.

GREECE

Crete

FINLAND

Helsinki

Murmansk

Leningrad

ESTONIA

LATVIA

LITHUANIA

Königsberg

Danzig

EAST PRUSSIA

Warsaw

POLAND

Vistula R.

Oder R.

ROMANIA

Ploesti

Bucharest

BULGARIA

Volga R.

Baltic Sea

SOVIET UNION

Moscow

Minsk

Voronezh

Stalingrad

Dnieper R.

Dniester R.

Black Sea

Istanbul

Ankara

TURKEY

Caspian Sea

IRAN

Cyprus

SYRIA (FR.)

IRAQ

PALESTINE (BR.)

TRANS-JORDAN (BR.)

SAUDI ARABIA

Nile R.

EGYPT

Tobruk

0   300   600 Miles
0   300   600 Kilometers

N

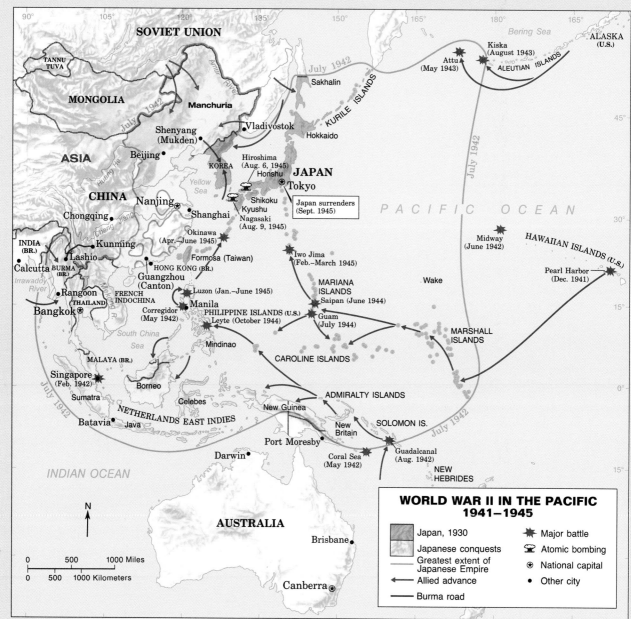

WORLD WAR II IN THE PACIFIC 1941–1945

Legend:
- Japan, 1930
- Japanese conquests
- Greatest extent of Japanese Empire
- ← Allied advance
- Burma road
- Major battle
- Atomic bombing
- National capital
- Other city

MERCATOR PROJECTION

Map labels:

SOVIET UNION

TANNU TUVA

MONGOLIA

Manchuria

ASIA

Amur River

Sakhalin

Bering Sea

Kiska (August 1943)

Attu (May 1943)

ALEUTIAN ISLANDS

ALASKA (U.S.)

Shenyang (Mukden)

Vladivostok

Hokkaido

KURILE ISLANDS

July 1942

Beijing

CHINA

KOREA

Hiroshima (Aug. 6, 1945)

Honshu

JAPAN

Tokyo

Nanjing

Hueng He

Yellow Sea

Shikoku

Kyushu

Nagasaki (Aug. 9, 1945)

Japan surrenders (Sept. 1945)

PACIFIC OCEAN

Chongqing

Shanghai

Cheng Jiang

Okinawa (Apr.–June 1945)

Midway (June 1942)

HAWAIIAN ISLANDS (U.S.)

INDIA (BR.)

Kunming

Lashio

Formosa (Taiwan)

Iwo Jima (Feb.–March 1945)

Calcutta

BURMA (BR.)

HONG KONG (BR.)

Guangzhou (Canton)

MARIANA ISLANDS

Wake

Pearl Harbor (Dec. 1941)

Irrawaddy River

Rangoon

THAILAND

FRENCH INDOCHINA

Luzon (Jan.–June 1945)

Manila

Saipan (June 1944)

Bangkok

Corregidor (May 1942)

PHILIPPINE ISLANDS (U.S.)

Leyte (October 1944)

Guam (July 1944)

MARSHALL ISLANDS

South China Sea

Mindinao

CAROLINE ISLANDS

MALAYA (BR.)

Singapore (Feb. 1942)

Borneo

Sumatra

Celebes

New Guinea

ADMIRALTY ISLANDS

July 1942

Batavia

Java

NETHERLANDS EAST INDIES

Port Moresby

New Britain

SOLOMON IS.

INDIAN OCEAN

Darwin

Coral Sea (May 1942)

Guadalcanal (Aug. 1942)

NEW HEBRIDES

N

AUSTRALIA

Brisbane

Canberra

0   500   1000 Miles

0   500   1000 Kilometers

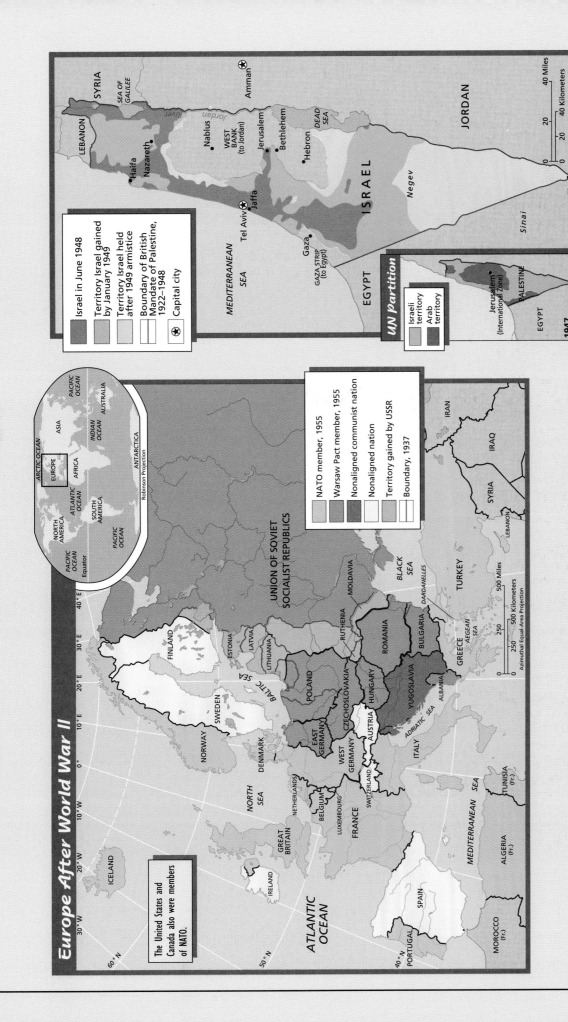

Israel, 1949

Israel, 1949 map legend:
- Israel in June 1948
- Territory Israel gained by January 1949
- Territory Israel held after 1949 armistice
- Boundary of British Mandate of Palestine, 1922–1948
- ✪ Capital city

Cities and places: SYRIA, LEBANON, SEA OF GALILEE, Amman, Nazareth, Haifa, Nablus, WEST BANK (to Jordan), Jerusalem, Bethlehem, Hebron, DEAD SEA, JORDAN, Jaffa, Tel Aviv, Gaza, GAZA STRIP (to Egypt), MEDITERRANEAN SEA, EGYPT, ISRAEL, Negev, Sinai, Elat, Jordan River

40 Miles / 40 Kilometers / 20 / Lambert Conformal Conic Projection

UN Partition

1947
- Israeli territory
- Arab territory

Jerusalem (International Zone), PALESTINE, EGYPT

Europe After World War II

The United States and Canada also were members of NATO.

Legend:
- NATO member, 1955
- Warsaw Pact member, 1955
- Nonaligned communist nation
- Nonaligned nation
- Territory gained by USSR
- Boundary, 1937

Inset globe: ARCTIC OCEAN, ASIA, EUROPE, AFRICA, PACIFIC OCEAN, INDIAN OCEAN, AUSTRALIA, ANTARCTICA, ATLANTIC OCEAN, NORTH AMERICA, SOUTH AMERICA, PACIFIC OCEAN, Equator, Robinson Projection

Countries and features: UNION OF SOVIET SOCIALIST REPUBLICS, FINLAND, ESTONIA, LATVIA, LITHUANIA, MOLDAVIA, RUTHENIA, ROMANIA, BULGARIA, POLAND, CZECHOSLOVAKIA, HUNGARY, YUGOSLAVIA, ALBANIA, GREECE, EAST GERMANY, AUSTRIA, WEST GERMANY, SWITZERLAND, ITALY, ADRIATIC SEA, AEGEAN SEA, BLACK SEA, DARDANELLES, TURKEY, SYRIA, IRAQ, IRAN, LEBANON, NETHERLANDS, BELGIUM, LUXEMBOURG, FRANCE, GREAT BRITAIN, IRELAND, ICELAND, NORWAY, SWEDEN, DENMARK, BALTIC SEA, NORTH SEA, ATLANTIC OCEAN, SPAIN, PORTUGAL, MEDITERRANEAN SEA, TUNISIA (Fr.), ALGERIA (Fr.), MOROCCO (Fr.)

30° W, 20° W, 10° W, 0°, 10° E, 20° E, 30° E, 40° E, 60° N, 50° N, 40° N

500 Miles / 500 Kilometers / 250 / Azimuthal Equal-Area Projection

97

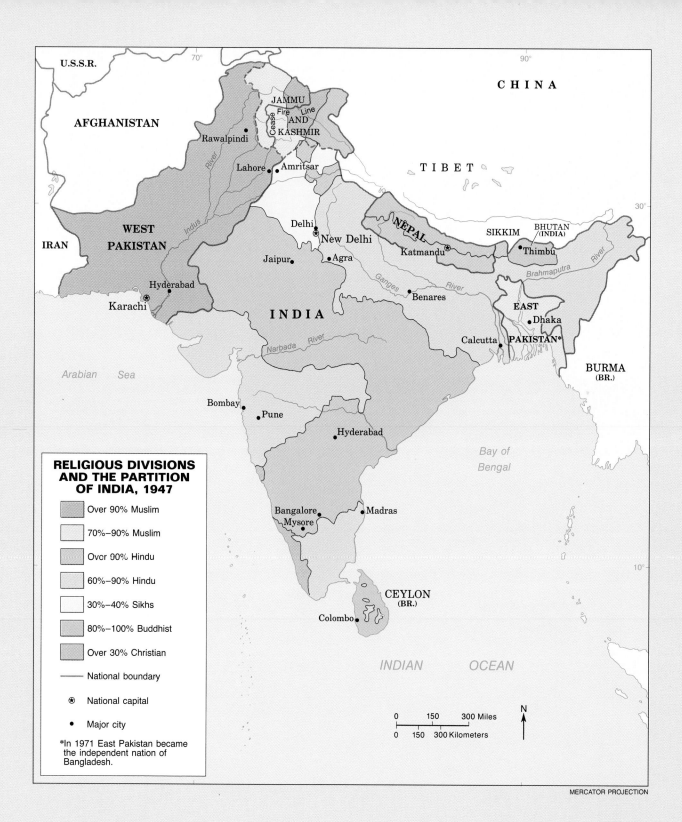

**RELIGIOUS DIVISIONS
AND THE PARTITION
OF INDIA, 1947**

Over 90% Muslim

70%–90% Muslim

Over 90% Hindu

60%–90% Hindu

30%–40% Sikhs

80%–100% Buddhist

Over 30% Christian

National boundary

⊛ National capital

• Major city

*In 1971 East Pakistan became
the independent nation of
Bangladesh.

MERCATOR PROJECTION

INDEPENDENT NATIONS IN SOUTHEAST ASIA, 1946–1984

⊛ National capital
• Other city
— National boundary
✳ Battle site
1945 Date of independence
▨ Continuously independent

0   250   500 Miles
0   250   500 Kilometers

N

MERCATOR PROJECTION

INDIA

CHINA

TAIWAN

BURMA
1948
• Mandalay

Dien Bien Phu
1954
⊛ Hanoi

Red R.

Irrawaddy
Salween R.

LAOS
1949

ANNAM CORDILLERA

⊛ Vientiane

Rangoon ⊛

THAILAND

Gulf of Tonkin

Mekong R.

Bangkok ⊛

VIETNAM
1945

CAMBODIA
1953

South China Sea

Luzon

Quezon City •
Manila ⊛

Andaman Sea

Gulf of Thailand

⊛ Phnom Penh
• Ho Chi Minh City
(Saigon)

Sulu Sea

PHILIPPINES
1946

PACIFIC OCEAN

MALAY PENINSULA

MALAYSIA
1957

Bandar Seri
Begawan
BRUNEI
1984

SABAH
(1963: Joined
Malaysia)

Mindanao

Kuala
Lumpur ⊛

SARAWAK
(1963: Joined Malaysia)

Celebes Sea

MOLUCCAS

• Singapore
1965

Strait of Malacca

Borneo

BARISAN MTS.

Sumatra

I N D O N E S I A
1 9 4 5

Molucca Sea

Ceram Sea

New Guinea

MAOKE MTS.

GREATER SUNDA IS.

Celebes

Banda Sea

IRIAN JAYA
(1963: Transferred
to Indonesia)

INDIAN OCEAN

Jakarta ⊛
Bandung • Java • Surabaya
Bali

Java Sea

LESSER SUNDA IS.

Timor PORT. TIMOR
(1975: Transferred
to Indonesia)

Arafura Sea

AUSTRALIA

100°   110°   120°   130°   140°
20°
10°
0°
10°

The Breakup of the Soviet Sphere, After 1989

Former Soviet republic
Former East European satellite of Soviet Union
Member of Commonwealth of Independent States
National capital
0 500 1,000 Miles
0 500 1,000 Kilometers
Lambert Conformal Conic Projection
0°
20° E
40° E
60° E
80° E
ARCTIC OCEAN
Eastern Europe, 1994
NORTH SEA
BALTIC SEA
ESTONIA
RUSSIA
LATVIA
LITHUANIA
RUSSIA
BELARUS
POLAND
GERMANY
CZECH REPUBLIC
SLOVAKIA
UKRAINE
MOLDOVA
AUSTRIA
SLOVENIA
HUNGARY
ROMANIA
CROATIA
ITALY
ADRIATIC SEA
SERBIA
BOSNIA AND HERZEGOVINA
BULGARIA
MONTENEGRO
ALBANIA
MACEDONIA
Azimuthal Equal-Area Projection
140°W
ALASKA (U.S.)
Bering Strait
180°
60° N
NORWAY
SWEDEN
BARENTS SEA
GERMANY
FINLAND
Murmansk
WHITE SEA
NOVAYA ZEMLYA
SEVERNAYA ZEMLYA
BALTIC SEA
POLAND
St. Petersburg
Minsk
BELARUS
Kyyiv (Kiev)
ROMANIA
Moscow
UKRAINE
Nizhniy Novgorod (Gorki)
Crimea
BLACK SEA
Yekaterinburg (Sverdlovsk)
RUSSIA
TURKEY
GEORGIA
CHECHNYA
Grozny
ARMENIA
Tbilisi
Yerevan
CASPIAN SEA
SIBERIA
AZERBAIJAN
Baki
ARAL SEA
KAZAKHSTAN
Lake Baykal
SEA OF OKHOTSK
Kamchatka Peninsula
SAKHALIN
160° E
TURKMENISTAN
UZBEKISTAN
Ashgabat
Toshkent
Bishkek
Almaty
KURIL IS.
IRAN
Dushanbe
Ulaanbaatar
MONGOLIA
CHINA
SEA OF JAPAN
40° N
PACIFIC OCEAN
AFGHANISTAN
KYRGYZSTAN
TAJIKISTAN
Vladivostok
JAPAN

Trade Organizations and Alliances, 1994

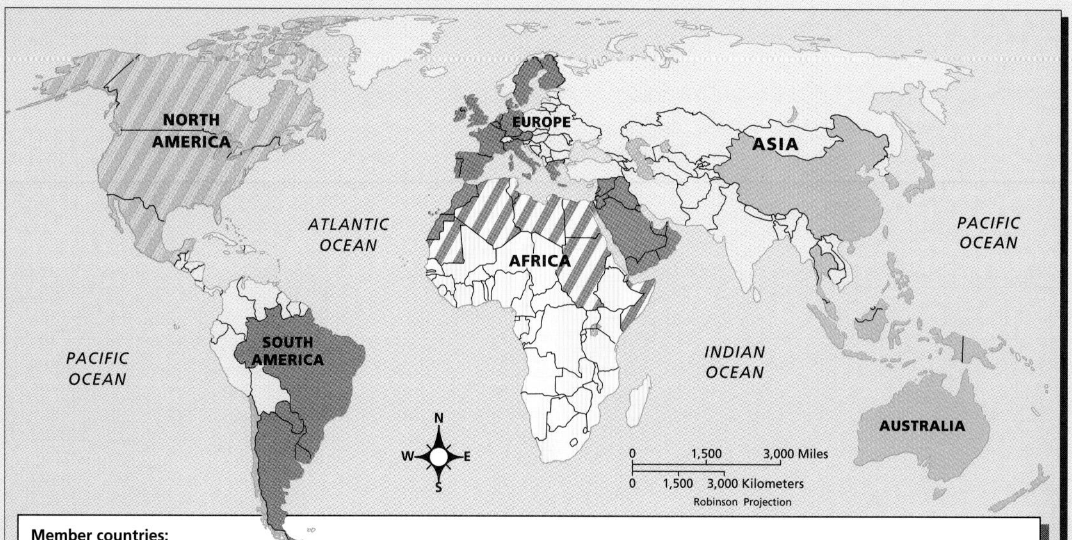

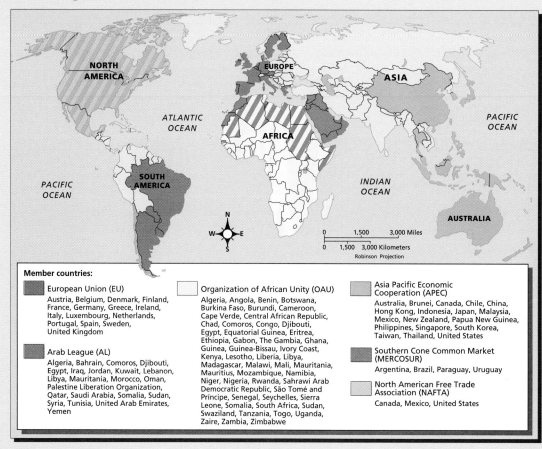

NORTH AMERICA
EUROPE
ASIA
ATLANTIC OCEAN
AFRICA
PACIFIC OCEAN
SOUTH AMERICA
PACIFIC OCEAN
INDIAN OCEAN
AUSTRALIA
0 1,500 3,000 Miles
0 1,500 3,000 Kilometers
Robinson Projection

Member countries:

European Union (EU)
Austria, Belgium, Denmark, Finland, France, Germany, Greece, Ireland, Italy, Luxembourg, Netherlands, Portugal, Spain, Sweden, United Kingdom

Arab League (AL)
Algeria, Bahrain, Comoros, Djibouti, Egypt, Iraq, Jordan, Kuwait, Lebanon, Libya, Mauritania, Morocco, Oman, Palestine Liberation Organization, Qatar, Saudi Arabia, Somalia, Sudan, Syria, Tunisia, United Arab Emirates, Yemen

Organization of African Unity (OAU)
Algeria, Angola, Benin, Botswana, Burkina Faso, Burundi, Cameroon, Cape Verde, Central African Republic, Chad, Comoros, Congo, Djibouti, Egypt, Equatorial Guinea, Eritrea, Ethiopia, Gabon, The Gambia, Ghana, Guinea, Guinea-Bissau, Ivory Coast, Kenya, Lesotho, Liberia, Libya, Madagascar, Malawi, Mali, Mauritania, Mauritius, Mozambique, Namibia, Niger, Nigeria, Rwanda, Sahrawi Arab Democratic Republic, São Tomé and Príncipe, Senegal, Seychelles, Sierra Leone, Somalia, South Africa, Sudan, Swaziland, Tanzania, Togo, Uganda, Zaire, Zambia, Zimbabwe

Asia Pacific Economic Cooperation (APEC)
Australia, Brunei, Canada, Chile, China, Hong Kong, Indonesia, Japan, Malaysia, Mexico, New Zealand, Papua New Guinea, Philippines, Singapore, South Korea, Taiwan, Thailand, United States

Southern Cone Common Market (MERCOSUR)
Argentina, Brazil, Paraguay, Uruguay

North American Free Trade Association (NAFTA)
Canada, Mexico, United States

AMERICAN HISTORY

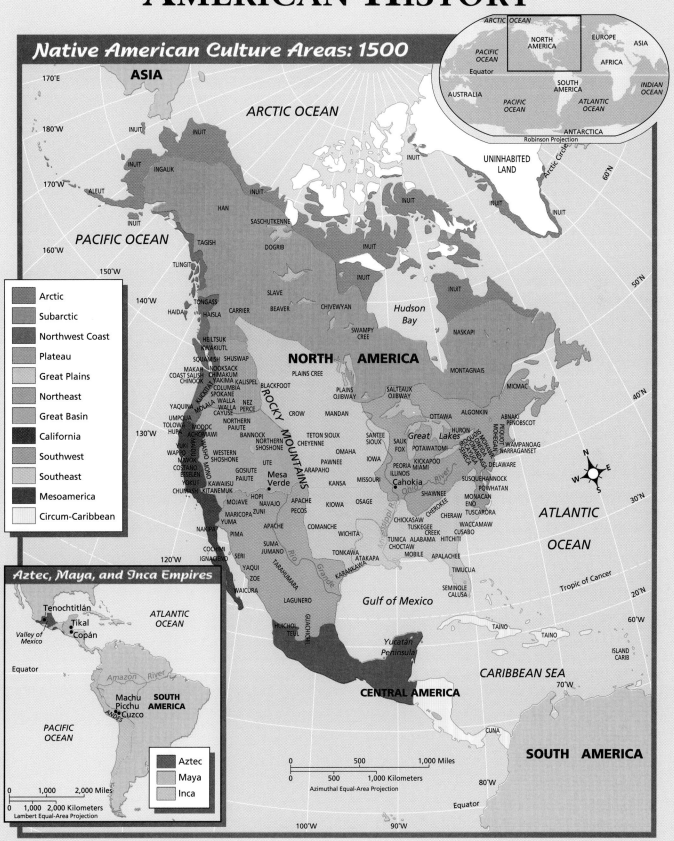

Native American Culture Areas: 1500

ASIA

ARCTIC OCEAN

170°E
180°W
170°W
160°W
150°W
140°W
130°W
120°W

PACIFIC OCEAN

INUIT
INUIT
INGALIK
ALEUT
INUIT
HAN
TAGISH
TLINGIT
HAIDA
TONGASS
HAISLA
HEILTSUK
KWAKIUTL
SQUAMISH SHUSWAP
MAKAH NOOKSACK
COAST SALISH CHIMAKUM
CHINOOK YAKIMA
KALISPEL
COLUMBIA
SPOKANE
YAQUINA WALLA
WALLA
UMPQUA MOLALA WALLA
TOLOWA NEZ
PERCE
CAYUSE
HUPA MODOC
ACHOMAWI
YUKI NORTHERN
WAPPO PAIUTE
MIWOK
WASHO WESTERN
COSTANO MONO SHOSHONE
ESSELEN GOSIUTE
YOKUT KAWAIISU PAIUTE
CHUMASH KITANEMUK
NAKIPA
MOJAVE
MARICOPA
YUMA
PIMA
COCHIMI
IGNACIENO SERI
YAQUI
ZOE
WAICURA

SASCHUTKENNE
DOGRIB
INUIT
SLAVE
CARRIER BEAVER CHIVEWYAN
SWAMPY
CREE
PLAINS CREE
BLACKFOOT
KUCKTA
COLUMBIA
NORTHERN
BANNOCK PAIUTE
SHOSHONE
UTE
ROCKY MOUNTAINS
CROW MANDAN
TETON SIOUX
CHEYENNE
OMAHA
PAWNEE
ARAPAHO IOWA
Mesa KANSA MISSOURI
Verde
HOPI
NAVAJO APACHE KIOWA OSAGE
ZUNI PECOS
APACHE COMANCHE
WICHITA
SUMA
JUMANO TONKAWA
TARAHUMARA KARANKAWA
LAGUNERO
HUICHOL
TEUL
GUACHICHIL

INUIT
INUIT
INUIT
Hudson Bay
NASKAPI
NORTH AMERICA
MONTAGNAIS
SALTEAUX
OJIBWAY
PLAINS
OJIBWAY
MICMAC
ALGONKIN
OTTAWA ABNAKI
HURON PENOBSCOT
Great Lakes MOHAWK
IROQUOIS ONEIDA
ONONDAGA MOHEGAN PEQUOT
SAUK CAYUGA WAMPANOAG
SANTEE FOX POTAWATOMI SENECA NARRAGANSET
SIOUX KICKAPOO DELAWARE
PEORIA MIAMI
ILLINOIS SUSQUEHANNOCK
Cahokia POWHATAN
SHAWNEE MONACAN
CHEROKEE ENO
CHICKASAW TUSCARORA
TUSKEGEE CHERAW WACCAMAW
CREEK CUSABO
TUNICA ALABAMA HITCHITI
CHOCTAW
MOBILE APALACHEE
TIMUCUA
SEMINOLE
CALUSA

Ohio River
Mississippi R.
Rio Grande

ATLANTIC OCEAN

Gulf of Mexico

Yucatán Peninsula

CARIBBEAN SEA

CENTRAL AMERICA

TAINO
TAINO
ISLAND CARIB
CUNA

SOUTH AMERICA

50°N
60°N
40°N
30°N
20°N
Tropic of Cancer
60°W
70°W
80°W

UNINHABITED LAND
Arctic Circle

Legend

- Arctic
- Subarctic
- Northwest Coast
- Plateau
- Great Plains
- Northeast
- Great Basin
- California
- Southwest
- Southeast
- Mesoamerica
- Circum-Caribbean

0   500   1,000 Miles
0   500   1,000 Kilometers
Azimuthal Equal-Area Projection

100°W   90°W

Equator

Aztec, Maya, and Inca Empires

Tenochtitlán
Valley of Mexico
Tikal
Copán
ATLANTIC OCEAN
Equator
Amazon River
Machu Picchu SOUTH
Cuzco AMERICA
ANDES
PACIFIC OCEAN

- Aztec
- Maya
- Inca

0   1,000   2,000 Miles
0   1,000   2,000 Kilometers
Lambert Equal-Area Projection

Inset (world locator)

ARCTIC OCEAN
NORTH AMERICA
EUROPE ASIA
PACIFIC OCEAN
AFRICA
Equator
SOUTH AMERICA
INDIAN OCEAN
AUSTRALIA PACIFIC OCEAN ATLANTIC OCEAN
ANTARCTICA
Robinson Projection

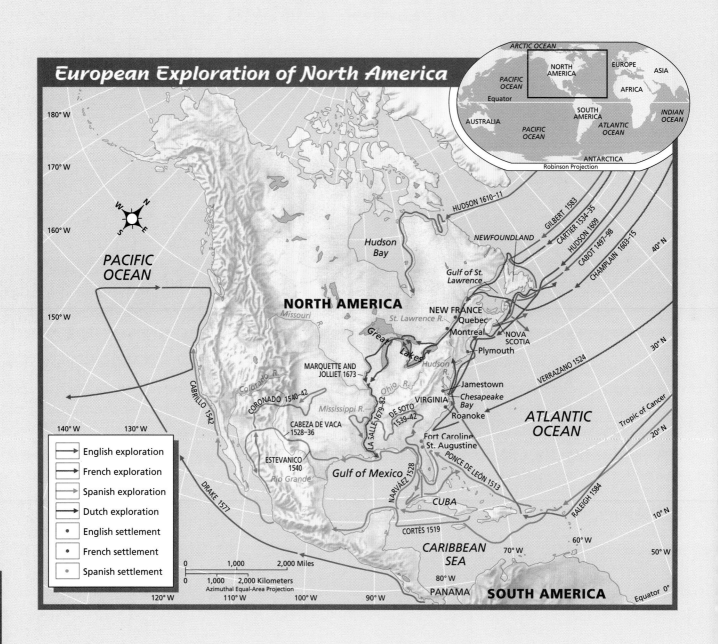

European Exploration of North America

ARCTIC OCEAN
NORTH AMERICA
EUROPE
ASIA
PACIFIC OCEAN
AFRICA
Equator
SOUTH AMERICA
INDIAN OCEAN
AUSTRALIA
PACIFIC OCEAN
ATLANTIC OCEAN
ANTARCTICA
Robinson Projection

180° W
170° W
160° W
150° W
140° W
130° W
120° W
110° W
100° W
90° W
80° W
70° W
60° W
50° W
40° N
30° N
20° N
10° N
Equator 0°
Tropic of Cancer

PACIFIC OCEAN

NORTH AMERICA

Hudson Bay

HUDSON 1610–11
GILBERT 1583
CARTIER 1534–35
HUDSON 1609
CABOT 1497–98
CHAMPLAIN 1603–15
NEWFOUNDLAND

Gulf of St. Lawrence

Missouri R.
St. Lawrence R.
NEW FRANCE
Quebec
Montreal
NOVA SCOTIA
Plymouth
Great Lakes
Hudson R.
VERRAZANO 1524

MARQUETTE AND JOLLIET 1673
Colorado R.
CORONADO 1540–42
Mississippi R.
Ohio R.
Jamestown
Chesapeake Bay
VIRGINIA
Roanoke

CABRILLO 1542
CABEZA DE VACA 1528–36
LA SALLE 1679–82
DE SOTO 1539–42

ATLANTIC OCEAN

ESTEVANICO 1540
Rio Grande
Fort Caroline
St. Augustine

Gulf of Mexico
NARVÁEZ 1528
PONCE DE LEÓN 1513

DRAKE 1577
RALEIGH 1584

CUBA

CORTÉS 1519

CARIBBEAN SEA

PANAMA
SOUTH AMERICA

Legend:
- English exploration
- French exploration
- Spanish exploration
- Dutch exploration
- English settlement
- French settlement
- Spanish settlement

0   1,000   2,000 Miles
0   1,000   2,000 Kilometers
Azimuthal Equal-Area Projection

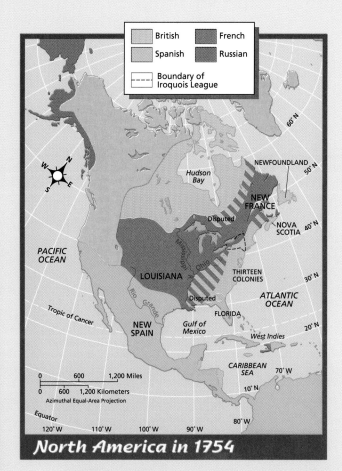

North America in 1754

Legend:
- British
- Spanish
- French
- Russian
- Boundary of Iroquois League

Labels: NEWFOUNDLAND, Hudson Bay, NEW FRANCE, Disputed, NOVA SCOTIA, PACIFIC OCEAN, Mississippi R., Ohio R., LOUISIANA, THIRTEEN COLONIES, ATLANTIC OCEAN, Disputed, Rio Grande, Tropic of Cancer, NEW SPAIN, Gulf of Mexico, FLORIDA, West Indies, CARIBBEAN SEA, Equator

Scale: 0 600 1,200 Miles / 0 600 1,200 Kilometers
Azimuthal Equal-Area Projection

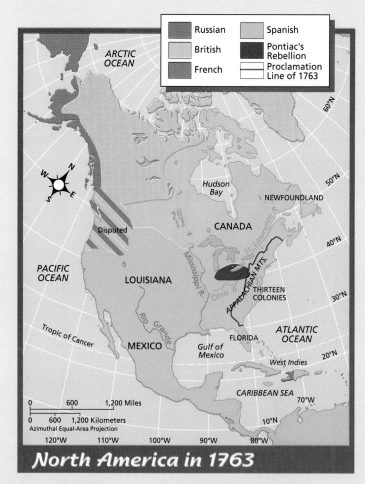

North America in 1763

Legend:
- Russian
- British
- French
- Spanish
- Pontiac's Rebellion
- Proclamation Line of 1763

Labels: ARCTIC OCEAN, Hudson Bay, NEWFOUNDLAND, CANADA, Disputed, PACIFIC OCEAN, Mississippi R., St. Lawrence R., LOUISIANA, APPALACHIAN MTS., THIRTEEN COLONIES, ATLANTIC OCEAN, Tropic of Cancer, Rio Grande, MEXICO, Gulf of Mexico, FLORIDA, West Indies, CARIBBEAN SEA

Scale: 0 600 1,200 Miles / 0 600 1,200 Kilometers
Azimuthal Equal-Area Projection

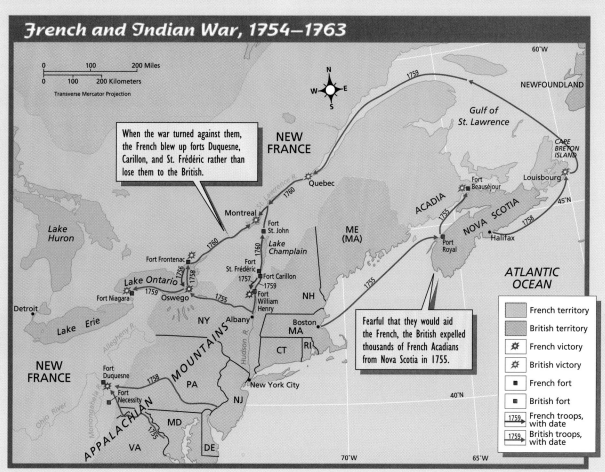

French and Indian War, 1754–1763

Scale: 0 100 200 Miles / 0 100 200 Kilometers
Transverse Mercator Projection

When the war turned against them, the French blew up forts Duquesne, Carillon, and St. Frédéric rather than lose them to the British.

Fearful that they would aid the French, the British expelled thousands of French Acadians from Nova Scotia in 1755.

Legend:
- French territory
- British territory
- French victory
- British victory
- French fort
- British fort
- 1759 French troops, with date
- 1759 British troops, with date

Labels: NEWFOUNDLAND, Gulf of St. Lawrence, NEW FRANCE, Quebec, Montreal, Fort St. John, Lake Champlain, Fort St. Frédéric, Fort Carillon, Lake Huron, Fort Frontenac, Lake Ontario, Fort Niagara, Oswego, Detroit, Lake Erie, Allegheny R., NY, Albany, NEW FRANCE, Fort Duquesne, Fort Necessity, APPALACHIAN, MOUNTAINS, PA, Monongahela R., Ohio River, VA, MD, DE, NJ, New York City, CT, RI, MA, Boston, NH, Hudson R., ME (MA), ACADIA, Fort Beauséjour, NOVA SCOTIA, Port Royal, Halifax, CAPE BRETON ISLAND, Louisbourg, ATLANTIC OCEAN, St. Lawrence R.

Dates on map: 1759, 1760, 1755, 1757, 1758, 1756, 1758

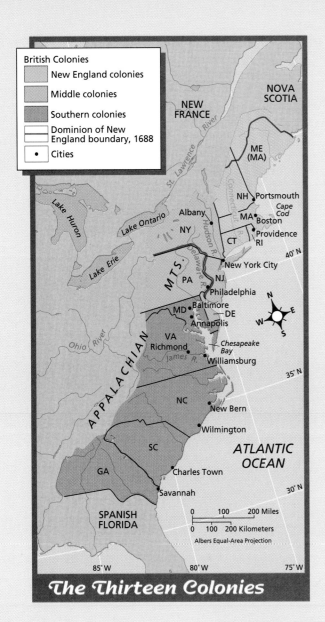

British Colonies

New England colonies

Middle colonies

Southern colonies

Dominion of New England boundary, 1688

• Cities

NEW FRANCE

NOVA SCOTIA

Lake Huron

Lake Ontario

Lake Erie

St. Lawrence River

Connecticut R.

Hudson R.

Delaware R.

ME (MA)

NH   Portsmouth

Cape Cod

Albany

MA   Boston

NY

CT   Providence

RI

New York City

APPALACHIAN MTS.

PA   NJ

Philadelphia

MD   Baltimore

DE

Annapolis

Ohio River

VA

Richmond

Chesapeake Bay

James R.

Williamsburg

NC

New Bern

Wilmington

SC

GA   Charles Town

Savannah

ATLANTIC OCEAN

SPANISH FLORIDA

40° N

35° N

30° N

85° W   80° W   75° W

0   100   200 Miles

0   100   200 Kilometers

Albers Equal-Area Projection

The Thirteen Colonies

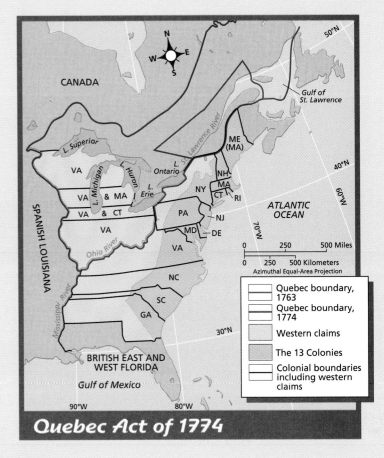

CANADA

L. Superior

L. Michigan

L. Huron

L. Ontario

L. Erie

St. Lawrence River

Gulf of St. Lawrence

50°N

ME (MA)

NH

NY   MA
CT
RI

VA

VA   & MA

VA   & CT

VA

PA

NJ

MD   DE

VA

SPANISH LOUISIANA

Ohio River

Mississippi R.

NC

SC

GA

ATLANTIC OCEAN

BRITISH EAST AND WEST FLORIDA

Gulf of Mexico

40°N

30°N

90°W   80°W

70°W

60°W

0   250   500 Miles

0   250   500 Kilometers

Azimuthal Equal-Area Projection

Quebec boundary, 1763

Quebec boundary, 1774

Western claims

The 13 Colonies

Colonial boundaries including western claims

Quebec Act of 1774

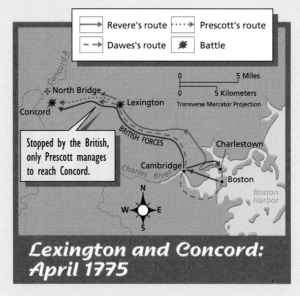

Revere's route

Dawes's route

Prescott's route

Battle

Concord River

North Bridge

Concord

Lexington

BRITISH FORCES

Charles River

Charlestown

Cambridge

Boston

Boston Harbor

Stopped by the British, only Prescott manages to reach Concord.

0   5 Miles

0   5 Kilometers

Transverse Mercator Projection

Lexington and Concord: April 1775

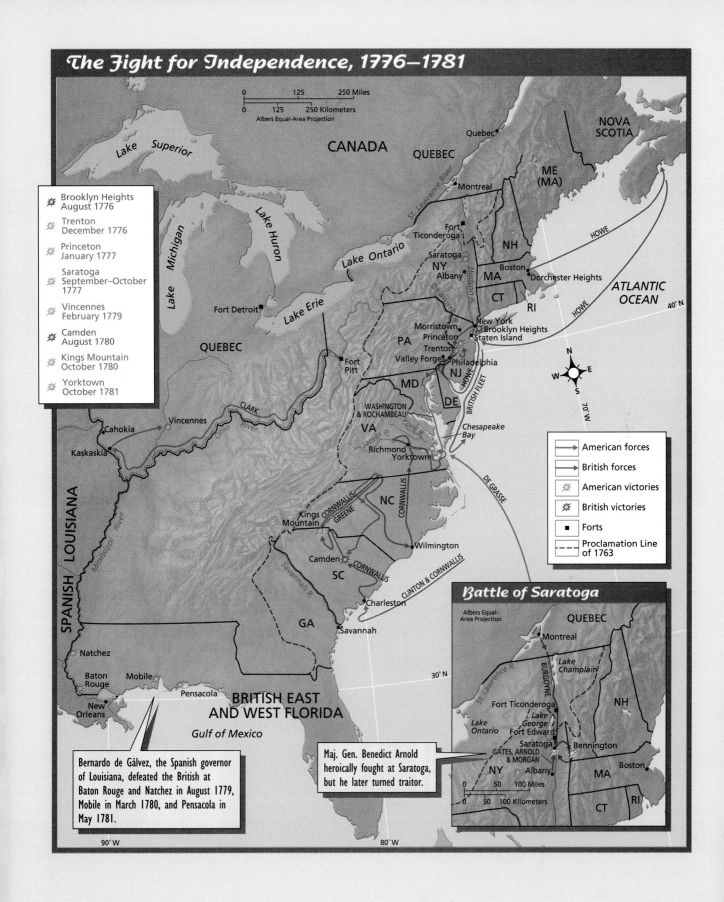

The Fight for Independence, 1776–1781

0   125   250 Miles
0   125   250 Kilometers
Albers Equal-Area Projection

Legend of battles:

- ✸ Brooklyn Heights August 1776
- ✸ Trenton December 1776
- ✸ Princeton January 1777
- ✸ Saratoga September–October 1777
- ✸ Vincennes February 1779
- ✸ Camden August 1780
- ✸ Kings Mountain October 1780
- ✸ Yorktown October 1781

Labels on main map:

CANADA
Lake Superior
Lake Michigan
Lake Huron
Lake Erie
Lake Ontario
QUEBEC
Quebec
Montreal
St. Lawrence River
ME (MA)
NH
NOVA SCOTIA
Fort Ticonderoga
Saratoga
NY
Albany
Hudson R.
Boston
MA
Dorchester Heights
CT
RI
ATLANTIC OCEAN
40° N
HOWE
Fort Detroit
Fort Pitt
Delaware R.
Morristown
New York
Brooklyn Heights
Staten Island
PA
Princeton
Trenton
Valley Forge
Philadelphia
NJ
MD
DE
BRITISH FLEET
CLARK
Vincennes
Cahokia
Kaskaskia
Ohio River
WASHINGTON & ROCHAMBEAU
VA
James R.
Richmond
York R.
Yorktown
Chesapeake Bay
DE GRASSE
70° W
Kings Mountain
CORNWALLIS
GREENE
NC
CORNWALLIS
Camden
CORNWALLIS
SC
Wilmington
CLINTON & CORNWALLIS
Charleston
GA
Savannah
Savannah R.
SPANISH LOUISIANA
Mississippi River
Natchez
Baton Rouge
Mobile
New Orleans
Pensacola
BRITISH EAST AND WEST FLORIDA
Gulf of Mexico
90° W
80° W
30° N

Map key:

- → American forces
- → British forces
- ✸ American victories
- ✸ British victories
- ■ Forts
- ---- Proclamation Line of 1763

Bernardo de Gálvez, the Spanish governor of Louisiana, defeated the British at Baton Rouge and Natchez in August 1779, Mobile in March 1780, and Pensacola in May 1781.

Maj. Gen. Benedict Arnold heroically fought at Saratoga, but he later turned traitor.

Battle of Saratoga

Albers Equal-Area Projection

QUEBEC
Montreal
St. Lawrence R.
Lake Champlain
BURGOYNE
Fort Ticonderoga
Lake Ontario
Lake George
Fort Edward
NH
Saratoga
GATES, ARNOLD & MORGAN
Bennington
NY
Albany
MA
Boston
CT
RI

0   50   100 Miles
0   50   100 Kilometers

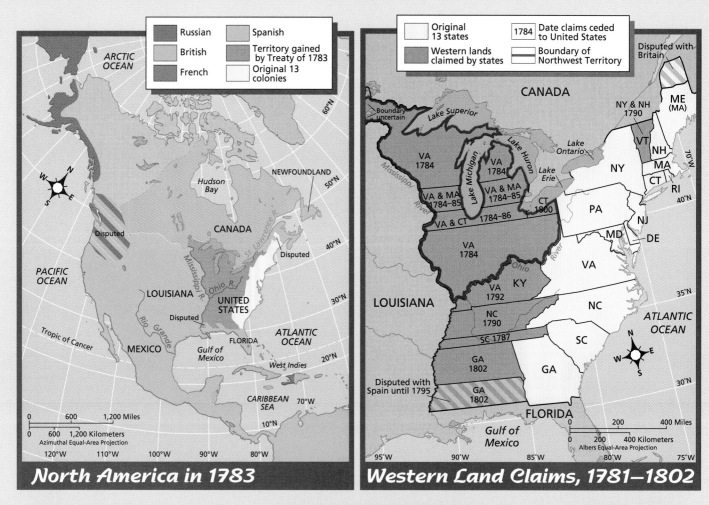

North America in 1783

Legend:
- Russian
- British
- French
- Spanish
- Territory gained by Treaty of 1783
- Original 13 colonies

ARCTIC OCEAN

Hudson Bay

NEWFOUNDLAND

CANADA

Disputed

Disputed

PACIFIC OCEAN

LOUISIANA

UNITED STATES

Disputed

Mississippi R.

Ohio R.

St. Lawrence R.

Rio Grande

Tropic of Cancer

MEXICO

Gulf of Mexico

FLORIDA

ATLANTIC OCEAN

West Indies

CARIBBEAN SEA

0   600   1,200 Miles
0   600   1,200 Kilometers
Azimuthal Equal-Area Projection

120°W   110°W   100°W   90°W   80°W   70°W

60°N   50°N   40°N   30°N   20°N   10°N

Western Land Claims, 1781–1802

Legend:
- Original 13 states
- Western lands claimed by states
- 1784 Date claims ceded to United States
- Boundary of Northwest Territory

CANADA

Boundary uncertain

Lake Superior

Lake Michigan

Lake Huron

Lake Ontario

Lake Erie

Mississippi River

Ohio River

Disputed with Britain

ME (MA)

NY & NH 1790

VT

NH

NY

MA

CT

RI

PA

NJ

MD

DE

VA 1784

VA 1784

VA & MA 1784-85

VA & MA 1784-85

VA & CT 1784-86

CT 1800

VA 1784

VA 1792

KY

VA

NC 1790

NC

SC 1787

SC

GA 1802

GA

Disputed with Spain until 1795

GA 1802

FLORIDA

LOUISIANA

ATLANTIC OCEAN

Gulf of Mexico

0   200   400 Miles
0   200   400 Kilometers
Albers Equal-Area Projection

95°W   90°W   85°W   80°W   75°W

40°N   35°N   30°N

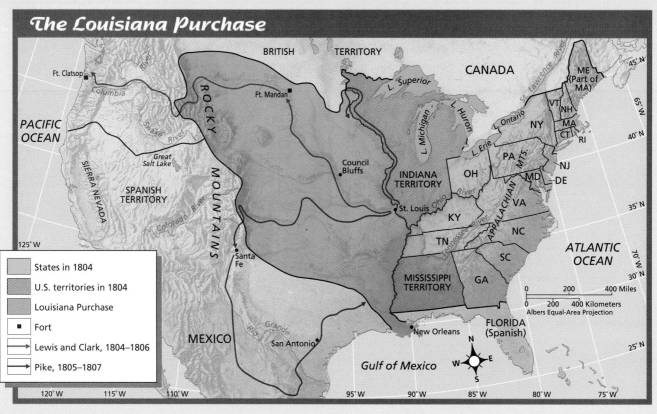

The Louisiana Purchase

Legend:
- States in 1804
- U.S. territories in 1804
- Louisiana Purchase
- ■ Fort
- Lewis and Clark, 1804–1806
- Pike, 1805–1807

BRITISH TERRITORY

CANADA

Ft. Clatsop

Columbia River

Ft. Mandan

Missouri River

Snake River

Great Salt Lake

ROCKY MOUNTAINS

SIERRA NEVADA

PACIFIC OCEAN

SPANISH TERRITORY

Colorado River

Platte River

Council Bluffs

St. Louis

Santa Fe

Red River

Rio Grande

San Antonio

MEXICO

New Orleans

Gulf of Mexico

L. Superior

L. Michigan

L. Huron

L. Ontario

L. Erie

INDIANA TERRITORY

OH

KY

TN

MISSISSIPPI TERRITORY

GA

Ohio River

Tennessee River

St. Lawrence River

ME (Part of MA)

VT

NH

NY

MA

CT

RI

PA

NJ

MD

DE

VA

APPALACHIAN MTS.

NC

SC

ATLANTIC OCEAN

FLORIDA (Spanish)

125° W   120° W   115° W   110° W   95° W   90° W   85° W   80° W   75° W

45° N   65° W   40° N   35° N   70° W   30° N   25° N

0   200   400 Miles
0   200   400 Kilometers
Albers Equal-Area Projection

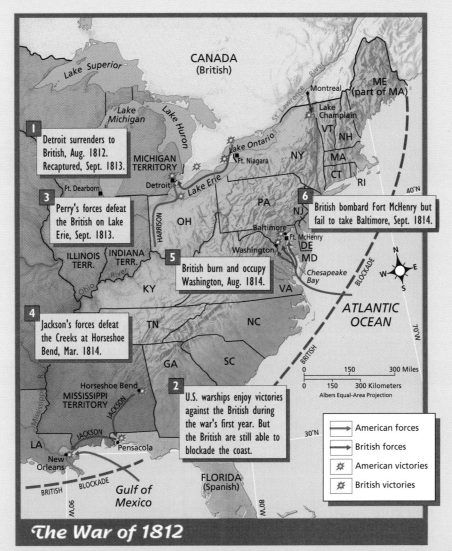

The War of 1812

CANADA (British)

Lake Superior

Lake Michigan

Lake Huron

Lake Ontario

1 Detroit surrenders to British, Aug. 1812. Recaptured, Sept. 1813.

MICHIGAN TERRITORY

Ft. Dearborn

Detroit

Ft. Niagara

Lake Erie

3 Perry's forces defeat the British on Lake Erie, Sept. 1813.

HARRISON

OH

PA

NJ

6 British bombard Fort McHenry but fail to take Baltimore, Sept. 1814.

ILLINOIS TERR.

INDIANA TERR.

Ohio River

5 British burn and occupy Washington, Aug. 1814.

Baltimore

Ft. McHenry

Washington

DE

MD

Chesapeake Bay

KY

VA

4 Jackson's forces defeat the Creeks at Horseshoe Bend, Mar. 1814.

TN

NC

Mississippi R.

JACKSON

Horseshoe Bend

MISSISSIPPI TERRITORY

GA

SC

JACKSON

LA

Pensacola

New Orleans

2 U.S. warships enjoy victories against the British during the war's first year. But the British are still able to blockade the coast.

BRITISH BLOCKADE

Gulf of Mexico

FLORIDA (Spanish)

ATLANTIC OCEAN

Montreal

St. Lawrence River

Lake Champlain

ME (part of MA)

VT

NH

NY

MA

CT

RI

40°N

70°W

BRITISH BLOCKADE

30°N

0   150   300 Miles
0   150   300 Kilometers
Albers Equal-Area Projection

→ American forces
➜ British forces
✳ American victories
✳ British victories

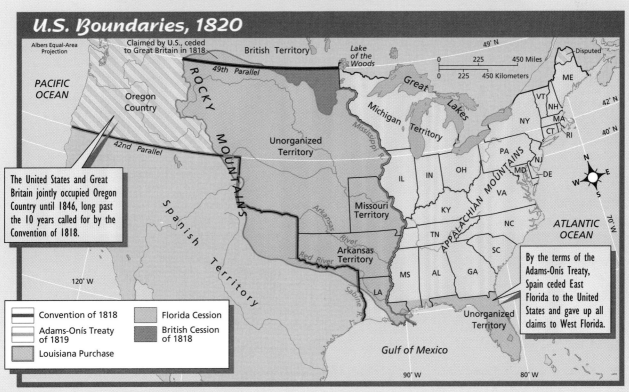

U.S. Boundaries, 1820

Albers Equal-Area Projection

Claimed by U.S., ceded to Great Britain in 1818

British Territory

Lake of the Woods

49°N

Disputed

ME

0   225   450 Miles
0   225   450 Kilometers

PACIFIC OCEAN

49th Parallel

ROCKY MOUNTAINS

Oregon Country

42nd Parallel

Great Lakes

Michigan Territory

Mississippi R.

VT

NH

NY

MA

CT

RI

42°N

40°N

The United States and Great Britain jointly occupied Oregon Country until 1846, long past the 10 years called for by the Convention of 1818.

Unorganized Territory

PA

OH

IL

IN

MD

DE

NJ

Spanish Territory

Arkansas River

Missouri Territory

VA

KY

APPALACHIAN MOUNTAINS

NC

ATLANTIC OCEAN

70°W

120°W

Red River

Arkansas Territory

TN

SC

By the terms of the Adams-Onís Treaty, Spain ceded East Florida to the United States and gave up all claims to West Florida.

Sabine R.

MS

AL

GA

LA

Unorganized Territory

Gulf of Mexico

90°W

80°W

■ Convention of 1818
▨ Adams-Onís Treaty of 1819
▨ Louisiana Purchase
▨ Florida Cession
▨ British Cession of 1818

Missouri Compromise: 1820

Free state
Free territory
Slave state
Slave territory

OREGON COUNTRY
MAINE
MISSOURI
Missouri Compromise Line
36° 30' N

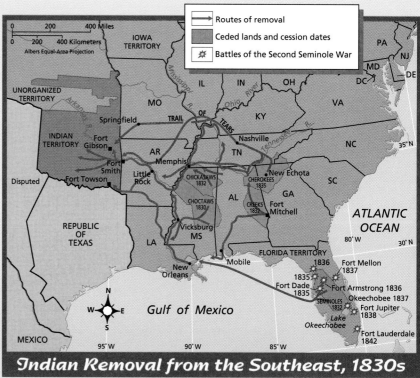

Indian Removal from the Southeast, 1830s

Routes of removal
Ceded lands and cession dates
Battles of the Second Seminole War

0 200 400 Miles
0 200 400 Kilometers
Albers Equal-Area Projection

IOWA TERRITORY
UNORGANIZED TERRITORY
INDIAN TERRITORY
Disputed
REPUBLIC OF TEXAS
MEXICO

Springfield
Fort Gibson
Fort Smith
Fort Towson
Little Rock
Memphis
Vicksburg
New Orleans
Mobile

TRAIL OF TEARS
Arkansas R.
Mississippi R.
Ohio River
Tennessee R.

IL IN OH
MO KY VA
AR TN NC
CHICKASAWS 1832
CHOCTAWS 1830
AL
CREEKS 1832
CHEROKEES 1835
New Echota
Fort Mitchell
GA SC
LA MS

Nashville

PA NJ
MD DE
DC
35° N

ATLANTIC OCEAN
80° W 30° N

FLORIDA TERRITORY
1836
Fort Mellon 1837
Fort Dade 1835
Fort Armstrong 1836
Okeechobee 1837
SEMINOLES 1832
Fort Jupiter 1838
Lake Okeechobee
Fort Lauderdale 1842
1835

Gulf of Mexico

95° W 90° W 85° W

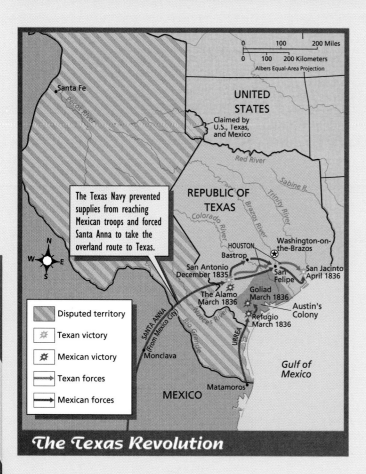

The Texas Revolution

The Texas Navy prevented supplies from reaching Mexican troops and forced Santa Anna to take the overland route to Texas.

Disputed territory
Texan victory
Mexican victory
Texan forces
Mexican forces

0 100 200 Miles
0 100 200 Kilometers
Albers Equal-Area Projection

Santa Fe
UNITED STATES
Claimed by U.S., Texas, and Mexico
Pecos River
Red River
Sabine R.
REPUBLIC OF TEXAS
Colorado River
Brazos River
Trinity River
Washington-on-the-Brazos
HOUSTON
Bastrop
San Felipe
San Antonio December 1835
San Jacinto April 1836
The Alamo March 1836
Goliad March 1836
Austin's Colony
Refugio March 1836
SANTA ANNA (from Mexico City)
URREA
Nueces River
Rio Grande
Monclava
Matamoros
MEXICO
Gulf of Mexico

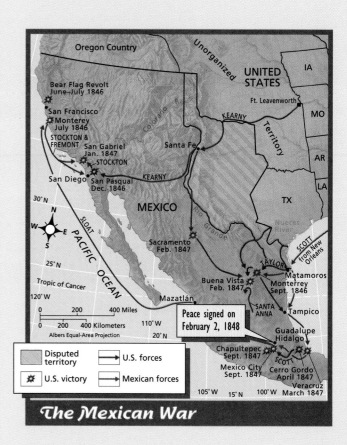

The Mexican War

Disputed territory
U.S. victory
U.S. forces
Mexican forces

Peace signed on February 2, 1848

0 200 400 Miles
0 200 400 Kilometers
Albers Equal-Area Projection

Oregon Country
Unorganized Territory
UNITED STATES
IA
MO
AR
LA
TX
Ft. Leavenworth
KEARNY
Santa Fe
KEARNY
Bear Flag Revolt June–July 1846
San Francisco
Monterey July 1846
STOCKTON & FREMONT
San Gabriel Jan. 1847
STOCKTON
San Diego
San Pasqual Dec. 1846
Colorado R.
Rio Grande
Nueces River
MEXICO
Sacramento Feb. 1847
Buena Vista Feb. 1847
SANTA ANNA
Mazatlán
SLOAT
PACIFIC OCEAN
Tropic of Cancer
30° N
25° N
120° W
110° W
105° W
100° W
20° N
15° N
TAYLOR
Matamoros
Monterrey Sept. 1846
Tampico
Guadalupe Hidalgo
Chapultepec Sept. 1847
Mexico City Sept. 1847
Cerro Gordo April 1847
Veracruz March 1847
SCOTT from New Orleans
SCOTT

U.S. Boundaries, 1853

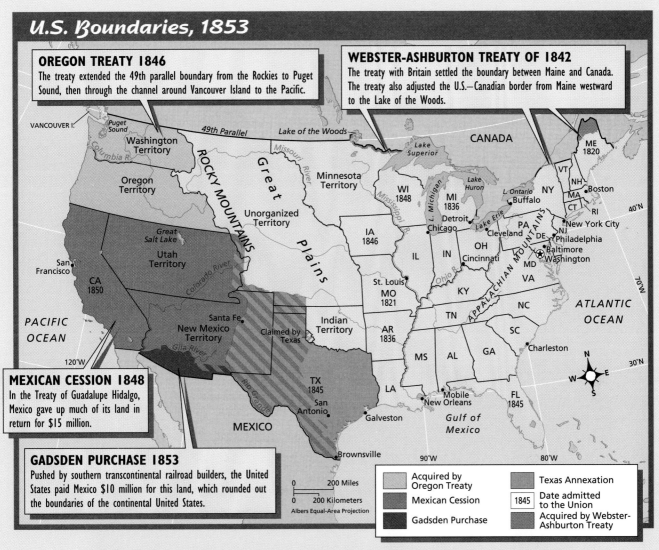

OREGON TREATY 1846
The treaty extended the 49th parallel boundary from the Rockies to Puget Sound, then through the channel around Vancouver Island to the Pacific.

WEBSTER-ASHBURTON TREATY OF 1842
The treaty with Britain settled the boundary between Maine and Canada. The treaty also adjusted the U.S.–Canadian border from Maine westward to the Lake of the Woods.

MEXICAN CESSION 1848
In the Treaty of Guadalupe Hidalgo, Mexico gave up much of its land in return for $15 million.

GADSDEN PURCHASE 1853
Pushed by southern transcontinental railroad builders, the United States paid Mexico $10 million for this land, which rounded out the boundaries of the continental United States.

Legend:
- Acquired by Oregon Treaty
- Mexican Cession
- Gadsden Purchase
- Texas Annexation
- 1845 Date admitted to the Union
- Acquired by Webster-Ashburton Treaty

0 200 Miles
0 200 Kilometers
Albers Equal-Area Projection

The Cotton Kingdom

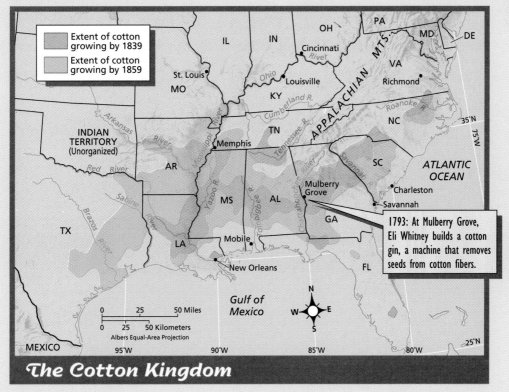

Legend:
- Extent of cotton growing by 1839
- Extent of cotton growing by 1859

1793: At Mulberry Grove, Eli Whitney builds a cotton gin, a machine that removes seeds from cotton fibers.

0 25 50 Miles
0 25 50 Kilometers
Albers Equal-Area Projection

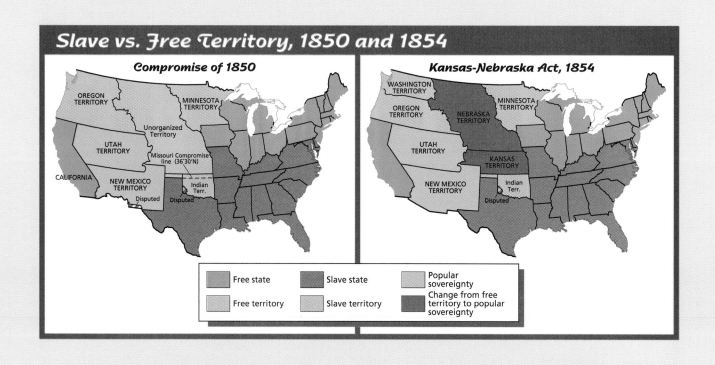

Slave vs. Free Territory, 1850 and 1854

Compromise of 1850

OREGON TERRITORY

MINNESOTA TERRITORY

Unorganized Territory

UTAH TERRITORY

Missouri Compromise line (36°30'N)

CALIFORNIA

NEW MEXICO TERRITORY

Indian Terr.

Disputed   Disputed

Kansas-Nebraska Act, 1854

WASHINGTON TERRITORY

OREGON TERRITORY

NEBRASKA TERRITORY

MINNESOTA TERRITORY

UTAH TERRITORY

KANSAS TERRITORY

NEW MEXICO TERRITORY

Indian Terr.

Disputed

Free state	Slave state	Popular sovereignty
Free territory	Slave territory	Change from free territory to popular sovereignty

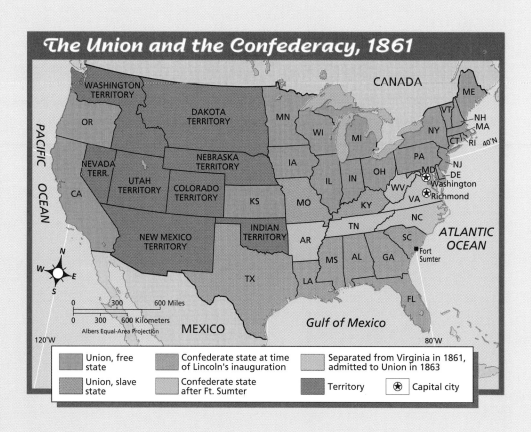

The Union and the Confederacy, 1861

CANADA

WASHINGTON TERRITORY

OR

DAKOTA TERRITORY

MN

ME

VT

NH

MA

NY

WI

MI

PACIFIC OCEAN

NEVADA TERR.

NEBRASKA TERRITORY

IA

PA

CT   RI   40°N

UTAH TERRITORY

COLORADO TERRITORY

CA

KS

IL   IN

OH

NJ

MD   DE

WV

Washington

VA   Richmond

MO

KY

NEW MEXICO TERRITORY

INDIAN TERRITORY

AR

TN

NC

SC

ATLANTIC OCEAN

TX

LA

MS   AL   GA

Fort Sumter

FL

0   300   600 Miles

0   300   600 Kilometers

Albers Equal-Area Projection

MEXICO

Gulf of Mexico

120°W

80°W

Union, free state	Confederate state at time of Lincoln's inauguration	Separated from Virginia in 1861, admitted to Union in 1863
Union, slave state	Confederate state after Ft. Sumter	Territory ⊛ Capital city

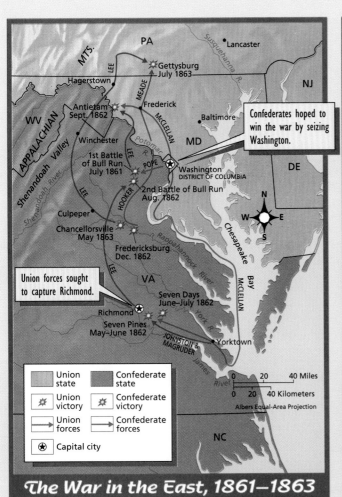

The War in the East, 1861–1863

Legend:
- Union state
- Confederate state
- Union victory
- Confederate victory
- Union forces
- Confederate forces
- ⊛ Capital city

MTS.
PA
• Lancaster
Susquehanna R.
LEE
✶ Gettysburg July 1863
Hagerstown
MEADE
NJ
Antietam Sept. 1862
McCLELLAN
Frederick
WV
APPALACHIAN
• Baltimore
Winchester
Shenandoah Valley
MD
DE
Potomac R.
1st Battle of Bull Run July 1861
LEE
POPE
Shenandoah River
HOOKER
⊛ Washington DISTRICT OF COLUMBIA
Confederates hoped to win the war by seizing Washington.
2nd Battle of Bull Run Aug. 1862
Culpeper •
Chancellorsville May 1863
Rappahannock River
Chesapeake Bay
N W E S
Fredericksburg Dec. 1862
VA
Union forces sought to capture Richmond.
McCLELLAN
LEE
Seven Days June–July 1862
Richmond ⊛
Seven Pines May–June 1862
York R.
• Yorktown
JOHNSTON & MAGRUDER
James River
0   20   40 Miles
0   20   40 Kilometers
Albers Equal-Area Projection
NC

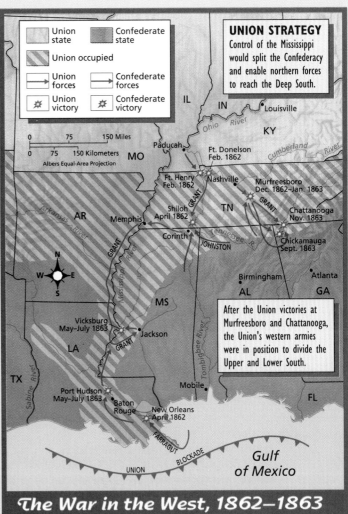

The War in the West, 1862–1863

Legend:
- Union state
- Confederate state
- Union occupied
- Union forces
- Confederate forces
- Union victory
- Confederate victory

UNION STRATEGY
Control of the Mississippi would split the Confederacy and enable northern forces to reach the Deep South.

0   75   150 Miles
0   75   150 Kilometers
Albers Equal-Area Projection

IL
IN
• Louisville
KY
Ohio River
Cumberland River
MO
• Paducah
Ft. Donelson Feb. 1862
Ft. Henry Feb. 1862
GRANT
Nashville •
Murfreesboro Dec. 1862–Jan. 1863
TN
Chattanooga Nov. 1863
GRANT
AR
Arkansas River
Memphis •
Shiloh April 1862
Tennessee R.
JOHNSTON
• Corinth
Chickamauga Sept. 1863
N W E S
GRANT
Birmingham •
• Atlanta
MS
AL
GA
Vicksburg May–July 1863
Jackson •
GRANT
Tombigbee River
After the Union victories at Murfreesboro and Chattanooga, the Union's western armies were in position to divide the Upper and Lower South.
LA
Mobile •
FL
TX
Sabine River
Port Hudson May–July 1863
Baton Rouge
New Orleans April 1862
FARRAGUT
UNION BLOCKADE
Gulf of Mexico

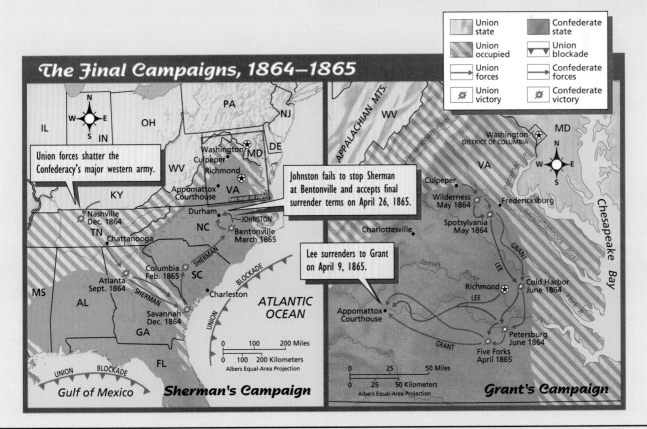

The Final Campaigns, 1864–1865

Legend:
- Union state
- Confederate state
- Union occupied
- Union blockade
- Union forces
- Confederate forces
- Union victory
- Confederate victory

Sherman's Campaign

N W E S
IL
IN
OH
PA
NJ
Union forces shatter the Confederacy's major western army.
Washington ⊛ MD
DE
Culpeper •
WV
Richmond •
Appomattox Courthouse
VA
See map at right
KY
Nashville Dec. 1864
JOHNSTON
TN
Chattanooga •
Durham •
Bentonville March 1865
Johnston fails to stop Sherman at Bentonville and accepts final surrender terms on April 26, 1865.
NC
Columbia Feb. 1865
SHERMAN
SC
MS
Atlanta Sept. 1864
SHERMAN
• Charleston
BLOCKADE
AL
ATLANTIC OCEAN
Savannah Dec. 1864
UNION
GA
0   100   200 Miles
0   100   200 Kilometers
Albers Equal-Area Projection
FL
UNION BLOCKADE
Gulf of Mexico

Grant's Campaign

APPALACHIAN MTS.
WV
Washington ⊛ MD
Rappahannock River
VA
Culpeper •
Wilderness May 1864
Fredericksburg •
GRANT
Chesapeake Bay
Charlottesville •
Spotsylvania May 1864
N W E S
Lee surrenders to Grant on April 9, 1865.
James River
Cold Harbor June 1864
LEE
Richmond •
York R.
Appomattox Courthouse
LEE
GRANT
Petersburg June 1864
Five Forks April 1865
0   25   50 Miles
0   25   50 Kilometers
Albers Equal-Area Projection

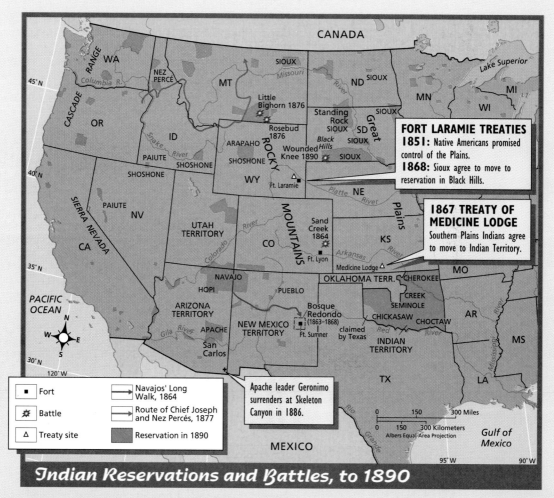

Indian Reservations and Battles, to 1890

FORT LARAMIE TREATIES
1851: Native Americans promised control of the Plains.
1868: Sioux agree to move to reservation in Black Hills.

1867 TREATY OF MEDICINE LODGE
Southern Plains Indians agree to move to Indian Territory.

Apache leader Geronimo surrenders at Skeleton Canyon in 1886.

Legend:
- ■ Fort
- ✷ Battle
- △ Treaty site
- Navajos' Long Walk, 1864
- Route of Chief Joseph and Nez Percés, 1877
- Reservation in 1890

0 150 300 Miles
0 150 300 Kilometers
Albers Equal-Area Projection

Railroads and Cattle Trails, 1870–1890

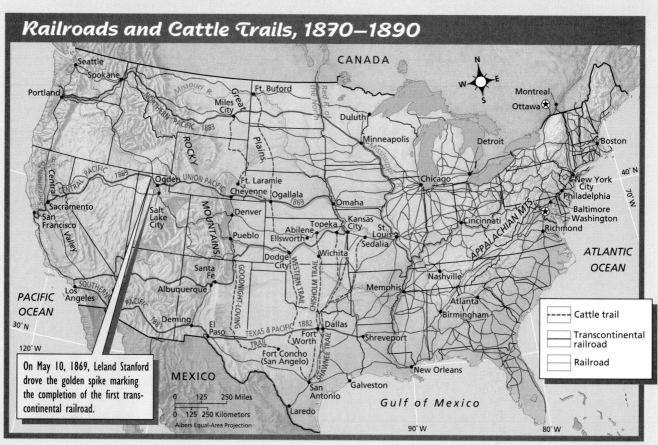

On May 10, 1869, Leland Stanford drove the golden spike marking the completion of the first transcontinental railroad.

Legend:
- Cattle trail
- Transcontinental railroad
- Railroad

0 125 250 Miles
0 125 250 Kilometers
Albers Equal-Area Projection

Labor Strikes, 1870–1900

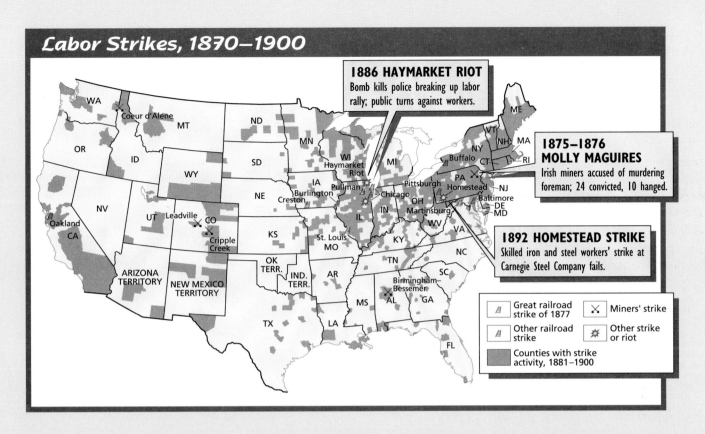

1886 HAYMARKET RIOT
Bomb kills police breaking up labor rally; public turns against workers.

1875–1876 MOLLY MAGUIRES
Irish miners accused of murdering foreman; 24 convicted, 10 hanged.

1892 HOMESTEAD STRIKE
Skilled iron and steel workers' strike at Carnegie Steel Company fails.

Legend:
- ▨ Great railroad strike of 1877
- ▨ Other railroad strike
- ▨ Counties with strike activity, 1881–1900
- ✕ Miners' strike
- ✳ Other strike or riot

Spanish-American War, 1898

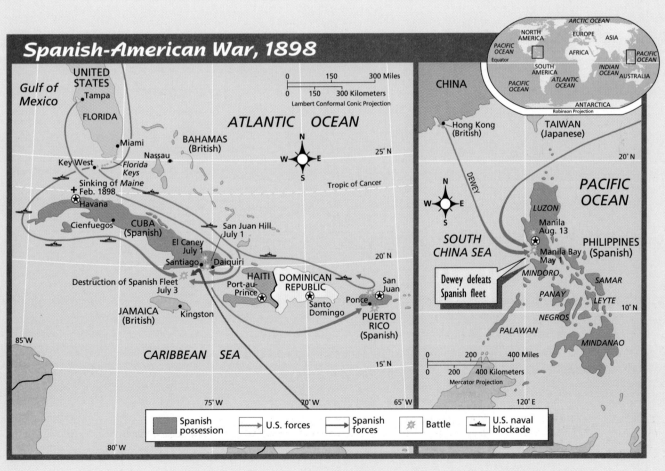

Legend:
- ▨ Spanish possession
- → U.S. forces
- → Spanish forces
- ✳ Battle
- ⛴ U.S. naval blockade

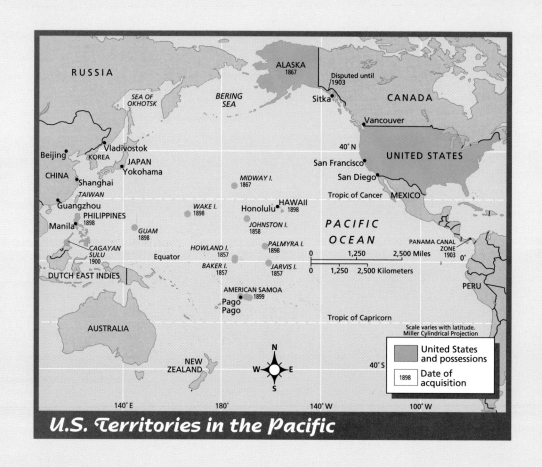

U.S. Territories in the Pacific

RUSSIA

SEA OF OKHOTSK

BERING SEA

ALASKA 1867

Disputed until 1903

Sitka

CANADA

Vancouver

Vladivostok

Beijing

KOREA

JAPAN

Yokohama

CHINA

Shanghai

TAIWAN

Guangzhou

PHILIPPINES 1898

Manila

CAGAYAN SULU 1900

DUTCH EAST INDIES

WAKE I. 1898

GUAM 1898

Equator

HOWLAND I. 1857

BAKER I. 1857

MIDWAY I. 1867

Honolulu

HAWAII 1898

JOHNSTON I. 1858

PALMYRA I. 1898

JARVIS I. 1857

AMERICAN SAMOA 1899

Pago Pago

AUSTRALIA

NEW ZEALAND

40° N

San Francisco

San Diego

Tropic of Cancer

MEXICO

PACIFIC OCEAN

0   1,250   2,500 Miles

0   1,250   2,500 Kilometers

PANAMA CANAL ZONE 1903

0°

PERU

Tropic of Capricorn

40° S

Scale varies with latitude.
Miller Cylindrical Projection

United States and possessions

1898 Date of acquisition

140° E   180°   140° W   100° W

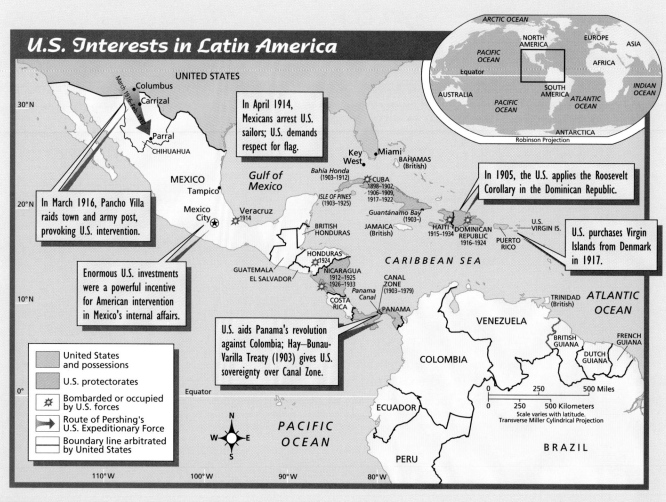

U.S. Interests in Latin America

ARCTIC OCEAN

NORTH AMERICA

EUROPE

ASIA

PACIFIC OCEAN

Equator

AFRICA

AUSTRALIA

PACIFIC OCEAN

SOUTH AMERICA

ATLANTIC OCEAN

INDIAN OCEAN

ANTARCTICA

Robinson Projection

UNITED STATES

30° N

Columbus

Carrizal

Parral

CHIHUAHUA

In April 1914, Mexicans arrest U.S. sailors; U.S. demands respect for flag.

Key West

Miami

BAHAMAS (British)

In 1905, the U.S. applies the Roosevelt Corollary in the Dominican Republic.

MEXICO

Tampico

Gulf of Mexico

Bahía Honda (1903–1912)

CUBA 1898–1902, 1906–1909, 1917–1922

20° N

Mexico City

Veracruz 1914

In March 1916, Pancho Villa raids town and army post, provoking U.S. intervention.

ISLE OF PINES (1903–1925)

Guantánamo Bay (1903–)

JAMAICA (British)

HAITI 1915–1934

DOMINICAN REPUBLIC 1916–1924

PUERTO RICO

U.S. VIRGIN IS.

U.S. purchases Virgin Islands from Denmark in 1917.

BRITISH HONDURAS

HONDURAS 1924

CARIBBEAN SEA

Enormous U.S. investments were a powerful incentive for American intervention in Mexico's internal affairs.

GUATEMALA

EL SALVADOR

NICARAGUA 1912–1925 1926–1933

Panama Canal

CANAL ZONE (1903–1979)

TRINIDAD (British)

ATLANTIC OCEAN

10° N

COSTA RICA

PANAMA

VENEZUELA

U.S. aids Panama's revolution against Colombia; Hay–Bunau-Varilla Treaty (1903) gives U.S. sovereignty over Canal Zone.

COLOMBIA

BRITISH GUIANA

DUTCH GUIANA

FRENCH GUIANA

United States and possessions

U.S. protectorates

Bombarded or occupied by U.S. forces

Route of Pershing's U.S. Expeditionary Force

Boundary line arbitrated by United States

0°

Equator

ECUADOR

0   250   500 Miles

0   250   500 Kilometers

Scale varies with latitude.
Transverse Miller Cylindrical Projection

PACIFIC OCEAN

PERU

BRAZIL

110° W   100° W   90° W   80° W

March 1916–February 1917

The Global Depression

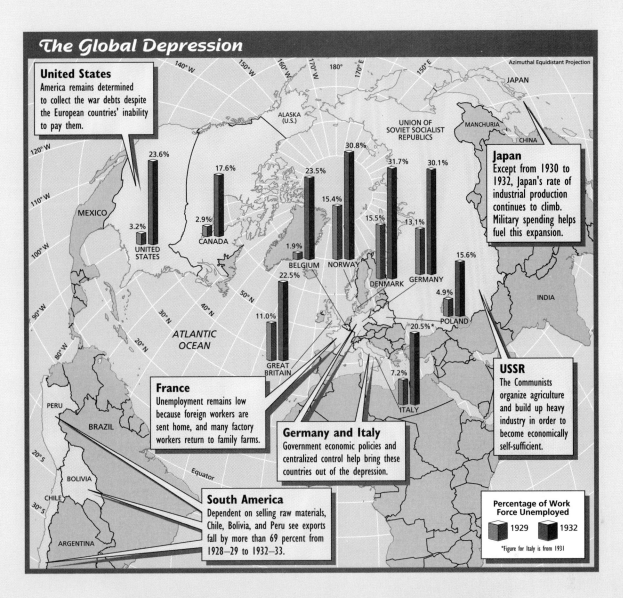

United States
America remains determined to collect the war debts despite the European countries' inability to pay them.

Japan
Except from 1930 to 1932, Japan's rate of industrial production continues to climb. Military spending helps fuel this expansion.

France
Unemployment remains low because foreign workers are sent home, and many factory workers return to family farms.

Germany and Italy
Government economic policies and centralized control help bring these countries out of the depression.

USSR
The Communists organize agriculture and build up heavy industry in order to become economically self-sufficient.

South America
Dependent on selling raw materials, Chile, Bolivia, and Peru see exports fall by more than 69 percent from 1928–29 to 1932–33.

Azimuthal Equidistant Projection

Percentage of Work Force Unemployed
1929 1932
*Figure for Italy is from 1931

Map values:
- UNITED STATES: 3.2% / 23.6%
- CANADA: 2.9% / 17.6%
- BELGIUM: 1.9% / 23.5%
- NORWAY: 15.4% / 30.8%
- DENMARK: 15.5% / 31.7%
- GERMANY: 13.1% / 30.1%
- POLAND: 4.9% / 15.6%
- GREAT BRITAIN: 11.0% / 22.5%
- ITALY: 7.2% / 20.5%*

Unemployment Relief: 1934

State values shown:
- ND: 29%
- SD: 41%
- NM: 31%
- OK: 28%

Percentage of Total State Population Receiving Unemployment Relief
- More than 25 percent
- 21-25 percent
- 16-20 percent
- 11-15 percent
- Less than 11 percent

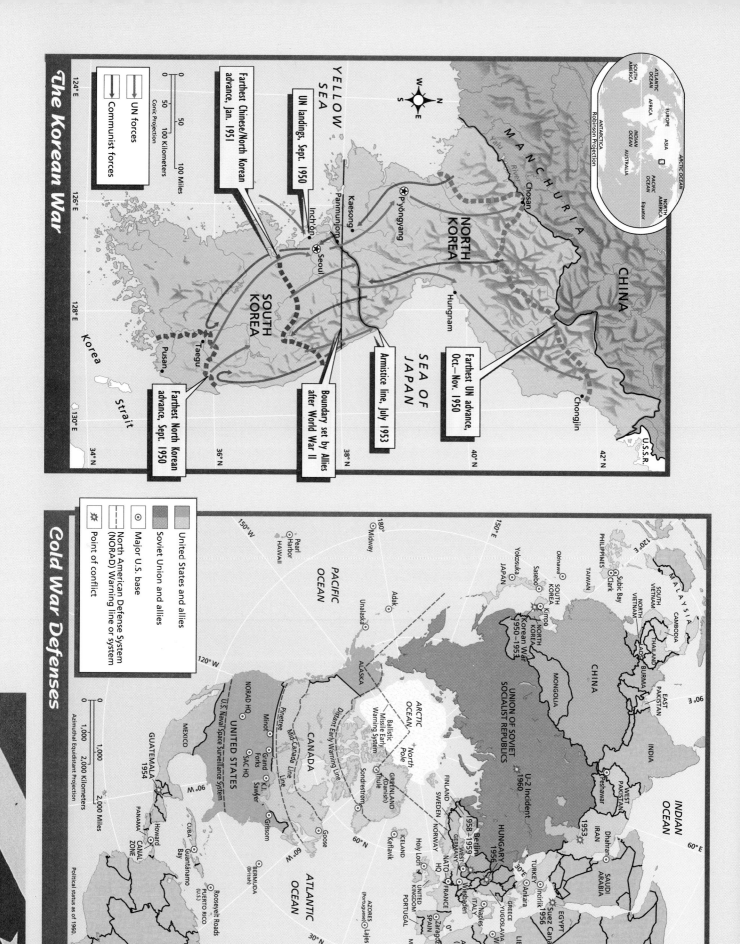

The Korean War

Cold War Defenses

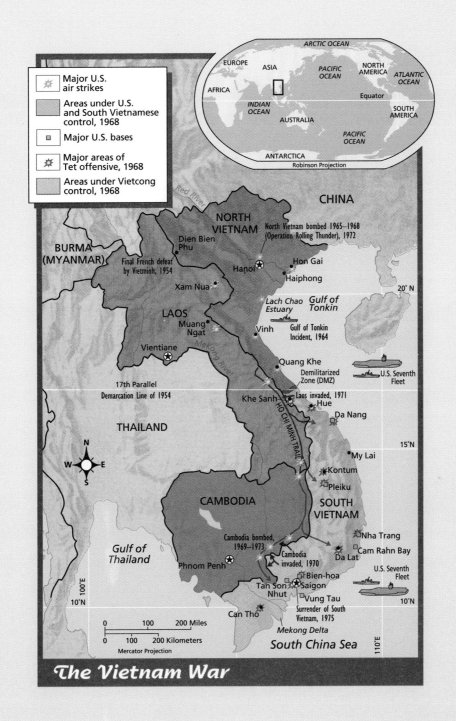

The Vietnam War

Legend:
- Major U.S. air strikes
- Areas under U.S. and South Vietnamese control, 1968
- Major U.S. bases
- Major areas of Tet offensive, 1968
- Areas under Vietcong control, 1968

ARCTIC OCEAN
EUROPE
ASIA
PACIFIC OCEAN
NORTH AMERICA
ATLANTIC OCEAN
AFRICA
Equator
INDIAN OCEAN
AUSTRALIA
SOUTH AMERICA
PACIFIC OCEAN
ANTARCTICA
Robinson Projection

CHINA

NORTH VIETNAM

North Vietnam bombed 1965–1968 (Operation Rolling Thunder), 1972

BURMA (MYANMAR)

Dien Bien Phu

Final French defeat by Vietminh, 1954

Hanoi

Hon Gai

Haiphong

Xam Nua

20° N

LAOS

Muang Ngat

Lach Chao Estuary

Gulf of Tonkin

Vientiane

Vinh

Gulf of Tonkin Incident, 1964

Mekong River

Quang Khe

Demilitarized Zone (DMZ)

U.S. Seventh Fleet

17th Parallel
Demarcation Line of 1954

Khe Sanh

Laos invaded, 1971

Hue

Da Nang

THAILAND

15° N

My Lai

N
W   E
S

Kontum

Pleiku

CAMBODIA

SOUTH VIETNAM

HO CHI MINH TRAIL

Gulf of Thailand

Cambodia bombed, 1969–1973

Nha Trang

Cam Rahn Bay

Da Lat

Phnom Penh

Cambodia invaded, 1970

U.S. Seventh Fleet

Tan Son Nhut

Bien-hoa

Saigon

100°E

Vung Tau

10° N

10° N

Can Tho

Surrender of South Vietnam, 1975

0   100   200 Miles
0   100   200 Kilometers
Mercator Projection

Mekong Delta

South China Sea

110°E

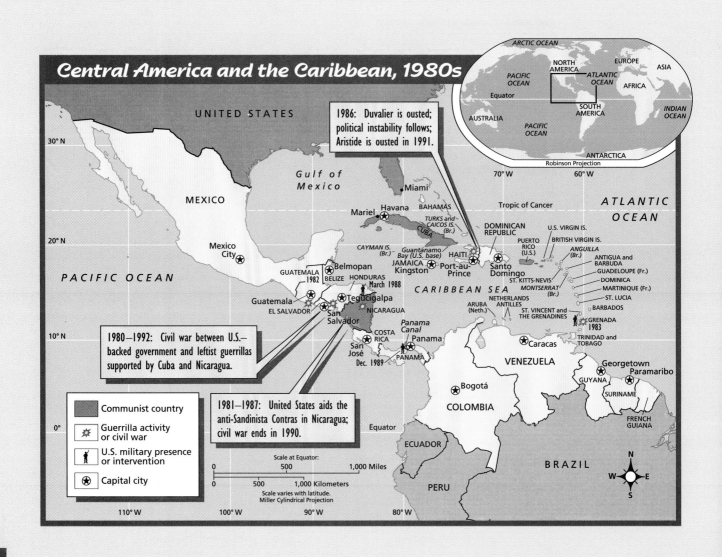

Central America and the Caribbean, 1980s

1986: Duvalier is ousted; political instability follows; Aristide is ousted in 1991.

1980–1992: Civil war between U.S.–backed government and leftist guerrillas supported by Cuba and Nicaragua.

1981–1987: United States aids the anti-Sandinista Contras in Nicaragua; civil war ends in 1990.

Legend:
- Communist country
- Guerrilla activity or civil war
- U.S. military presence or intervention
- Capital city

Scale at Equator:
0 — 500 — 1,000 Miles
0 — 500 — 1,000 Kilometers
Scale varies with latitude.
Miller Cylindrical Projection

Map labels:
UNITED STATES
Gulf of Mexico
MEXICO
Mexico City
PACIFIC OCEAN
Miami
Mariel · Havana · BAHAMAS
CUBA
TURKS and CAICOS IS. (Br.)
CAYMAN IS. (Br.)
Guantánamo Bay (U.S. base)
GUATEMALA 1982
Guatemala
EL SALVADOR
San Salvador
Belmopan
BELIZE
HONDURAS
March 1988
Tegucigalpa
NICARAGUA
COSTA RICA
San José
Dec. 1989
Panama Canal
Panama
PANAMA
JAMAICA
Kingston
HAITI
Port-au-Prince
DOMINICAN REPUBLIC
Santo Domingo
PUERTO RICO (U.S.)
U.S. VIRGIN IS.
BRITISH VIRGIN IS.
ANGUILLA (Br.)
ANTIGUA and BARBUDA
GUADELOUPE (Fr.)
DOMINICA
MARTINIQUE (Fr.)
ST. LUCIA
BARBADOS
ST. KITTS-NEVIS
MONTSERRAT (Br.)
ST. VINCENT and THE GRENADINES
GRENADA 1983
NETHERLANDS ANTILLES
ARUBA (Neth.)
TRINIDAD and TOBAGO
CARIBBEAN SEA
ATLANTIC OCEAN
Tropic of Cancer
Caracas
VENEZUELA
COLOMBIA
Bogotá
Georgetown
GUYANA
Paramaribo
SURINAME
FRENCH GUIANA
Equator
ECUADOR
PERU
BRAZIL

30° N
20° N
10° N
0°
110° W
100° W
90° W
80° W
70° W
60° W

Inset globe (Robinson Projection):
ARCTIC OCEAN
NORTH AMERICA
EUROPE
ASIA
PACIFIC OCEAN
ATLANTIC OCEAN
AFRICA
Equator
SOUTH AMERICA
AUSTRALIA
PACIFIC OCEAN
INDIAN OCEAN
ANTARCTICA

Compass rose: N W E S

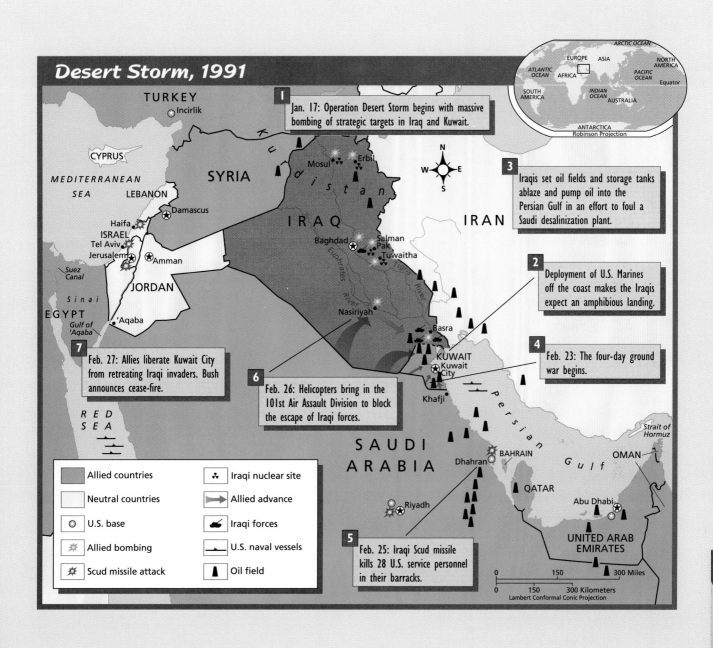

Desert Storm, 1991

TURKEY
Incirlik

1 Jan. 17: Operation Desert Storm begins with massive bombing of strategic targets in Iraq and Kuwait.

CYPRUS

MEDITERRANEAN SEA

SYRIA

Mosul • Erbil

IRAN

3 Iraqis set oil fields and storage tanks ablaze and pump oil into the Persian Gulf in an effort to foul a Saudi desalinization plant.

LEBANON
Damascus

Haifa
ISRAEL
Tel Aviv
Jerusalem

IRAQ

Baghdad
Salman Pak
Tuwaitha

Amman

2 Deployment of U.S. Marines off the coast makes the Iraqis expect an amphibious landing.

Suez Canal

JORDAN

Sinai

EGYPT

Nasiriyah

Basra

4 Feb. 23: The four-day ground war begins.

Gulf of 'Aqaba

'Aqaba

7 Feb. 27: Allies liberate Kuwait City from retreating Iraqi invaders. Bush announces cease-fire.

KUWAIT
Kuwait City

Khafji

6 Feb. 26: Helicopters bring in the 101st Air Assault Division to block the escape of Iraqi forces.

RED SEA

Persian Gulf

Strait of Hormuz

SAUDI ARABIA

Dhahran
BAHRAIN

OMAN

QATAR

Riyadh

Abu Dhabi

UNITED ARAB EMIRATES

5 Feb. 25: Iraqi Scud missile kills 28 U.S. service personnel in their barracks.

Legend

Allied countries	Iraqi nuclear site
Neutral countries	Allied advance
U.S. base	Iraqi forces
Allied bombing	U.S. naval vessels
Scud missile attack	Oil field

0   150   300 Miles
0   150   300 Kilometers
Lambert Conformal Conic Projection

Locator map
ARCTIC OCEAN
EUROPE ASIA
ATLANTIC OCEAN
AFRICA
NORTH AMERICA
PACIFIC OCEAN
SOUTH AMERICA
INDIAN OCEAN
AUSTRALIA
Equator
ANTARCTICA
Robinson Projection

A MULTI-CULTURAL COUNTRY

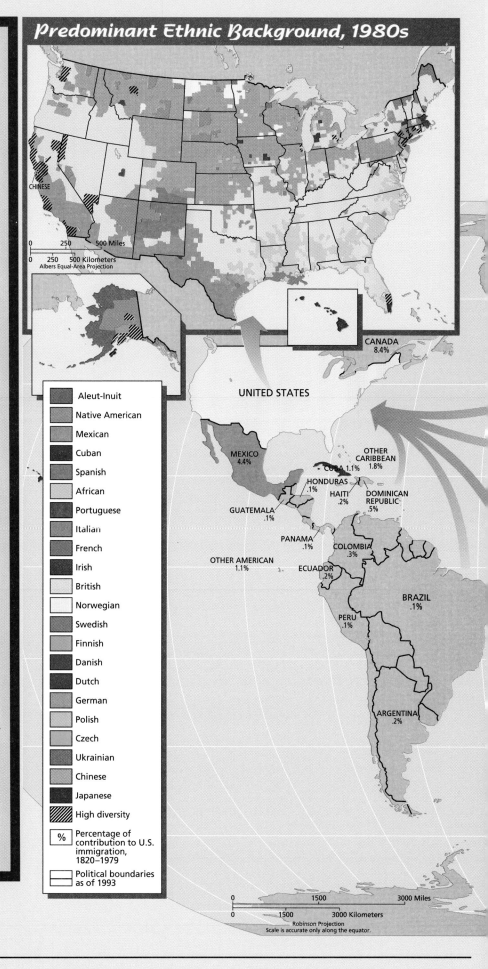

Predominant Ethnic Background, 1980s

CHINESE

0   250   500 Miles
0 250 500 Kilometers
Albers Equal-Area Projection

EVEN before the founding of the United States, immigrants flocked to America from around the world. The origins of the immigrants have changed over time, however. The original Native Americans emigrated from Asia across Beringia. In colonial times the vast majority of immigrants came from Europe and Africa. Although Europe continued to provide the bulk of immigrants throughout the 19th century, more and more were from southern and eastern Europe. After World War II, immigration patterns changed dramatically as more people began to come from Latin America and from Asia. All of these immigrant groups have contributed to the diversity of American culture.

Legend:
- Aleut-Inuit
- Native American
- Mexican
- Cuban
- Spanish
- African
- Portuguese
- Italian
- French
- Irish
- British
- Norwegian
- Swedish
- Finnish
- Danish
- Dutch
- German
- Polish
- Czech
- Ukrainian
- Chinese
- Japanese
- High diversity
- % Percentage of contribution to U.S. immigration, 1820–1979
- Political boundaries as of 1993

CANADA 8.4%

UNITED STATES

MEXICO 4.4%

CUBA 1.1%

OTHER CARIBBEAN 1.8%

HONDURAS .1%

HAITI .2%

DOMINICAN REPUBLIC .5%

GUATEMALA .1%

PANAMA .1%

COLOMBIA .3%

OTHER AMERICAN 1.1%

ECUADOR .2%

BRAZIL .1%

PERU .1%

ARGENTINA .2%

0   1500   3000 Miles
0   1500   3000 Kilometers
Robinson Projection
Scale is accurate only along the equator.

Every day new residents arrive in the United States from throughout the world. In recent years many very small countries, such as Jamaica and El Salvador, have been huge contributors to U.S. immigration. Between 1981 and 1990, some 213,800 Jamaicans immigrated to the U.S.—close to 10 percent of Jamaica's total population in 1982!

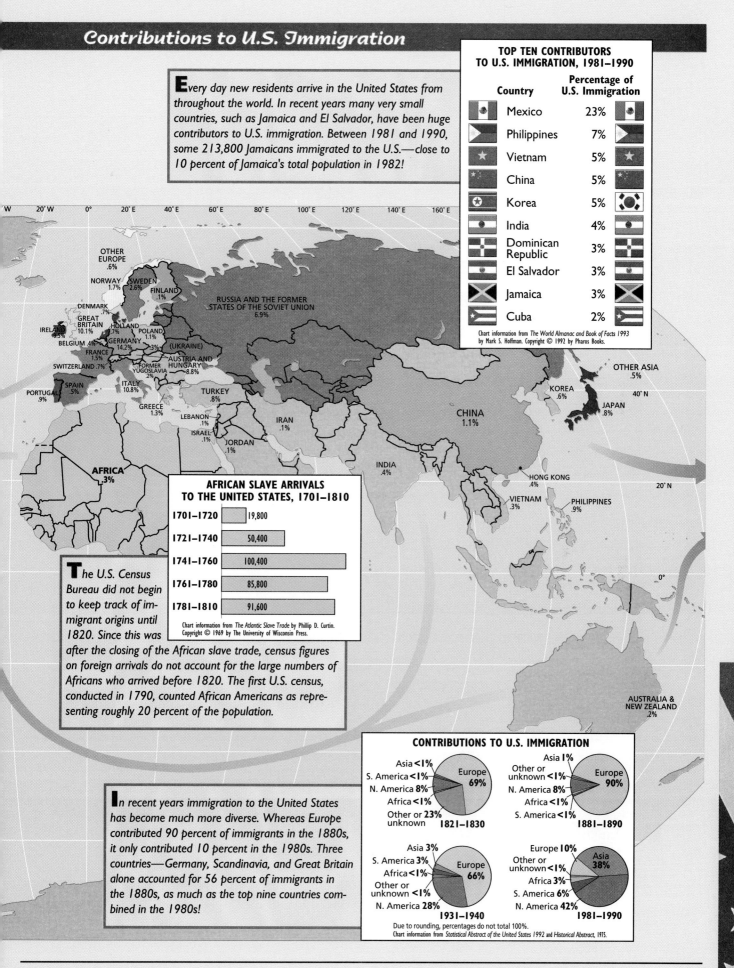

TOP TEN CONTRIBUTORS TO U.S. IMMIGRATION, 1981–1990

Country	Percentage of U.S. Immigration
Mexico	23%
Philippines	7%
Vietnam	5%
China	5%
Korea	5%
India	4%
Dominican Republic	3%
El Salvador	3%
Jamaica	3%
Cuba	2%

Chart information from *The World Almanac and Book of Facts 1993* by Mark S. Hoffman. Copyright © 1992 by Pharos Books.

Map labels:

OTHER EUROPE .6%
NORWAY 1.7%
SWEDEN 2.6%
FINLAND .1%
DENMARK .7%
GREAT BRITAIN 10.1%
IRELAND 5.5%
HOLLAND .7%
BELGIUM .4%
GERMANY 14.2%
POLAND 1.1%
(UKRAINE)
FRANCE 1.5%
.3%
AUSTRIA AND HUNGARY 8.8%
FORMER YUGOSLAVIA .2%
SWITZERLAND .7%
PORTUGAL .9%
SPAIN .5%
ITALY 10.8%
GREECE 1.3%
TURKEY .8%
LEBANON .1%
ISRAEL .1%
IRAN .1%
JORDAN .1%
RUSSIA AND THE FORMER STATES OF THE SOVIET UNION 6.9%
AFRICA .3%
INDIA .4%
CHINA 1.1%
HONG KONG .4%
VIETNAM .3%
PHILIPPINES .9%
KOREA .6%
JAPAN .8%
OTHER ASIA .5%
AUSTRALIA & NEW ZEALAND .2%

AFRICAN SLAVE ARRIVALS TO THE UNITED STATES, 1701–1810

Period	Arrivals
1701–1720	19,800
1721–1740	50,400
1741–1760	100,400
1761–1780	85,800
1781–1810	91,600

Chart information from *The Atlantic Slave Trade* by Phillip D. Curtin. Copyright © 1969 by The University of Wisconsin Press.

The U.S. Census Bureau did not begin to keep track of immigrant origins until 1820. Since this was after the closing of the African slave trade, census figures on foreign arrivals do not account for the large numbers of Africans who arrived before 1820. The first U.S. census, conducted in 1790, counted African Americans as representing roughly 20 percent of the population.

In recent years immigration to the United States has become much more diverse. Whereas Europe contributed 90 percent of immigrants in the 1880s, it only contributed 10 percent in the 1980s. Three countries—Germany, Scandinavia, and Great Britain alone accounted for 56 percent of immigrants in the 1880s, as much as the top nine countries combined in the 1980s!

CONTRIBUTIONS TO U.S. IMMIGRATION

1821–1830
Asia <1%
S. America <1%
N. America 8%
Africa <1%
Other or unknown 23%
Europe 69%

1881–1890
Asia 1%
Other or unknown <1%
N. America 8%
Africa <1%
S. America <1%
Europe 90%

1931–1940
Asia 3%
S. America 3%
Africa <1%
Other or unknown <1%
N. America 28%
Europe 66%

1981–1990
Europe 10%
Other or unknown <1%
Africa 3%
S. America 6%
N. America 42%
Asia 38%

Due to rounding, percentages do not total 100%.
Chart information from *Statistical Abstract of the United States 1992* and *Historical Abstract, 1975.*

APPENDIX

Metric Conversion Table

	If you have	multiply by	to get
LENGTH	miles	1.609	kilometers
	kilometers	.62	miles
	feet	.3048	meters
	meters	39.37, then divide by 12	feet
	inches	2.54	centimeters
	centimeters	.39	inches
WEIGHT	pounds	.454	kilograms
	kilograms	2.2046	pounds
AREA	acres	.405	hectares
	hectares	2.47	acres
	square miles	2.59	square kilometers
	square kilometers	.3861	square miles
CAPACITY	quarts	.946	liters
	liters	1.057	quarts
TEMPERATURE	degrees Fahrenheit	subtract 32, then multiply by $5/9$	degrees Celsius
	degrees Celsius	multiply by $9/5$, then add 32	degrees Fahrenheit

Country ★ Capital	Population (1994)	Land Area (1994)	Principal Languages
THE UNITED STATES AND CANADA			
United States ★ Washington, D.C.	260,713,585	3,618,765 sq. mi. 9,372,610 sq. km	English, Spanish, Native American languages, other languages of the world
Canada ★ Ottawa	28,113,997	3,851,788 sq. mi. 9,976,140 sq. km	English, French
MIDDLE AND SOUTH AMERICA			
Antigua and Barbuda ★ St. John's	64,762	170 sq. mi. 440 sq. km	English, local dialects
Argentina ★ Buenos Aires	33,912,994	1,068,296 sq. mi. 2,766,890 sq. km	Spanish, English, Italian, German, French

Country ★ Capital	Population (1992)	Land Area (1992)	Principal Languages
Bahamas ★ Nassau	273,055	5,382 sq. mi. 13,940 sq. km	English, Creole
Barbados ★ Bridgetown	255,827	166 sq. mi. 430 sq. km	English
Belize ★ Belmopan	208,949	8,865 sq. mi. 22,960 sq. km	English, Spanish, Maya, Garifuna (Carib)
Bolivia ★ La Paz ★ Sucre	7,719,445	424,162 sq. mi. 1,098,580 sq. km	Spanish, Quechua, Aymara,
Brazil ★ Brasília	158,739,257	3,286,470 sq. mi. 8,511,965 sq. km	Portuguese, Spanish, English, French
Chile ★ Santiago	13,950,557	292,258 sq. mi. 756,950 sq. km	Spanish
Colombia ★ Bogotá	35,577,556	439,733 sq. mi. 1,138,910 sq. km	Spanish
Costa Rica ★ San José	3,342,154	19,730 sq. mi. 51,100 sq. km	Spanish, English
Cuba ★ Havana	11,064,344	42,803 sq. mi. 110,860 sq. km	Spanish
Dominica ★ Roseau	87,696	290 sq. mi. 750 sq. km	English, French patois
Dominican Republic ★ Santo Domingo	7,826,075	18,815 sq. mi. 48,730 sq. km	Spanish
Ecuador ★ Quito	10,677,067	109,483 sq. mi. 283,560 sq. km	Spanish, Quechua and other Native American languages
El Salvador ★ San Salvador	5,552,511	8,124 sq. mi. 21,040 sq. km	Spanish, Nahuatl
Grenada ★ St. George's	94,109	131 sq. mi. 340 sq. km	English, French patois
Guatemala ★ Guatemala City	10,721,387	42,042 sq. mi. 108,890 sq. km	Spanish, Native American dialects
Guyana ★ Georgetown	729,425	83,000 sq. mi. 214,970 sq. km	English, Native American dialects
Haiti ★ Port-au-Prince	6,491,450	10,714 sq. mi. 27,750 sq. km	French, Creole

Country ★ Capital	Population (1994)	Land Area (1994)	Principal Languages
Honduras ★ Tegucigalpa	5,314,794	43,278 sq. mi. 112,090 sq. km	Spanish, Native American dialects
Jamaica ★ Kingston	2,555,064	4,243 sq. mi. 10,990 sq. km	English, Creole
Mexico ★ Mexico City	92,202,199	761,602 sq. mi. 1,972,550 sq. km	Spanish, Mayan dialects
Nicaragua ★ Managua	4,096,689	49,998 sq. mi. 129,494 sq. km	Spanish, English, Native American languages
Panama ★ Panama City	2,630,000	30,193 sq. mi. 78,200 sq. km	Spanish, English
Paraguay ★ Asunción	5,213,772	157,046 sq. mi. 406,750 sq. km	Spanish, Guaraní
Peru ★ Lima	23,650,671	496,223 sq. mi. 1,285,220 sq. km	Spanish, Quechua, Aymara
St. Kitts and Nevis ★ Basseterre	40,671	104 sq. mi. 269 sq. km	English
St. Lucia ★ Castries	145,090	239 sq. mi. 620 sq. km	English, French patois
St. Vincent and the Grenadines ★ Kingstown	115,437	131 sq. mi. 340 sq. km	English, French patois
Suriname ★ Paramaribo	422,840	63,039 sq. mi. 163,270 sq. km	Dutch, English, Surinamese, Hindi, Javanese
Trinidad and Tobago ★ Port-of-Spain	1,328,282	1,981 sq. mi. 5,130 sq. km	English, Hindi, French, Spanish
Uruguay ★ Montevideo	3,198,910	68,039 sq. mi. 176,220 sq. km	Spanish
Venezuela ★ Caracas	20,562,405	352,143 sq. mi. 912,050 sq. km	Spanish, Native American dialects

EUROPE

Country ★ Capital	Population (1994)	Land Area (1994)	Principal Languages
Albania ★ Tiranë	3,374,085	11,100 sq. mi. 28,750 sq. km	Albanian, Greek
Andorra ★ Andorra la Vella	63,930	174 sq. mi. 450 sq. km	Catalan, French, Castilian

	Country ★ Capital	Population (1994)	Land Area (1994)	Principal Languages
	Austria ★ Vienna	7,954,974	32,374 sq. mi. 83,850 sq. km	German
	Belgium ★ Brussels	10,062,836	11,780 sq. mi. 30,510 sq. km	Flemish (Dutch), French, German
	Bosnia and Herzegovina ★ Sarajevo	4,651,485	19,781 sq. mi. 51,233 sq. km	Serbo-Croatian
	Bulgaria ★ Sofia	8,799,986	42,822 sq. mi. 110,910 sq. km	Bulgarian, Turkish
	Croatia ★ Zagreb	4,697,614	21,829 sq. mi. 56,538 sq. km	Serbo-Croatian
	Czech Republic ★ Prague	10,408,280	30,387 sq. mi. 78,703 sq. km	Czech, Slovak
	Denmark ★ Copenhagen	5,187,821	16,629 sq. mi. 43,070 sq. km	Danish, Faroese, Greenlandic, German
	Estonia ★ Tallinn	1,616,882	17,413 sq. mi. 45,100 sq. km	Estonian, Latvian, Lithuanian, Russian
	Finland ★ Helsinki	5,068,931	130,127 sq. mi. 337,030 sq. km	Finnish, Swedish, Lapp, Russian
	France ★ Paris	57,840,445	211,208 sq. mi. 547,030 sq. km	French, regional dialects and languages
	Germany ★ Berlin	81,087,506	137,803 sq. mi. 356,910 sq. km	German
	Greece ★ Athens	10,564,630	50,942 sq. mi. 131,940 sq. km	Greek, English, French
	Hungary ★ Budapest	10,319,113	35,919 sq. mi. 93,030 sq. km	Hungarian
	Iceland ★ Reykjavik	263,599	39,768 sq. mi. 103,000 sq. km	Icelandic
	Ireland ★ Dublin	3,539,296	27,135 sq. mi. 70,280 sq. km	English, Irish (Gaelic)
	Italy ★ Rome	58,138,394	116,305 sq. mi. 301,230 sq. km	Italian, German, French, Slovene
	Latvia ★ Riga	2,749,211	24,749 sq. mi. 64,100 sq. km	Lettish, Lithuanian, Russian

Country ★ Capital	Population (1994)	Land Area (1994)	Principal Languages
Liechtenstein ★ Vaduz	30,281	62 sq. mi. 160 sq. km	German, Alemannic dialect
Lithuania ★ Vilnius	3,848,389	25,174 sq. mi. 65,200 sq. km	Lithuanian, Polish, Russian
Luxembourg ★ Luxembourg	401,900	998 sq. mi. 2,586 sq. km	Luxembourgisch, German, French, English
Macedonia ★ Skopje	2,213,785	9,781 sq. mi. 25,333 sq. km	Macedonian, Albanian, Turkish, Serbo-Croatian
Malta ★ Valletta	366,767	124 sq. mi. 320 sq. km	Maltese, English
Monaco ★ Monaco	31,278	.73 sq. mi. 1.9 sq. km	French, English, Italian, Monegasque
Netherlands ★ Amsterdam ★ The Hague	15,367,928	14,413 sq. mi. 37,330 sq. km	Dutch
Norway ★ Oslo	4,314,604	125,181 sq. mi. 324,220 sq. km	Norwegian, Lapp, Finnish
Poland ★ Warsaw	38,654,561	120,726 sq. mi. 312,680 sq. km	Polish
Portugal ★ Lisbon	10,524,210	35,552 sq. mi. 92,080 sq. km	Portuguese
Romania ★ Bucharest	23,181,415	91,699 sq. mi. 237,500 sq. km	Romanian, Hungarian, German
San Marino ★ San Marino	24,091	23 sq. mi. 60 sq. km	Italian
Slovakia ★ Bratislava	5,403,505	18,859 sq. mi. 48,845 sq. km	Slovak, Hungarian
Slovenia ★ Ljubljana	1,972,227	7,836 sq. mi. 20,296 sq. km	Slovenian, Serbo-Croatian
Spain ★ Madrid	39,302,665	194,884 sq. mi. 504,750 sq. km	Castilian Spanish, Catalan, Galician, Basque
Sweden ★ Stockholm	8,778,461	173,731 sq. mi. 449,964 sq. km	Swedish, Lapp, Finnish
Switzerland ★ Bern	7,040,119	15,942 sq. mi. 41,290 sq. km	German, French, Italian, Romansh

Country ★ Capital	Population (1994)	Land Area (1994)	Principal Languages
United Kingdom ★ London	58,135,110	94,525 sq. mi. 244,820 sq. km	English, Welsh, Scottish Gaelic
Vatican City ★ Vatican City	821	0.169 sq. mi. 0.44 sq. km	Italian, Latin, other languages of the world
Yugoslavia (Serbia and Montenegro) ★ Belgrade	10,759,897	39,517 sq. mi. 102,350 sq. km	Serbo-Croatian, Albanian

RUSSIA AND NORTHERN EURASIA

Country ★ Capital	Population (1994)	Land Area (1994)	Principal Languages
Armenia ★ Yerevan	3,521,517	11,506 sq. mi. 29,800 sq. km	Armenian, Russian
Azerbaijan ★ Baki	7,684,456	33,436 sq. mi. 86,600 sq. km	Azeri, Russian, Armenian
Belarus ★ Minsk	10,404,862	80,154 sq. mi. 207,600 sq. km	Belorussian, Russian
Georgia ★ T'bilisi	5,681,025	26,911 sq. mi. 69,700 sq. km	Georgian, Russian, Armenian, Azeri
Kazakhstan ★ Almaty	17,267,554	1,049,150 sq. mi. 2,717,300 sq. km	Kazak, Russian
Kyrgyzstan ★ Bishkek	4,698,108	76,641 sq. mi. 198,500 sq. km	Kyrgyz, Russian
Moldova ★ Chişinău	4,473,033	13,012 sq. mi. 33,700 sq. km	Moldovan, Romanian, Russian, Turkish dialect
Russia ★ Moscow	149,608,953	6,592,735 sq. mi. 17,075,200 sq. km	Russian
Tajikistan ★ Dushanbe	5,995,469	55,251 sq. mi. 143,100 sq. km	Tajik, Russian
Turkmenistan ★ Ashgabat	3,995,122	188,455 sq. mi. 488,100 sq. km	Turkmen, Russian, Uzbek
Ukraine ★ Kyyiv	51,846,958	233,089 sq. mi. 603,700 sq. km	Ukrainian, Russian, Romanian, Polish, Hungarian
Uzbekistan ★ Toshkent	22,608,866	172,741 sq. mi. 447,400 sq. km	Uzbek, Russian, Tajik

SOUTHWEST ASIA

Country ★ Capital	Population (1994)	Land Area (1994)	Principal Languages
Afghanistan ★ Kabul	16,903,400	250,000 sq. mi. 647,500 sq. km	Pashtu, Afghan Persian, Uzbek, Turkmen

Country ★ Capital	Population (1994)	Land Area (1994)	Principal Languages
Bahrain ★ Manama	585,683	239 sq. mi. 620 sq. km	Arabic, English, Farsi, Urdu
Cyprus ★ Nicosia	730,084	3,571 sq. mi. 9,250 sq. km	Greek, Turkish, English
Iran ★ Tehran	65,615,474	636,293 sq. mi. 1,648,000 sq. km	Persian and Persian dialects, Turkic dialects, Kurdish, Luri, Baloch, Arabic, Turkish
Iraq ★ Baghdad	19,889,666	168,753 sq. mi. 437,072 sq. km	Arabic, Kurdish, Assyrian, Armenian
Israel ★ Jerusalem	5,050,850	8,019 sq. mi. 20,770 sq. km	Hebrew, Arabic, English
Jordan ★ Amman	3,961,194	34,445 sq. mi. 89,213 sq. km	Arabic, English
Kuwait ★ Kuwait City	1,819,322	6,880 sq. mi. 17,820 sq. km	Arabic, English
Lebanon ★ Beirut	3,620,395	4,015 sq. mi. 10,400 sq. km	Arabic, French, Armenian, English
Oman ★ Muscat	1,701,470	82,031 sq. mi. 212,460 sq. km	Arabic, English, Balochi, Urdu, Indian dialects
Qatar ★ Doha	512,779	4,447 sq. mi. 11,000 sq. km	Arabic, English
Saudi Arabia ★ Riyadh	18,196,783	756,981 sq. mi. 1,960,582 sq. km	Arabic
Syria ★ Damascus	14,886,672	71,498 sq. mi. 185,180 sq. km	Arabic, Kurdish, Armenian, Aramaic, Circassian, French
Turkey ★ Ankara	62,153,898	301,382 sq. mi. 780,580 sq. km	Turkish, Kurdish, Arabic
United Arab Emirates ★ Abu Dhabi	2,791,141	29,182 sq. mi. 75,581 sq. km	Arabic, Persian, English, Hindi, Urdu
Yemen ★ Sanaa	11,105,202	203,849 sq. mi. 527,970 sq. km	Arabic

AFRICA

Country ★ Capital	Population (1994)	Land Area (1994)	Principal Languages
Algeria ★ Algiers	27,895,068	919,590 sq. mi. 2,381,740 sq. km	Arabic, French, Berber dialects

Country ★ Capital	Population (1994)	Land Area (1994)	Principal Languages
Angola ★ Luanda	9,803,576	481,351 sq. mi. 1,246,700 sq. km	Portuguese, Bantu, other African languages
Benin ★ Porto-Novo	5,341,710	43,483 sq. mi. 112,620 sq. km	French, Fon, Yoruba, other local languages
Botswana ★ Gaborone	1,359,352	231,803 sq. mi. 600,370 sq. km	English, Setswana
Burkina Faso ★ Ouagadougou	10,134,661	105,869 sq. mi. 274,200 sq. km	French, local languages
Burundi ★ Bujumbura	6,124,747	10,745 sq. mi. 27,830 sq. km	Kirundi, French, Swahili
Cameroon ★ Yaoundé	13,132,191	183,567 sq. mi. 475,440 sq. km	English, French, African languages
Cape Verde ★ Praia	423,120	1,556 sq. mi. 4,030 sq. km	Portuguese, Crioulo
Central African Republic ★ Bangui	3,142,182	240,533 sq. mi. 622,980 sq. km	French, Sangho, Arabic, Hunsa, Swahili
Chad ★ N'Djamena	5,466,771	495,752 sq. mi. 1,284,000 sq. km	French, Arabic, Sara, Sango, other dialects
Comoros ★ Moroni	530,136	838 sq. mi. 2,170 sq. km	Arabic, French, Comoran
Congo ★ Brazzaville	2,446,902	132,046 sq. mi. 342,000 sq. km	French, Lingala, Kikongo, other African languages
Côte d'Ivoire ★ Yamoussoukro	14,295,501	124,502 sq. mi. 322,460 sq. km	French, Dioula, native dialects
Democratic Republic of Congo ★ Kinshasa	42,684,091	905,563 sq. mi. 2,345,410 sq. km	French, Lingala, Swahili, Kingwana, Kikongo, Tshiluba
Djibouti ★ Djibouti	412,599	8,494 sq. mi. 22,000 sq. km	French, Arabic, Somali, Afar
Egypt ★ Cairo	60,765,028	386,660 sq. mi. 1,001,450 sq. km	Arabic, English, French
Equatorial Guinea ★ Malabo	409,550	10,830 sq. mi. 28,050 sq. km	Spanish, pidgin English, Fang, Bubi, Ibo
Eritrea ★ Asmara	3,782,543	46,842 sq. mi. 121,320 sq. km	Tigre and Kunama, Tigre, Nora Bana, Arabic, other dialects

Country ★ Capital	Population (1994)	Land Area (1994)	Principal Languages
Ethiopia ★ Addis Ababa	54,927,108	435,184 sq. mi. 1,127,127 sq. km	Amharic, Tigrinya, Orominga, Guaraginga, Somali, Arabic, English
Gabon ★ Libreville	1,139,006	103,347 sq. mi. 267,670 sq. km	French, Fang, Myene, Bateke, Bapounou/Eschira, Bandjabi
Gambia ★ Banjul	959,300	4,363 sq. mi. 11,300 sq. km	English, Mandinka, Wolof, Fula, other local dialects
Ghana ★ Accra	17,225,185	92,100 sq. mi. 238,540 sq. km	English, Akan, Moshi-Dagomba, Ewe, Ga
Guinea ★ Conakry	6,391,536	94,927 sq. mi. 245,860 sq. km	French, local languages
Guinea-Bissau ★ Bissau	1,098,231	13,946 sq. mi. 36,120 sq. km	Portuguese, Criolo, African languages
Kenya ★ Nairobi	28,240,658	224,961 sq. mi. 582,650 sq. km	English, Swahili, local languages
Lesotho ★ Maseru	1,944,493	11,718 sq. mi. 30,350 sq. km	Sesotho, English, Zulu, Xhosa
Liberia ★ Monrovia	2,972,766	43,000 sq. mi. 111,370 sq. km	English, Niger-Congo languages
Libya ★ Tripoli	5,057,392	679,358 sq. mi. 1,759,540 sq. km	Arabic, Italian, English
Madagascar ★ Antananarivo	13,427,758	226,656 sq. mi. 587,040 sq. km	French, Malagasy
Malawi ★ Lilongwe	9,732,409	45,745 sq. mi. 118,480 sq. km	English, Chichewa, other regional languages
Mali ★ Bamako	9,112,950	478,764 sq. mi. 1,240,000 sq. km	French, Bambara, African languages
Mauritania ★ Nouakchott	2,192,777	397,953 sq. mi. 1,030,700 sq. km	Hasaniya Arabic, Pular, Soninke, Wolof
Mauritius ★ Port Louis	1,116,923	718 sq. mi. 1,860 sq. km	English, Creole, French, Hindi, Urdu, Hakka, Bojpoori
Morocco ★ Rabat	28,558,635	172,413 sq. mi. 446,550 sq. km	Arabic, Berber dialects, French
Mozambique ★ Maputo	17,346,280	309,494 sq. mi. 801,590 sq. km	Portuguese, many local dialects

Country ★ Capital	Population (1994)	Land Area (1994)	Principal Languages
Namibia ★ Windhoek	1,595,567	318,694 sq. mi. 825,418 sq. km	English, Afrikaans, German, local languages
Niger ★ Niamey	8,971,605	489,189 sq. mi. 1,267,000 sq. km	French, Hausa, Djerma
Nigeria ★ Abuja	98,091,097	356,668 sq. mi. 923,770 sq. km	English, Hausa, Yoruba, Ibo, Fulani
Rwanda ★ Kigali	8,373,963	10,170 sq. mi. 26,340 sq. km	Kinyarwanda, French, Kiswahili
São Tomé and Príncipe ★ São Tomé	136,780	371 sq. mi. 960 sq. km	Portuguese
Senegal ★ Dakar	8,730,508	75,749 sq. mi. 196,190 sq. km	French, Wolof, Pulaar, Diola, Mandingo
Seychelles ★ Victoria	72,113	176 sq. mi. 455 sq. km	English, French, Creole
Sierra Leone ★ Freetown	4,630,037	27,699 sq. mi. 71,740 sq. km	English, Mende, Temne, Krio
Somalia ★ Mogadishu	6,666,873	246,201 sq. mi. 637,660 sq. km	Somali, Arabic, Italian, English
South Africa ★ Pretoria	43,930,631	471,008 sq. mi. 1,219,912 sq. km	Afrikaans, English, Ndebele, Pedi, Sotho, Swati, Tsonga, Tswana, Venda, Xhosa, Zulu
Sudan ★ Khartoum	29,419,798	967,493 sq. mi. 2,505,810 sq. km	Arabic, Nubian, Ta Bedawie, various other dialects, English
Swaziland ★ Mbabane	936,369	6,703 sq. mi. 17,360 sq. km	English, siSwati
Tanzania ★ Dar es Salaam	27,985,660	364,899 sq. mi. 945,090 sq. km	Swahili, English, local languages
Togo ★ Lomé	4,255,090	21,927 sq. mi. 56,790 sq. km	French, Ewe, Mina, Dagomba, Kabye
Tunisia ★ Tūnis	8,726,562	63,170 sq. mi. 163,610 sq. km	Arabic, French
Uganda ★ Kampala	19,121,934	91,135 sq. mi. 236,040 sq. km	English, Luganda, Swahili, other Bantu and Nilotic languages

Country ★ Capital	Population (1994)	Land Area (1994)	Principal Languages
Zambia ★ Lusaka	9,188,190	290,583 sq. mi. 752,610 sq. km	English, local languages
Zimbabwe ★ Harare	10,975,078	150,803 sq. mi. 390,580 sq. km	English, Shona, Sindebele

EAST AND SOUTHEAST ASIA

Country ★ Capital	Population (1994)	Land Area (1994)	Principal Languages
Brunei ★ Bandar Seri Begawan	284,653	2,228 sq. mi. 5,770 sq. km	Malay, English, Chinese
Burma (Myanmar) ★ Rangoon (Yangon)	44,277,014	261,969 sq. mi. 678,500 sq. km	Burmese, local languages
Cambodia ★ Phnom Penh	10,264,628	69,900 sq. mi. 181,040 sq. km	Khmer, French
China ★ Beijing	1,190,431,106	3,705,386 sq. mi. 9,596,960 sq. km	Mandarin Chinese, other Chinese dialects
Indonesia ★ Jakarta	200,409,741	741,096 sq. mi. 1,919,440 sq. km	Bahasa Indonesia, English, Dutch, Javanese and other local dialects
Japan ★ Tokyo	125,106,937	145,882 sq. mi. 377,835 sq. km	Japanese
Laos ★ Vientiane	4,701,654	91,428 sq. mi. 236,800 sq. km	Lao, French, English
Malaysia ★ Kuala Lumpur	19,283,157	127,316 sq. mi. 329,750 sq. km	Malay, English, Chinese dialects, Tamil, local dialects
Mongolia ★ Ulaanbaatar	2,429,762	604,247 sq. mi. 1,565,000 sq. km	Khalkha Mongol, Russian, Chinese, Turkic languages
North Korea ★ P'yŏngyang	23,066,573	46,540 sq. mi. 120,540 sq. km	Korean
Philippines ★ Manila	69,808,930	115,830 sq. mi. 300,000 sq. km	Pilipino, English
Singapore ★ Singapore	2,859,142	244 sq. mi. 633 sq. km	Chinese, Malay, Tamil, English
South Korea ★ Seoul	45,082,880	38,023 sq. mi. 98,480 sq. km	Korean, English
Taiwan ★ T'aipei	21,298,930	13,892 sq. mi. 35,980 sq. km	Mandarin Chinese, Taiwanese (Min), Hakka dialects

Country ★ Capital	Population (1994)	Land Area (1994)	Principal Languages
Thailand ★ Bangkok	59,510,471	198,455 sq. mi. 514,000 sq. km	Thai, English, regional dialects
Vietnam ★ Hanoi	73,103,898	127,243 sq. mi. 329,560 sq. km	Vietnamese, French, Chinese, English, Khmer, local languages

SOUTH ASIA

Country ★ Capital	Population (1994)	Land Area (1994)	Principal Languages
Bangladesh ★ Dhaka	125,149,469	55,598 sq. mi. 144,000 sq. km	Bangla, English
Bhutan ★ Thimphu	716,380	18,147 sq. mi. 47,000 sq. km	Dzongkha, Tibetan dialects, Nepalese dialects
India ★ New Delhi	919,903,056	1,269,338 sq. mi. 3,287,590 sq. km	Hindi, English, Hindustani, local languages
Maldives ★ Male	252,077	116 sq. mi. 300 sq. km	Divehi, English
Nepal ★ Kathmandu	21,041,527	54,363 sq. mi. 140,800 sq. km	Nepali, local dialects
Pakistan ★ Islamabad	128,855,965	310,401 sq. mi. 803,940 sq. km	English, Punjabi, Sindhi, Pashtu, Balochi, Urdu
Sri Lanka ★ Colombo	18,129,850	25,332 sq. mi. 65,610 sq. km	Sinhala, Tamil, English

THE PACIFIC WORLD

Country ★ Capital	Population (1994)	Land Area (1994)	Principal Languages
Australia ★ Canberra	18,077,419	2,967,893 sq. mi. 7,686,850 sq. km	English, local languages
Fiji ★ Suva	764,382	7,054 sq. mi. 18,270 sq. km	English, Fijian, Hindustani
Kiribati ★ Tarawa	77,853	277 sq. mi. 717 sq. km	English, Gilbertese
Marshall Islands ★ Majuro	54,031	70 sq. mi. 181 sq. km	English, Marshallese dialects, Japanese
Micronesia, Federated States of ★ Palikir	120,347	271 sq. mi. 702 sq. km	English, Trukese, Pohnpeian, Yapese, Kosrean
Nauru ★ Yaren District	10,019	8 sq. mi. 21 sq. km	Nauruan, English

	Country ★ Capital	Population (1994)	Land Area (1994)	Principal Languages
	New Zealand ★ Wellington	3,388,737	103,737 sq. mi. 268,680 sq. km	English, Maori
	Palau ★ Koror	16,366	177 sq. mi. 458 sq. km	English, Palauan, Japanese, Sonsorolese, other local languages
	Papua New Guinea ★ Port Moresby	4,196,806	178,259 sq. mi. 461,690 sq. km	local languages, English, pidgin English, Motu
	Solomon Islands ★ Honiara	385,811	10,985 sq. mi. 28,450 sq. km	local languages, Melanesian pidgin, English
	Tonga ★ Nuku'alofa	104,778	289 sq. mi. 748 sq. km	Tongan, English
	Tuvalu ★ Funafuti	9,831	10 sq. mi. 26 sq. km	Tuvaluan, English
	Vanuatu ★ Port-Vila	169,776	5,699 sq. mi. 14,760 sq. km	English, French, pidgin
	Western Samoa ★ Apia	204,447	1,104 sq. mi. 2,860 sq. km	Samoan (Polynesian), English

THE UNITED STATES

State	Capital	Date entered Union	State	Capital	Date entered Union
Alabama	Montgomery	1819	**Montana**	Helena	1889
Alaska	Juneau	1959	**Nebraska**	Lincoln	1867
Arizona	Phoenix	1912	**Nevada**	Carson City	1864
Arkansas	Little Rock	1836	**New Hampshire**	Concord	1788
California	Sacramento	1850	**New Jersey**	Trenton	1787
Colorado	Denver	1876	**New Mexico**	Santa Fe	1912
Connecticut	Hartford	1788	**New York**	Albany	1788
Delaware	Dover	1787	**North Carolina**	Raleigh	1789
Florida	Tallahassee	1845	**North Dakota**	Bismarck	1889
Georgia	Atlanta	1788	**Ohio**	Columbus	1803
Hawaii	Honolulu	1959	**Oklahoma**	Oklahoma City	1907
Idaho	Boise	1890	**Oregon**	Salem	1859
Illinois	Springfield	1818	**Pennsylvania**	Harrisburg	1787
Indiana	Indianapolis	1816	**Rhode Island**	Providence	1790
Iowa	Des Moines	1846	**South Carolina**	Columbia	1788
Kansas	Topeka	1861	**South Dakota**	Pierre	1889
Kentucky	Frankfort	1792	**Tennessee**	Nashville	1796
Louisiana	Baton Rouge	1812	**Texas**	Austin	1845
Maine	Augusta	1820	**Utah**	Salt Lake City	1896
Maryland	Annapolis	1788	**Vermont**	Montpelier	1791
Massachusetts	Boston	1788	**Virginia**	Richmond	1788
Michigan	Lansing	1837	**Washington**	Olympia	1889
Minnesota	St. Paul	1858	**West Virginia**	Charleston	1863
Mississippi	Jackson	1817	**Wisconsin**	Madison	1848
Missouri	Jefferson City	1821	**Wyoming**	Cheyenne	1890

INDEX